In Malay Forests

In Malaya Forests

IN MALAY FORESTS

by
SIR GEORGE MAXWELL
K.B.E., C.M.G.

GRAHAM BRASH

SINGAPORE

First published in Great Britain in 1907

This edition published in 1989 by
Graham Brash (Pte) Ltd
227, Rangoon Road
Singapore 0821

ISBN 9971-49-148-6

Cover design by Choy Yeen Kheng
Printed by Ocean Colour Printing (Pte) Ltd

PREFACE.

———

Six of the articles in this volume have appeared before, and for permission to reprint them my thanks are due to the editors of 'Blackwood's,' 'The Pall Mall,' 'Macmillan's,' and 'Temple Bar.'

The first article is intended to be an introduction to, or setting for, the others, regarding which I need say no more than that they are accounts of personal incidents, and they range through different States of the Malay Peninsula, and cover many years.

GEORGE MAXWELL.

PENANG,
January 1907.

CONTENTS

CONTENTS

IN MALAY FORESTS

THE FOREST.

To most people the Malay Peninsula is only known as the long narrow strip that, on the map of Asia, runs down into the sea beyond the bulky V-shaped projection of India, and divides the Indian Ocean from the China Sea.

Passengers by the mail-boats for the Far East, though they approach it at the islands of Penang and Singapore, see of its length during their voyage down the warm smooth waters of the Straits of Malacca but little save a continuous range of distant mountains bathed in a haze of purple, blue, and grey.

He whose business or pleasure takes him on one of the local steamers sees a little more. In the foreground there is, on the west coast, an unbroken line, level as that of the sea, of dark-green forest. This is the mangrove belt, which grows on the alluvial soil brought down and silted up by the rivers, and which ends where the sea begins. Behind this line rises a range of heavily-timbered mountains, and behind this yet another range; and on all sides the horizon is bounded either by forest-covered mountains or by forest-covered plains.

It is almost the literal truth that the whole peninsula is covered with forest. It is not that the country is un-inhabited, for it has a population of some hundreds of thousands: but it is that the inhabited area, every yard of which has been won from, and hacked out of the forest, is infinitesimal in comparison with the extent of the forest that remains untouched.

Throughout its hundreds of miles of length and breadth the Malay Peninsula is practically one vast forest. The great alluvial tin-fields of Kinta, Larut, Selangor, and Seremban, where tens of thousands of Chinese coolies strip the surface to lay bare the ore, are really mere patches; and the towns, palatial and magnificent though the buildings of some of them are, are nothing more than specks in an expanse that sweeps from one Sultanate to another, and is only limited by the sea.

Our railways and roads run through forest, and our mines, plantations, and towns are bounded by it.

It is, however, difficult at first to realise the environment of the forest. When the newcomer has left his steamer, and the railway has taken him to the town which is his destination, it is possible that he may fail to appreciate the most wonderful of all the new sights around him; he may, and most frequently does, accept the dense mass of trees and vegetation that shuts in the railway line as " the jungle," and consider the timber-clad mountains merely in the light of scenery.

In a Malay village one may better realise the manner in which the forest hems in the cultivated area. The settlement is generally situated on the banks of a river. By the water's edge are the houses, built under the shade of fruit-trees, and behind them are the flat, irrigated padi-fields. On all sides this area is shut in by a dark heavy line that uprears itself, around and above it, like the walls of a prison. This line is the forest edge; and thence the forest spreads in every direction, miles upon miles, until some other village is reached; there it opens out again, and sweeping round the clearing, as a wave encircles some ocean rock, closes in again behind it and continues, over mountains, over plains, until the sea is reached.

But it is when he views it from a mountain peak that the stranger can best see the extent of the forest. He will then discover, what the Malay can never for a minute forget, that he lives his life in the midst of a forest which is as much apart from him as it is around him. The fact that it extends, interminable, far beyond the horizon on every side, then for the first time makes its indelible impression upon his mind.

This other wonderful thing he will perhaps first realise: the forest is an evergreen; the season, whose changes in the cultivated area turn brown soil to the tender green of the young padi shoots, to the richness of the colour of the swelling plants, and to the golden wealth of the ripened grain, fails to touch the forest. Neither the season, nor the flight of time, leaves a mark upon the forest; virgin in the days of which we cannot guess the morn, virgin in our days, virgin it will remain in the days of generations yet unborn.

On the slopes of the nearest spur each individual tree stands clear, each giant form showing the swelling roundness of its wealth of bough and leaf. Tier upon tier, the trees stand thickly massed, without a break, from the level of the plain to the height of the topmost trees that show their heads against the sky-line. Deep, dark, sombre green is the colour of this near range; here and there one may catch glimpses of lighter shades, a few scattered patches perhaps of sage green where some trees, after fruiting, are putting forth a new flush of leaves; possibly there may be a speck of vivid red that marks a tree whose young shoots assume an unusual colour. But the contrast only accentuates the prevailing tone.

Beyond these hills, which are not perhaps more than a few miles away, rises a range that is clad in purple. At this distance the mass of tree shows through the clear atmosphere, not with the shape of each individual tree, but with a uniform raised and rounded roughness that covers alike mountain crag and mountain ravine.

In some places in the plains between the two ranges one may perhaps see the lighter green that marks a

cultivated area, or a gleam of white sand where alluvial
tin-mines show like islands in the sea.

Beyond the purple mountains rise other ranges, and
though, of course, you cannot see it, you know that the
forest sweeps on through wide hidden valleys and wonderful places rarely trodden by man, until it reappears in
sight upon another range.

The mountain-chains melt from purple to blue, and as
they recede the roughness of the forest covering becomes
a velvety pile, and then an even softer texture; and finally,
where grey mists melt and dissolve in the distant haze, it
is not easy to know which is forest and which is sky.

Such is the view that lies beneath your eyes as you
stand upon a mountain peak some four or five thousand
feet above the plain. But so deep, so soft is the mantle of
forest, that you may fail to realise the grandeur of the
mountains. They have not the austerity that belongs to
nakedness. To right and to left, where the mountain spurs
run out and down to the plain, your eyes rest on slopes
which, though steep perhaps, are softly undulating. Each
tree melts gently into its neighbour, or partly hides it;
all is green and harmonious, and the mountain offers a
face which appears to be as smooth and unbroken as a
pasture land. But sometimes you may see how deceptive
this appearance is. It has been raining, and a great
cloud comes slowly swimming landward from the sea.
The direction that it takes will bring it within a mile of
you. As it approaches the mountain you wonder what
will happen,—whether it will rest against the mountain-
side, or whether it will roll upwards through the trees.
But to your amazement, when the cloud edge touches the
mountain it does not stop. Then you see that the whole
cloud is swimming on into the mountain. What has
happened is that a mountain ravine has acted as the
channel up which a current of air is rushing skywards
from the plain, and into the ravine the cloud is being
slowly sucked. As the cloud enters, its shape and size
and colour help your eye to see both sides of the ravine,

and you may vaguely estimate the depth and width of the valley that had been strangely invisible although so close. But as soon as the cloud is past and gone, the trees on both sides of the ravine seem to leap together; and, though you now know exactly where to look, waving branches and woven leaves defy your efforts to say where the entrance is. You then wonder how many similar places are hidden around you, and picture to yourself the great sea cloud hemmed in by the sides of the ravine and still swimming farther landward.

There is another time when you may have a revelation. A few minutes after sunset the westward facing mountains blaze with the refulgent glory of an afterglow. A rosy light probes the secrets that the forest hides from the noonday sun—the grandeur of wide valleys that wind an intricate way into the inmost heart of the mountains; the mystery of little deeply-shaded tributaries that fall into them on either side; the vastness of untrodden ravines and gorges; the majesty of unscaleable precipices; the terror of long straight scars that tell of landslides where trees and soil and rock have slipped in hideous disaster, leaving a wound that has cut to the very bone. For a moment all is revealed—the mantle of forest does not avail against this searching light, and you may well think that it is in the sweet exposure that the mountains blush.

But come down from the mountain peak, and walk alone along a forest path. Though it is midday it is very sombre. The sun cannot pierce the dense foliage of the branches of the giant trees, and so heavily do shadows lie upon shadows that the very green seems almost black. The sheltered air is fresh and cool, and there is an almost perfect stillness. Underfoot, except where the path is trodden bare, is a matting of dead leaves and of sweet damp moss. The track upon which you stand is a foot or perhaps a foot and a half wide, and at the height of your body the width of the open way is perhaps three feet. The daily passage of the Malays keeps back the encroachment of brambles and forest creepers. But the track is only wide enough and the opening only high enough to allow a man to pass. You could not ride even the smallest and handiest of ponies along it.

To right and left of the path the forest appears to be almost impenetrable. The trees grow so thickly together that you are closed in by a small but unbroken circle of tree-trunks. Between the trees there are tangled masses of bushes, briers, and saplings. Rattans and creepers of every kind crawl along the ground and among the trees, sometimes hanging in heavy festoons and sometimes tense with the pressure that they exert. So thick and strong is the mass of creepers that when a wood-cutter has hacked through a tree-trunk it is often kept upright by the ligaments that bind it to the surrounding trees. After an hour's walk along a forest path, a casual observer might say that, so far as he could see, the forest contained no flowers, no butterflies, no birds, no life of any kind. But if you sit upon a fallen tree-trunk and look around, you may see a little more. High in a tree, and almost out of sight, you may see an occasional flower, and lower down perhaps, your eye may light upon an inconspicuous spray of blossoms that a careful scrutiny shows to be a miniature orchid. There are few butterflies in the forest, but now and then, if you are by one of the openings among the trees, which are to the winged creatures what the paths are to us, you may see a moth or butterfly pass by flapping its heavy velvet wings. You seldom hear a bird, but if you are quiet and wait long enough some tiny sun-bird may come your way, or, perhaps some weird bird with light-blue eyes and an enormous tail; or a jungle-hen may creep out from under a bush, and scratch for ants' eggs in an open space where a tree has fallen. The only other thing that you will see, except an occasional lizard, will be ants, and perhaps a millepede. If you know where to look for them, you will see the tracks of four-footed animals, but you will not see the animals themselves.

But in a forest which you know to be so vast and so boundless you have a right to expect more than you have seen. Ants, a butterfly, even a bird, do not and cannot represent the life of this great gloomy place. But more you cannot see. You are the centre of a small circle whose radius varies from fifteen to thirty yards. Inside this circle you can see more or less distinctly; outside it everything is hidden. Even so huge an animal as an elephant is sometimes invisible at fifteen yards, and almost always invisible at thirty yards. Wherever you go you carry with you that little circle outside which lies the unknown. The path that lies behind you is, as soon as it passes outside that circle, as full of the unknown as the path before you or the tangle on either side. So little do you see that the feeling comes over you that you are alone in the midst of mysterious, hidden things. The feeling that immediately follows this is that these mysterious things are not merely hidden, but are specially hidden from you. The circle that moves with you is the veil built up against you. You could imagine that you were a trespasser, or at all events were regarded as such. Then you have the horrible feeling that from behind the tree-trunks watching eyes are looking upon you. It is bad enough at any time if you are alone and all is quiet; it is worse as the sun sinks and light fades; it is worst if by any ill chance you happen to know that you have lost not only your way but your sense of direction.

At all times you may see things happen of which the reason is hard to divine. Though not a breath of air can be felt to move, a frond of a palm may begin to sway gently and rhythmically backwards and forwards while all the other fronds of the same tree remain as motionless as the trees around. You examine the palm to see if there is possibly a rat or some other animal at its base, but can discover nothing. Sometimes one single leaf amidst the numbers on a branch may begin without apparent cause to be violently agitated, and will as suddenly stop.

The Malays always consider themselves as intruders when they enter the forest, and never forget their awe of and reverence for it. They seldom go into the forest alone; and when one man asks another to accompany him, the reason that he is going into the forest is always considered to be sufficient in itself. While it is true that the forest lies almost at their doors, they never forget not merely that no man knows its extent, but that it actually is without bound or limit.

To the Malays the great enveloping forest is full of supernatural powers. There are the wonderful *Jin Tanah*, the Earth Spirits; *Gergasi*, the great tusked giants; *Orang Bunyi*, the invisible Voice Folk. There are individual creatures—such as *Hantu Pemburu*, the Spectral Hunter; mountain-top and river pool have their local spirits; and there are classes innumerable of ghosts, goblins, and demons.

They are known as *Hantu Hutan*—the Spirits of the Forest,—and are as real to the Malays and as much dreaded as the tigers and other wild animals of the forest.

Men, such as rattan-cutters or gutta-hunters, whose vocations take them into the forest, repeat a short charm to avert the wrath or displeasure of these spirits; and the farther they go from home the more careful are they to make use of due ceremony and incantation.

The forest envelops their homes and their lives; but, as with the fisherfolk and the sea, the more they explore it the more they know that it is a world apart. That it is so near and extends so far adds to it majesty and terror. In order to realise something of what the Malay forest is, one may perhaps look at it for a moment from the point of view of the Malays, who know it better than any one else. And in the charms, which have been handed down from generation to generation, and which the Malays repeat to this day when they enter the forest, one may have some perception of the sentiment that inspires them. A rattan-cutter, though he may find plenty of canes within

easy call of his home, repeats this invocation to the spirits
of the forest—

> "Peace [1] unto ye all!
> I come as a friend, not as an enemy.
> I come to seek my living, not to make war.
> May no harm come to me, nor mine,
> To my wife, my children, or my home.
> Because I intend no harm, nor evil,
> I ask that I may come, and go, in peace.

It is worthy of notice that, though the Malays have
been staunch Muhammadans for centuries, their aboriginal fear of the forest is so deeply rooted that it is to the
spirits and not to Allah that they apply for protection.

Similarly, when a party of Malays sets out to drive
deer, the commonest of all game, they may go no more
than a few hundred yards away from the village; but
none the less the leader of the party will utter this preface
to his prayer to the spirits—

> "Hail!   All hail!
> We crave permission to enter on this domain
> And to tie our nooses to these trees."

---

1. The original Malay of the various invocations quoted in
these pages will be found in the Appendix.

THE PINJIH RHINO.

An old rhinoceros, that made its abode in the Pinjih valley in the Kinta district, was for many years the most famous animal in the native State of Perak.

In the first place, it was *kramat*: that is to say, the Malays credited it with supernatural powers, and imagined it to be protected against all danger by a guardian spirit. It often happens that an animal which attaches itself to one locality and establishes a reputation for daring or cunning, and which is fortunate enough to escape a few ill-directed bullets, comes in a few years to be considered *kramat*, and is in many cases imagined to be a reincarnation of a deceased celebrity. It is generally recognised that animals under the protection of another world will treat the human inhabitants of the district honoured by their presence with a benign consideration bordering on condescension; thus a *kramat* elephant will walk by the rice-fields leaving the crops untouched, and a child might drive away a *kramat* tiger that strayed too near the cattle-folds.

But this rhinoceros was extraordinarily savage; and it was this combination of *kramat* power and savagery that constituted its second claim to distinction. It was known to have killed three men on three separate occasions, and in each case the attack was said to have been entirely unprovoked. At an inquest held on the terribly mangled body of a Malay named Japaringonen, the evidence proved that two men had been walking quietly along a forest path when, without any warning, the great brute had rushed upon them. In many other cases men had been attacked, but had escaped with their lives. It would turn aside for no one, so it was said; on the contrary, if met in the forest, it would either stand its ground and then slowly and deliberately advance in the direction from which it had been disturbed, or it would charge without warning.

It had been a terror in the Pinjih valley long before the British occupation of Perak (1874), and twenty-five years later, at the time of this narrative, it was only in large and armed parties that the wood-cutters and rattan-collectors ventured into the less frequented parts of the forest.

On more than one occasion the headman of the district had organised expeditions to kill the animal, and once a party of five picked Malays had met the rhinoceros and had fired fifty shots at it. I heard the headman tell the story once. "It was no child's play," the old man said, turning fiercely on one of an audience who had criticised the shooting. "If a bullet felled the brute, it picked itself up at once; and if a shot missed, it charged forthwith. A hundred men might have fired more shots, but they could not have done more to kill it. And," he added with a scowl, "the end of the matter is, that you cannot kill an animal that will not die."

The animal's third claim to distinction lay in its horn, which was said to be of exceptional length and girth, and also to be blue. Malays divide rhinoceroses into four classes, according to their horns. There is the one known as *sumbu lilin*, the "wax-coloured horn"; *sumbu api*, "the flame-coloured horn"; *sumbu nila*, "the blue horn"; and lastly, *sumbu itam*, the ordinary everyday "black horn."

Rhinoceros' horns are considered to have the most marvellous efficacy as remedies for almost every kind of disease, and even shavings of a horn are carefully prized. In a case where the most appalling wounds were inflicted by this particular rhinoceros upon a man named Kanda Daud, the whole credit of the man's recovery was ascribed to the alleged fact that some of the blue of the animal's horn had come off on the man's hands as he sought to

defend himself, and that this blue had been used by the
native doctors as the antidote to the wounds.

The fact that made this rhinoceros so well-known
among the Europeans of Kinta was not so much the
colour of its horn, or that it was *kramat*, or was savage,
as that it was of the large one-horned variety known as
Rhinoceros Sondaicus, which is somewhat rare, and that
it seldom left an area of some forty square miles, circumscribed by bridle-paths, and within close reach of the
headquarters of the district. By comparison with the
boundless extent of the forest on all sides, and with the
roving propensities of most big-game animals, this made
it easily accessible; and many efforts were made to bring
it to account. But (partly on account of the native
trackers being afraid to bring their men up to the brute)
something always went wrong. Once the District Magistrate managed to get on terms with it, but was charged
so often and so determinedly in very thick scrub that he
had to beat a retreat and leave the rhinoceros master of
the field. In the dull record of failures there was, however, one light spot. The attendant spirit of *kramat*
animals has power to deceive the hunter by altering the
appearance of the hunted animal or by giving its shape
to one of the hunters or their attendants, and on one occasion a gallant officer in the N—— Regiment fell its victim.
Leaving his pad elephant in the forest with a Malay in
charge, he proceeded one day to set off on foot to look for
fresh tracks. He walked for hours, until suddenly his
tracker stopped him and silently pointed out the outline
of a huge animal in front of them. M. took a steady
aim and fired: a scream from a sorely-stricken elephant
and a yell from a terrified Malay were his answer. He
had walked in a circle and had fired at his own elephant.
As the smoke cleared he caught a glimpse of the elephant
rushing madly through the forest and had a full view of
the Malay bellowing on the ground. The wretched man
had been quietly smoking his cigarette on the elephant's
neck, and now, lying where he fell, was only in doubt

whether a bullet-wound or a broken neck was the cause of his death. Both elephant and man recovered, the Malay the quicker of the two, for the elephant, though the wound healed, was never fit for work again; but both had a lucky escape, for the bullet, which hit the elephant high on the shoulder, had gone perilously near the man's leg. It will be some time before M. hears the last of the shot; but the chaff of the clubs does not carry the bite of the smiles of the Malays, who give the credit of the whole occurrence to "old *kramat*" and his guardian spirit.

Such, briefly, was the history of the animal, and Malias was by no means keen on tackling him. Malias was a local Malay who drew a regular salary from me, and who wandered round the country seeking for, and as far as possible verifying, news of game. He was not particularly bright, and, like all Malays, was inclined to be lazy; on fresh tracks, however, he was as keen as possible, and he would follow up a wounded tiger without his pulse giving a stroke above its normal beat. Chance brought us an ally: this was an old man named Pa' Senik, a foreigner from one of the northern unprotected States. He was of another type to Malias, who was a mere villager; for Pa' Senik's youth had been spent at the court of a petty raja, and had been such as might be expected from his surroundings, full of conspiracy and intrigue, love and lust, fair fight and cold-blooded murder. At last he had fallen upon bad days, for another raja ruled in the place of the man he had served, and he had had to fly for his life. He came to Perak, where he was shrewdly suspected of complicity in a carefully planned and well-executed dacoity, and then settled down quietly in the Pinjih valley, where until his eyesight failed him he had made a living by shooting deer. He was now old and poor, but despite his age was keen to go after the rhinoceros, and, knowing its haunts and wallows, assured us that he could bring me up with it. But this was no ordinary quest, he said; if without preliminary preparations we went in search of tracks, we were foredoomed to the failure that had attended all previous efforts. We must first "ask" for the rhinoceros from the *Jin Tanah*, or Earth Spirits, who have power over the forest and all its inhabitants, and to whom the attendant spirits of *kramat* animals are vassals. Pa' Senik, who was a *pawang*,[1] proposed to make a feast and invoke the spirits, and to ask them to give us the rhinoceros and to accept compensation. We should not have to pay much, he said, for the spirit, if it accepted the offer, would probably ask for something to eat, a fowl perhaps, or some eggs, and a lime or two. Of course, if the spirits proved obdurate, nothing could be done, and we must not think of any act of defiance; but, if made with skill and address, our application would, he thought, be favourably considered. The exchange value of a rhinoceros in the spirit world seemed to be extremely moderate, and I gave the old man a dollar (all he asked for) with which to prepare the feast preliminary to the invocation, and arranged to go to his house to witness the ceremony.

The following Saturday was the day agreed upon, and a few miles by railway to the next station, and a walk of a couple of miles took me to his village, where a house has been set aside for me. After dinner I was invited into the adjoining house, where Pa' Senik had made his preparations. Like all Malay houses it was divided into three parts: the front room or verandah, absolutely public; the middle room, where the men eat and sleep, reserved for intimates; and the kitchen, where the unmarried women sleep, absolutely private. The ceremony was to take place in the centre room, and here I was introduced to Che Mat, a brother pawang, whom Pa' Senik had called in to assist him. After a few minutes' conversation the proceedings began, and while they sat down and faced one another over a brass bowl

---

1. A *pawang* is a man who, by ceremony, incantation, or charm, propitiates or invokes the assistance of the spirits. He figures in every enterprise and festival of the Malay community. For a fuller account see the last article.

containing burning charcoal, I made myself as comfortable as I could upon the floor within a few feet of them, and round us such men and women and children as had obtained admission ranged themselves in a semi-circle. Various bowls of water, in which floated leaves and flowers, were set about the floor, and twigs and sprays of leaves and blossoms were fixed to the posts and walls. Each bowl and leaf and flower had its definite significance, and to each were spells and charms attached. Pa' Senik then took up an *arbab*, a three-stringed instrument, in shape somewhat like a banjo, but played with a bow. After a tentative essay or two he struck up a monotonous chant to a tune a degree more monotonous. Much of his music was improvised to meet the special conditions of the present instance; but the greater portion of it was part of his traditional craft. It was lengthy and full of repetitions: but the gist of it was that here was a white man, who came to ask the assistance of the spirits; and here were Malias, Che Mat, and Pa' Senik, the servants and followers of the white man, and they too craved the assistance of the spirits; and in the forest was the rhinoceros whom they desired to take, and whom they now besought the spirits to give them. What answer would the spirits give us, and by what means could we ensure their assistance in the enterprise? Such, in a few words, was the meaning of an invocation that lasted twenty minutes. The chant ended, Pa' Senik laid aside his bow, and asked one of the company to recite from the Koran. A man at once began to intone some verses, while the whole audience joined in the usual responses and replies, and the protection of the Islam religion was thus called in upon proceedings utterly at variance with the teaching of Muhammad. When this was over, a tray containing rice and various kinds of curry was brought up to Che Mat, who had hitherto remained silent and motionless, in pose of entire abstraction. He now roused himself, and throwing some gum benjamin into the censer over which he faced Pa' Senik, moved the tray in and out of the thick

smoke until it was thoroughly fumigated.   Then he took
a saucer of rice from an attendant, and passed it in a
similar manner through the smoke, and after placing a
lighted candle on the edge of the saucer, put it on a tray
suspended from the roof between the two men.   Finally,
a plate of parched rice was purified from all mortal taint
by smoke, and then, also with a lighted candle on its rim,
carried out of the house by Che Mat, and hung on a tree.
This marked the conclusion of the opening stage of the
proceedings.   The rice on the tray between the two men
was of a peculiar kind, considered a delicacy, which is
used in sweetmeats, and was intended to attract the
attention of the spirits we desired to invoke. The parched
rice outside the house was for any of the thousand and
one wandering demons who might appear, and who, unless
thus provided for, might mar the proceedings. The curry
and rice was for the audience, most of whom at once
followed it to a corner of the room, and devoted an un-
divided attention to it.

   After an interval both men stripped to the waist, and
Pa' Senik took up his instrument, and to the same drear
chant reiterated the purpose for which we met.   Che Mat
in the meantime undoing the handkerchief that Malays
bind round their heads, let a mass of long hair fall down
upon his shoulders, and carefully combed it out and
anointed it with cocoanut-oil. He then bound his handkerchief round the long glistening hair, and rolled it
scarf-wise round his head. When this was done he brought
forward more saucers of rice, and held them in the smoke
of the censer, and passed his hands, his head, his breast,
his knees, and his back through the pungent incense,
ending by moving the censer three times round himself.
He bowed to the four cardinal points, took some of the
rice in his hand, and, muttering a spell over it, blew upon
it in the professional manner known as *jampi*.   Another
candle was lit, and Pa' Senik again began to play his
instrument.   Suddenly Che Mat broke in upon the monotonous music of the *arbab*, clapped his hands wildly above

his head, shook his hair free from the handkerchief that bound it round his forehead, and, with a quick twist of his neck, swung his long locks in a sweeping circle round his head. The suddenness of the interruption was startling. Round whirled the black glistening mane, followed by the gaze of every eye in the room, and as it completed the circle, another short jerk of the muscles of the neck sent it again madly flying round his head. Again and again, and more quickly each succeeding time, was the stream made to revolve round him, until at last all that was to be seen of the man seated on the floor was his short bare body, with an occasional glimpse of white compressed features, surmounted by a black, rushing, whirling halo that filled and fanned the room. For some minutes this extraordinary muscular effort continued, until suddenly Che Mat fell forward in a state of collapse. There was perfect silence for a few moments, while all the spectators held their breath, and then Pa' Senik, picking up some rice, threw it over the supine figure, and asked him who he was. There was no answer, and Pa' Senik was forced to have recourse to his *arbab*. After a considerable interval Che Mat announced that he was Pran Ali, meaning thereby that he was possessed by a spirit of that name. In answer to questions put by Pa' Senik, the spirit Pran Ali expressed himself as friendly to us, and a natural enemy of the earth spirits and the guardian spirits, but declared that he was unable to help us in the quest of the rhinoceros; deer were the animals over which he had power, not rhinoceroses. If it had been a deer now——

Pran Ali could help us no further, and thereupon left, and Che Mat was no longer possessed of him. There was another interval of singing and playing by Pa' Senik, who called on various spirits to come to our assistance, and repeated innumerable charms to prevent the rhinoceros from hearing or scenting us as we approached it, to prevent it from charging, or from recovering from any wound that might be inflicted upon it. "If all the dead return to life and walk this world again, then, and not till then, may this animal turn upon us; if the bottom-most of the three layers of stone that support the earth reappear upon the surface, then, and not till then, may this animal attack us." But to repeat one-tenth of the incantations and invocations would fill many pages, and would interest but very few. Che Mat stopped the long tale by again evincing signs of another demoniacal posses-sion. Again his attitude of abstraction fell from him, and his weird hair-swinging held the room. After the pause that followed his collapse he inquired what we wanted of him, and when Pa' Senik offered him a bowl of parched rice, he at once seized it and swallowed a handful of the contents; when a plantain was produced, he gulped it, skin and all, and then announced that he was Sang Kala Raja Megang Rimba, one of the guardian spirits. Pa' Senik thereupon humbly inquired whether we might be allowed to follow the rhinoceros (which, by the way, was throughout the evening spoken of as a buffalo), and the spirit's immediate reply was a downright refusal, saying that on no account would he lose the animal. This caused a sensation amongst the audience, and there was much shaking of heads, but Pa' Senik was not to be beaten. He began with cajolery, and when that had no effect tried what is vulgarly known as bounce. Who was this spirit that he should take this defiant atti-tude? To this the spirit answered that he was a thousand years old: Pa' Senik declared that he was a thousand years older. "Ten thousand years old," replied the spirit, "Ten thousand years older," retorted Pa' Senik, who thereupon challenged his adversary to a contest as to which was the stronger. When the challenge was accepted, Pa' Senik seized a handful of parched rice and threw it full in the face of his adversary, and then leant forward, glaring at him over the smouldering censer. His opponent immediately seized a huge bowl of rice and raised it in the act to hurl; but when his arm reached the topmost point above his shoulder from which it would turn to throw, he suddenly stiffened, and the whole of his body became rigid. For a few seconds he sat there living and motionless as the statue of a discobolus: and then the bowl dropped from his nerveless fingers and fell crashing to the floor. Sang Kala Raja Megang Rimba was beaten in contest. He cast himself forth, and Che Mat was thrown into a third frenzy, becoming possessed of a spirit named Awang Mahat. Unfortunately Awang Mahat belongs to that unhappy class, whether in this world or the other, of creatures who mean well: his intentions are excellent, but he is powerless for good or evil, and the consideration he meets with is, therefore, such as might be expected. Little was asked of him, and he could tell us less: beyond saying that if our quarry were wounded near water it would come to life again (a pleasing prospect, as we had to seek it in swamp and marsh), he could not help us. He remained but a few minutes, and then craved leave to depart. When he left, Che Mat was nearly fainting, and to allow him to recover there was a long interval of playing and singing by Pa' Senik. Che Mat's wife, herself no unskilled disciple in witchcraft, in the meantime occupied herself in attending to her husband, breathing upon him, rubbing, kneading, and massaging him. When attention was called and the proceedings resumed, Che Mat fell into a fourth frenzy, more violent than any that had preceded it. He had undergone his previous attacks in silence, but this time he gave vent to scream after scream, short sharp yells of pain. When the succeeding exhaustion had somewhat passed, he declared that he was the Jin Kepala Gunong Api—the Jin of the Volcano's Summit—one of the *Jin Tanah*, the Earth Spirits, whom we had to fear in this enterprise. He was most violent at first, but soon became quiet, and then friendly, and finally asked what we would give him if he allowed us to "take" the rhinoceros. Various gifts were suggested, but rejected as valueless in the Spirit World, until finally the offer of an egg, some parched rice, and the rice I have mentioned as a delicacy, was accepted.

This, Pa' Senik was careful to explain to me the next morning, was not in this case to be considered as representing the exchange value of the rhinoceros; it was tendered and accepted only in the sense of a propitiatory offering. All that was vouchsafed was that, as far as the Earth Spirits were concerned, we were at liberty to follow the rhinoceros; whether we succeeded or not was another thing, and to that the Jin would not commit himself. But we were given an omen, and told that if we met a tiger's tracks crossing those of the rhinoceros, we were to return at once, and not to make another attempt; when we made our offering at the entrance of the forest, certain signs in the flame of a candle would tell us the disposition of the guardian spirit; and, thirdly, we were to be guided by our dreams that night. The Jin then threw Che Mat into a final frenzy and left. This ended the night's work.

We were astir early the next morning. Pa' Senik was ready with his offering, and soon he, Malias, and I set off for a walk in the forest. We had no news of the whereabouts of the rhinoceros, for, as I have said, no one would go to look for this animal's tracks; but a day would be well spent in learning as much as possible of the country. Pa' Senik had been directed by the Earth Spirit to make his offering at "the gateway of the forest," which is the Malay term for the place where the village foot-track leaves the open cultivated land and plunges into the virgin forest. At the "gateway," then, Pa' Senik made his offering. Splitting into four the end of a bamboo, and deftly weaving the stem of a creeper through the split ends, he improvised a censer, which a couple of green leaves and a handful of earth made fire-proof. Some dry leaves and a dead twig or two made a fire, upon which he sprinkled incense. The stipulated offering was passed through the smoke, and then carefully placed on an open spot. Pa' Senik lit a candle, and placed it on the edge of the censer, and, after due invocation, stepped back and keenly watched the flames. In doing this one has to stay beside the lighted candle, calling upon the spirits to attend until one feels one's skin move, then step back and watch the flame: if it flickers, it betokens the arrival of the spirits; if, after breaking and wavering, it burns true, straight, and upright—success; extinction is failure; if it blows to the right or toward you, hope; to the left or away from you, the chances are against you. In the wind-protected corner Pa' Senik had chosen the candle burnt true and bright, and as we started hope ran high. We had a long day's walk through the forest, but to find fresh tracks was too much to expect. Old tracks, however, and abandoned wallows gave proof of "old *kramat's*" existence; and the next morning I returned to my quarters well satisfied at having got through the opening stages of the campaign.

Though no result was seen that day, Pa' Senik's offering had not been without its effect, for not many days later a Malay came hot-foot in search of Malias, and told him that he had that morning seen the fresh tracks of the rhinoceros crossing a native path some twelve miles away. Pa' Senik was sent for, kit and provisions packed, and that night we all slept in our informant's house. It stood in a small clearing, in the depths of the forest. A few hundred yards away from the door a precipitous limestone hill rose sheer out of the level plain, and towered some seven hundred feet above our heads. At sunset numbers of jungle-fowl crowed and called on every side as they came down to drink at a little stream behind the house; and a party of black gibbons made the echoes ring with their ear-piercing whoops. The wild goat lived on this limestone hill, our host Hussein informed us; one could hear them bleat at night, and they often came down from the precipitous heights to feed round his clearing, but they were very rarely seen. We went to sleep early, and the next morning I woke my men at half-past four. A tiger had roared close to the house during the night, and this made Pa' Senik rather apprehensive of the omen regarding the tiger tracks crossing the rhinoceros tracks.

While the first jungle-cock was shrilling his clear challenge and the gibbons went whooping through the tree-tops in search of food, we started to make a wide cast through the forest to find fresh tracks of the rhinoceros. Without doubt the heart of the Jin had been softened, for we had not gone more than two or three miles before we came on tracks made early the previous evening.

Pa' Senik had explained to me overnight that his "work" of the evening I have described would remain effectual for a month, and that an offering each time we entered the forest anew was all that was now required. He was provided with his censer and propitiatory gift, and in half an hour we were ready to proceed. Malias and I then went on alone, instructing Pa' Senik, Hussein, and another local Malay, to follow us slowly, and to keep, so far as they could judge, a quarter of a mile behind us. We followed a well-beaten track, and it seemed from the manner in which the animal had walked steadily on, without stopping to feed on the way, that he was making for another part of the country, and that many miles lay between him and us. We were therefore taken entirely by surprise when, before we had gone more than half a mile, a turn in the path brought us suddenly upon him. He was lying at full length in a wallow; but I was unable to make use of the disadvantage at which we held him, for as I threw up my 10-bore a hanging creeper caught the barrels, and I had to lower the rifle and disengage it before I could bring it fairly to my shoulder. By this time the rhinoceros had lurched out of the pool, and I only had time for a hasty shot at his shoulder, hitting him, as I subsequently discovered, too high up and too far forward. The thick smoke of the black powder prevented me from getting a second shot before the animal disappeared in the dense forest growth. An examination of the tracks explained the suddenness of the encounter, for they showed that the rhinoceros had stayed the whole night long in the wallow, and the footprints proved that it really was "old *kramat*" that we had

met. This Malias was at first inclined to doubt, for we had
seen the animal plainly, and his horn was not the cubit's
length of cerulean blue that every one said "old *kramat*"
carried, but only a short, black, shapeless stump; nor had
he in the least degree acted up to his reputation for pugna-
city. The only fact in favour of the theory that it was
he whom we had met was that there was not a sign
of blood. This rather disconcerted the Malays; but I
had before followed a wounded rhinoceros for three
miles without finding a drop of blood (until the Malays
had openly grumbled at my following an animal that had
obviously been missed), and had found it when I did
come up with it on the point of death—dying, I believe,
from internal hemorrhage. We made but a short pause
by the wallow to examine the tracks, and then pushed on.
At once we were covered from head to foot, and our rifles
from stock to muzzle, with the wet clay that clung to the
bushes through which the rhinoceros had made its way.
Slimy branches dripping with mire slapped our faces, and
oozy drops of mud fell upon our heads and clotted in
our hair. Then before we had worked more than a hundred yards of our way along the track a mass of white glittering clay caught my eye, and as I squatted on my heels
Malias reached forward to make an excited tug at my
coat. What we saw was on slightly higher ground than
that on which we stood, and appeared to be least seven
feet high; it was perfectly motionless. An "ant-hill,"
whispered Malias, for it was covered with the same
substance as that with which we were smeared. An ant-
hill, of course, I thought, and the rhinoceros had rubbed
against it in passing. And so I nodded and prepared to
move forward, but as I did so the mass moved and disappeared behind the brown pile of a real ant-hill. "Allah!
that was he," groaned Malias. But before I could express
my feelings the animal reappeared on the other side of
the covering heap, and walked slowly away from us.
Though his back was well exposed, a careful aim at the
base of the spine produced no effect, and (the smoke

hung terribly) I had no time for a second shot; nor
perhaps would I have risked it, for I felt sure that this
time at all events he would charge. However, the rhinoceros went straight away, nor did we see him again for
many hours. For perhaps a mile we followed him
through virgin forest, where, though rattans and creepers
obstructed the path, the great trees afforded a shelter
from the sun. But then the rhinoceros turned aside into
a clearing where two seasons before the Malays or the
aboriginal Sakeis had felled the timber to grow a crop
of hill-rice. The scrub that had grown up since they had
reaped their harvest and abandoned the place was some
ten feet high, and here the difficulty of making one's way
was increased a hundredfold, and moreover we were
exposed to the full force of the tropical sun. Bowing
and bending to avoid the interlacing creepers, twisting
and turning to free our rifles from the branches that,
despite our efforts, caught their projecting muzzles, we
had of course to move in perfect silence. The sun struck
fair on our rounded backs, and we were surrounded by
myriads of flies. They flew into our eyes, imprisoned
themselves in our ears, or crawled clog-footed over our
glistening faces. We pushed on extremely slowly, for we
had no desire to come up with the rhinoceros in this
horrible tangle, where we had but little chance of self-
defence. There was no alternative, however, but to stick
to the tracks. We could not say what line the animal
intended to take, and to make a detour was therefore
out of the question. The only thing to do was to give
the rhinoceros time to move on, and to trust to meeting
him in more favourable country. At first the track
showed that he could not decide whether to go straight
away or whether to refuse to leave the advantage the thick
scrub gave, or, thirdly, whether to wait in the path and
fight. This, of course, necessitated extreme caution, but
at last after some two or three hours we emerged from the
scrub and re-entered the forest. Soon afterwards we saw
a few scanty drops of blood, and Malias was much

reassured thereby. Then the rhinoceros took a definite line across country, and at about one o'clock we came to a small stream that it had crossed. Here we waited for Pa' Senik and the men. When they came up they informed us that we were close to the place where Japaringonen had been killed by this animal. After our meal and a cigarette we pushed on again. Before we had gone another mile a snort and rush showed that we had come up with "old *kramat*" again. His behaviour was most extraordinary: from a distance perhaps of some fifty yards away he charged headlong towards us, passing within fifteen or twenty yards of our position. The sound of saplings crashing and breaking, and creepers rending and snapping, filled the place and testified to the enormous bulk and power of the animal. When he had gone fifty yards behind us, he stopped. Here he paused a few seconds, and then with a snort charged back again at an acute angle to the last direction he had taken. He again passed close enough for us to catch a glimpse of him and to see the bushes moving, but not close enough for one to aim with any certainty. Again he stopped, paused, and then with a snort came back on another line that passed us no nearer than the others. What his intention was I cannot say; whether it was that he could not discover our exact position, or whether his wounds had knocked the inclination for real fighting out of him, I do not know; but I am inclined to believe that he did not want to fight, and think that it was what tacticians term a demonstration. He made five such rushes, but no time did he come close enough for me to take more than a snap-shot, and this, thinking that I should require my cartridges for close quarters, I refused to risk.

At last, however, Malias pointed out a stationary black object some twenty-five or thirty yards away. I could see that it was the rhinoceros, but could not make out what part of him it was. Nevertheless, thinking that I might not get a better opportunity, I fired; in another wild charge he rushed headlong through the forest straight away from us, bursting or tearing a path through every obstacle. Again we followed, and after another mile came up with him for the fourth time, when, after a series of similar demonstrations, he gave me a clear shot at twenty-five yards at the base of his spine. He again went straight away; but the blood showed that both this bullet and the one before had taken effect, and when we came on a place where the poor brute had lain down we made certain of him. Though we followed the tracks until four o'clock we failed, however, to come up with him again. It was now within two hours of sundown, and as we had only a rough idea of where we were, it was necessary to think of getting back. Before we left the tracks we marked a tree or two, so as to be able to start the next morning where we now left off, and then made our way in the direction of Hussein's house, which we reached before sun-set. The actual distance we had followed the rhinoceros all day was not more than fifteen miles (from point to point it was perhaps seven); but these miles had been covered step by step—carrying the weight of a heavy rifle under a tropical sun, bent double to evade the thorns that clutched at everything, stepping delicately to avoid the dead leaves that crackled underfoot; and, with every nerve on the alert, we did not estimate the distance by miles.

Early the next morning we went back at the spot where we had left the tracks the evening before. We found that the rhinoceros had lain down and slept the night not far from where we had left him: he had eaten but very little, and had not wallowed. He had now, of course, many hours' start of us, and we had to make such speed as we could in order to overtake him, and yet to exercise extreme caution that we might not stumble upon him and be charged unawares. We had to move in perfect silence or we should not come up with him, and at the same time we had to keep our eyes on the tracks step by step. The difficulty of following the tracks even of a rhinoceros is extraordinary. One would imagine

that an animal weighing perhaps two tons, and whose
footprints are nearly twelve inches across, would be easy
to follow; but time after time we had to stop, retrace
our steps, or make a cast through the forest. On hard
dry ground covered with leaves only the barest impression was left: we had often to lift the leaves to look for
the mark of a toe-nail dinting perhaps the undermost leaf
to the ground. Often, too, the tracks appeared to go
straight on, and it might not be for some time that we
found that we were on old tracks and must turn back.
Traces of blood were extremely scanty, and it was only
from time to time that one or the other of us would
silently point to a single drop of clotted blood on a leaf
or twig. The difficulty, too, and the physical exertion of
moving in silence through the thick vegetation of the
forest, must be undergone to be fully realised. While
one hand is perhaps disengaging a thorny creeper from
the shoulder, the other hand holding a heavy rifle, and
one foot suspended in the air to avoid some crackling
leaf, every muscle of the body is called upon to maintain
the equilibrium. Moving thus in silence, we saw in the
forest animals that would otherwise have been alarmed
long before we came in sight. Mousedeer repeatedly
allowed us to approach within a few feet of them; twice
we got among a sounder of sleeping pig before they
awoke; and once an agitated tapir dashed across the
track only a few yards away from me. A danger, however, there is of this silence. Malias and I had followed
a wrong track for a few yards before we discovered our
mistake; retracing our footsteps, we saw that beside the
path lay a green puff-adder còiled and ready to strike,
and that each of us had unwittingly set foot down within
six inches of its head. It was slowly thus that we made
our way, and it was past one o'clock on an intensely hot
day that we came up with the rhinoceros again. I then
saw him some thirty yards away standing broadside on
to us. His head was hidden by foliage, and it was impossible to say at which end of the formless mass it was.

I made the inevitable mistake, and a careful aim at the spot where I imagined the heart to be only hit him far back in the quarters.   As on the preceding day, he rushed away on receiving the bullet, and the country in which the tracks took us was extremely dangerous.   This was another clearing made for the cultivation of hill-rice such as that we had passed through the day before: but this was younger, and therefore worse.   That of yesterday was some two years old, and through it one could see a few yards; this was only seven months old, and an object a foot away was invisible.   Of course, I repeat, no sane man would seek an encounter with any dangerous animal in either place.   But the younger growth is really wonderful: it is a mass of tangled vegetation—for here the giant *lalang* grass, that grows some six feet high, fights for its life with the horrible creepers that bind and choke it, and with the scrub-bushes that send their roots down into the earth to undermine it.   Here, like wrestlers, they strain and pull, and the victory is to the one that can endue the longest.   The loser dies, and giant grass, creepers, and scrub fight interlocked at death-grips.

Through this almost impenetrable thicket the rhinoceros made his way, and, to use a homely simile, his track looked like a double cutting on a railway line.   It was necessary, therefore, to give him time to quit such desperate country, for in a patch of such wide extent a detour was out of the question.   We therefore sat down for half an hour and then followed on; but soon we found that what appeared to be a double cutting had developed into something more like a tunnel, through which it was necessary to make our way on hands and knees.   It was impossible to see more than a foot in any direction, impossible to stand, and, except with one hand on the ground, impossible to fire.   I therefore again gave the order to retreat, and for another half hour we waited on the edge of the thicket.   Then we heard an uproar among some monkeys on the far side of the scrub.   "They are chattering at the rhinoceros," I said.

"Let us see," said Malias. And on we went again.
Happily the tracks led straight on through the scrub; and
as there was none of the twisting and turning we had
met the day before, we were emboldened by the calls we
had heard from the monkeys, and pushed on in hopes
that the rhinoceros was now in more open country.
Suddenly a few heat drops, generated from a steaming
ground and a blazing sky, fell pattering around and on us.
Malias at once seized my coat and looked on every side
with perturbation. *"Hujan panas,"* he whispered, for
"hot rain" is the sign of a bloody death.

"Perhaps," I suggested, "it is a sign that the rhinoceros will die to-day."

"That is not certain," he retorted. "It may be the
rhinoceros that will die, and perhaps it may not."

And then he added, very slowly and sententiously,
"It is the Malay custom to be very careful when this
happens."

His nerve seemed shaken for the moment, and more
carefully than ever we crept along on hands and knees.
The heat in the open scrub was terrific. The tangled
vegetation we were crawling through afforded our spines
and necks no protection from the sun, and the air was
bound a prisoner by the giant grass and bushes that
throttled one another. Waves of heat were rising from
the sweltering ground in quivering lines, and more than
half we breathed there was steam: this filled the throat,
but, though they hammered against our ribs, could not
fill the lungs. The perspiration dripped from every pore
of the body, but the mouth and tongue were clogged with
drought, and salt with moisture from our lips; and worse
than anything else was the drumming of the nearly bursting blood-vessels behind our ears and temples. Time
after time I was deceived into thinking that I heard the
rhinoceros move.

At last we reached the edge of the forest in safety,
and threw ourselves down in utter exhaustion. We lay
there gasping until the other men came up with us, and

then found that the help we had expected from them had failed us. They produced sandwiches, cigarettes, my small flask of neat whisky, but for some extraordinary reason had forgotten the bottle of cold tea. I could not touch the whisky, and without something to drink it was impossible to eat or smoke. The only thing to do was to go on. On, on, and on therefore we pushed, without finding a drop of water to alleviate our thirst and to enable us to touch the mockery of refreshment we carried.

There was not a sign of the big beast that led the way, except the three round dents that marked his toes, and occasionally in softer ground the impression of his sole. At last, at four o'clock, as we were thinking of giving up for the day, we came on a path that Malias recognised as one leading to the village of Pinjih. We therefore waited for the other men, and after marking the place, made our way to the village. There we arrived at sunset, and a house was quickly put at our disposal. Then after a swim in the river, rice, grilled chicken, chillies, and salt fish—all that the village could offer—were ready for us.

Malias was openly despondent. Had not every one failed in this quest? And how was it that bullets that would kill an elephant dead on the spot failed to knock this animal over? The Jin was playing with us: we were safe from his displeasure perhaps, but it did not seem that he had any intention of allowing us to kill the rhinoceros. Though Pa' Senik was more cheerful, his prognostications were even worse. The animal, he said, was making for a hill called Changkat Larang, and if it once reached that spot its wounds would immediately be healed. We had left the tracks within three miles of the hill, and our only chance was to come up with it the next day before it reached this hill of healing. Both were so down-hearted that I reminded them of the portent of the "hot rain," and suggested that the rhinoceros had returned to die by the stream and the village from which he had taken his name for so many years. But without avail. Both shook their heads in doubt, and I went to sleep, to hope for better luck the next day.

By sunrise the next morning we had finished our meal of rice and chicken, and set off to pick up the tracks of the day before. We were soon on the ground, and then proceeded in the same order as on the two previous days. Soon we came on the spot where "old *kramat*" had spent the night. He had fed heavily on lush grass and young shrubs, and had wallowed for some hours. This was bad, very bad indeed, for the night before he had barely eaten a few mouthfuls, and had not wallowed at all; and now it seemed as though he were better and stronger after the second day than he had been after the first. Pa' Senik, who was close behind, came up, shook his old head, and intimated that he had told us overnight that if the rhinoceros reached Changkat Larang his wounds would heal: the hill was now not far off, and then——I cut him short, and, picking up the tracks, pressed on. In a few minutes a rush some twenty yards ahead of us showed that our quarry was again afoot. This was worse than ever. Hitherto every time that we had come up with him we had managed to catch a glimpse of him; but now he would not let us come within sight of him, and I felt inclined to give up hope. To-day was my last chance, for I had to be back at my head-quarters the next morning. The brute was stronger and better than he had been the day before, and now he refused to allow us to come to close quarters, and—climax of despair—he was heading straight for Changkat Larang.

One ray of hope remained. The rush we had heard seemed but a short one—seemed, I say; for even so huge a brute as an elephant, after its first startled rush, can settle down to so silent a walk that a man may be pardoned for imagining it to be standing still, whereas it is really rapidly putting a lot of ground between it and its pursuer. Hoping, therefore, that the rhinoceros might really have remained stationary after the rush we had heard, I moved as rapidly and as noiselessly as possible round to the right, in the hope of cutting him off, and after a detour of a few hundred yards, had the extraordinarily good luck of finding myself close behind him. The wind was in my favour, and I was able to get within some twenty-five yards. He was looking down the path he had come up, and I had made an exact semicircle in my detour, and was diametrically behind him. I had misjudged him when I had thought a few minutes before that he would not allow me to come to close quarters, for now his every attitude meant fighting. Hustled and harried for the last two days, poor brute, he could stand it no longer, and was now determined to run no farther. Malias, crouching close on my heels, urged me in whisper to shoot at the leg, and aim to break the bone. But I hoped for a better chance than that, and squatted down to await developments. Then a slant of our wind must have reached the rhinoceros, for he very slowly began to slew round. The huge hideous head lifted high in the air and swung slowly over the shoulder, the dumpy squat horn showed black, the short hairy ears pricked forward, and a little gleam showed in the small yellow eyes; the nostrils were wrinkled high, and the upper lip curled right back over the gums, as he sought to seek the source of the tainted air. Pain and wrath were pictured in every ungainly action and hideous feature. High in the air he held his head as he turned round, high above us as we squatted close to the ground; and his neck was fairly exposed to a shot, but I waited to let him show yet more. Then—how slowly it was I cannot say, but very slowly it seemed—his shoulder swung round, and at last I was afforded a quartering shot at the heart and lungs. I fired, and knew that he was mine. A short rush of some thirty yards, and he fell in an open grassy glade, never to rise, and never again to see Changkat Larang.

Though he could not rise, the poor brute was not dead; and as he moved his head lizard-like from side to side in his efforts to raise his ponderous body, he seemed more like a prehistoric animal than one of our times. The head of a lizard it was exactly, and the body of an elephant was joined on to it. Another shot killed it. When the other men came up, the two local Malays were wildly excited. Malias was nearly off his head. He examined the feet whose tracks we had followed so long and so far, the skin, the head, the teeth that killed Japaringonen and the two other men who had died so long ago that their names had been forgotten, the horn that was said to carry the famous blue which cured Kanda Daud. He touched and handled every part of the animal, and returned to touch and handle it with fresh interest— in fact, he behaved exactly like a terrier puppy with its first rabbit. But old Pa' Senik, when he had uttered a short charm over the body to preserve us all from the consequences of its death, stood back a little space and looked on with folded arms. It was not in the company of such mere mortals as Malias and myself that he had been hunting: for the last three days he had been in the mighty presence of the Earth Spirit, who step for step had been with us in the forest. In Pa' Senik's eyes the day's success was the result of the promise made when Che Mat had been possessed, and only a line at the corner of his mouth and a gleam in his old eyes showed the grim satisfaction with which he viewed the victim of the compact.

After a short rest I sent Pa' Senik and the two Malays to the house where we had slept three nights before to fetch my servants, my clothes, and my camera, and ordered Malias to follow me to Pinjih village to get some pack-elephants to carry the rhinoceros' head and feet.

It was with the greatest difficulty that I induced Malias to leave the body.

"Some one must stay and look after it," he said.

"But it's dead now," I objected.

"Yes," he said with firm conviction; "but it was dead after Kanda Daud shot it. and it came to life again and nearly killed him."

And he then asked to be allowed to stay behind, to shoot it again if it showed any symptoms of returning vitality.

It was with some trouble that he was finally persuaded to come away; but not even then would he move until he had hacked one of the hind-feet nearly off.

"If he does go, he will go lame," he said.

We found Pinjih village seething with excitement. My shots had been heard, and the entire population was waiting for news of an event that meant more to the villagers than it is easy to realise.

By noon I had collected three elephants, and on the arrival of the men with my camera and impedimenta we returned to take some snap-shots (which were not a success), and to cut off the head and feet of the rhinoceros.

Between two upright posts at the shoulder and fore-feet I made out its height to be 5 feet 5½ inches. I am certain, however, that the measurement did not do it justice: it had fallen in a cramped position, and it was impossible to stretch it out. Measurement between uprights is the best way of taking records of dead game, but it is a poor way: one can imagine the difference between measuring a horse standing up and a horse lying down. When I caught my second glimpse of the animal, it appeared to be nearly seven feet high. I am sure that it was but little short of six feet high.

The horn was disappointingly small, the more so because it had been said to be so extraordinarily fine. It was a short shapeless lump, only some seven or eight inches high; but I think that it had once been much longer. The tip had been broken off, and the base was much worn and splintered.

Through the crowd that collected round us as we cut off the feet, a lame old man pushed his way up to the headman, who brought him up to me and explained that this was one of the rhinoceros' victims. He was Kanda Daud, to whom I have already referred, and the story of his adventure was briefly as follows: Years before, "in

the days when the white man had not yet come into the
country," and when he was a young man, he had felled a
patch of forest in the Pinjih valley to make a plantation
of hill padi. The crop was nearing the harvest, and he
was sitting at night with his gun to keep away the pigs
and deer, when this rhinoceros came out of the forest
and fed close up to his house. He fired, and heard the
brute rush away and fall at the forest's edge. The next
morning he went with a youngster to hack off its horn,
when the animal threw off the semblance of death and
charged him. He fell, and the rhinoceros did not gore
him with his horn, as is the custom of the African animal,
but bit him with its enormous razor-edged teeth. The
boy ran away, and in a few minutes returned with some
ten men, whose approach frightened the brute. Kanda
Daud appeared to be dead when they picked him up and
took him to his house. Though the wretched man had
been bitten in almost every part of his body, he recovered,
and as he limped beside me to see the dead body of his
old enemy, he showed me the cicatrices of his wounds.
The calf and the fleshy part of the thigh of the left leg
had atrophied; they had been bitten away; and the ball
of his toe reached the ground in a painful hobble. On
his ribs and under one arm were great drawn lines of
hideous white, such as one associates with the idea of a
scald. The muscles of an arm had disappeared, and
there only remained a bone. It was marvellous that he
had recovered; but when I told him so he replied that
when he was picked up and taken home, his hands and
arms were found to be stained with an indigo blue.
This was the dye of the rhinoceros' horn, which he had
seized with both hands in his efforts to free himself from
the brute as it held him the ground. His hands and arms
had been carefully washed, and the stained water was the
only medicine that he was given. Part he drank, and
with part his wounds were washed. It was indeed a
marvellous recovery. And the poor old man talked ex-
citedly, as he limped along, of the result he expected from

getting more of this remedy: perhaps with a further supply a skilled pawang might make the flesh grow on his withered limbs. Didn't we think so? A very little had served to heal his wounds, surely an unlimited supply would bring a perfect cure. For more than twenty—perhaps thirty—years the old man had been waiting for this event, and at last the day had come. Bitter was his disappointment, and pitiable to see, when he reached the carcass, for no amount of rubbing and washing would yield a sign of the desired blue from that black stumpy horn. The Malays stood back and whispered in little groups. All felt sorry for him, but it was difficult to know what to do. Finally I touched him on the shoulder.

"The rhinoceros is very old, Kanda Daud", I said, "and now in his old age the blue stain he carried has disappeared."

He stood up and looked at me in silence for a moment. "And I am very old too," he said; and then he added as he turned away, "and now I shall never recover."

A DEER-DRIVE.

IN the corner of many Malay houses one may often see a curious bundle of rattan. It is coiled into great loops in the manner that a sailor coils a rope, and the inquirer is told that it is a *sidin*. If he inquires further, he will be told that it is used in deer-drives; and if he is still curious, it may be exhibited for his inspection. The great ring of rattan opens out into a straight line some twenty-five or thirty yards long. The main line is of plaited and twisted rattans, and is about an inch thick, and from this line hangs a series of nooses. Each noose is made of three fine rattans plaited together, and forms, when spread, a circle about three and a half feet in diameter. They hang from the main line at intervals of eighteen inches, and therefore overlap considerably; the catch is the ordinary running knot. In a deer-drive the *sidins* are stretched in a long line in some favourably situated part of the forest, and the deer are driven in that direction. The number of *sidins* used depends, of course, upon the locality. Ten are generally enough, for they form, when tied end to end, a line nearly 300 yards long, with 600 nooses; but sometimes twenty; or even thirty, are used.

The Malays use *sidins*, rather than more sporting methods, in a deer-drive for many reasons. The forest is often a featureless wilderness of trees and undergrowth, in which an unbroken line of nooses some hundreds of yards long has a better chance of stopping a deer than a few men armed with guns; and two or three guns is generally all that a village can produce. Then the undergrowth beneath the trees is almost always so dense that a deer may pass unseen between two men not more than fifty yards apart, and under the most favourable circumstances it is rare to get more than a snapshot.

A deer-drive with *sidins* is perhaps the favourite form of sport among the Malays; and if deer are known to be in any patch of forest that can be beaten out, a suggestion to have a hunt is generally welcomed. Rusa (the sambar deer of India) are fairly common everywhere throughout the peninsula, and often do considerable damage by their depredations in the rice-fields when the crops are ripening.

Let me describe an imaginary deer-drive. For the past two or three nights a couple of deer have been feeding in the rice-fields, and lying up by day in an adjoining patch of secondary forest. The injured cultivators go to the village headman, who at their suggestion decides to have a deer-drive on the following day. Messages are sent from mouth to mouth on all sides, and before many hours elapse every one knows that he is expected to be at the headman's house the next morning at daybreak, and to bring his *sidin*, if he chances to have one, with him.

While still a star or two shines whitely through the grey morning light, and while the night-jars are still wheeling and calling te-te-goh, te-te-goh, the Malays leave their homes and begin to gather round the headman's house.

Those that own *sidins* bring them slung on their shoulders, and every man is armed. The majority have spears, others carry a dagger or *kris* in their belt, and the remainder have the long-bladed knife called a *parang*. This last is the everyday companion of the Malay, and he carries one from the day that he can toddle, gradually emerging from the state of cutting himself with it to that of cutting everything else. With a sharpened edge nearly two feet long, it is equally useful for cutting down a small tree or for putting an edge to a copper fish-hook or extracting a thorn. It will slice a man nearly in two, and more than one tiger has been brought in for the

Government reward by a Malay who had nothing else
with which to defend himself.

The gathering increases momentarily, and there is a
violent barking and yapping of the headman's house-
dogs as some strange dogs are brought forward and tied
up to separate trees. Unhappy-looking brutes are these
last—small yellow animals, with sharp noses and prick
ears: they are, I believe, direct descendants of the wild
dog. They are generally much better than they look, and
the most insignificant in appearance has perhaps a reputation that extends throughout the district. While some
men are overhauling the *sidins* for flaws, a small circle
surrounds a man who is loading his muzzle-loader. The
only other men with guns are an old *haji*,[1] who has a
snider, and the headman's son, who carries a double-
barrelled shot-gun.

The old man squatting at the foot of a coconut-tree
and tracing figures in the sand with his finger is the
pawang, on whose skill the success of the drive will
depend. In addition to a belief that certain animals are
protected by attendant spirits, the Malays believe that the
death of any animal is avenged by influences known as
bahdi, jinggi, and *genaling.* The *bahdi* have, they
believe, the power of bringing sickness, blindness, or
madness upon the hunter, and an attack of fever after
unwonted exertion in a malarial forest is always ascribed
to them. The *jinggi* can let the deer pass by the un-
witting hunter in the form of a mouse or attack him in
the form of a tiger. They can also give the hunter the
appearance of the hunted, and thus expose him to the
fire of his friends. The *genaling* can kill the hunter outright; but being the strongest, are perhaps the most
merciful, for I have never heard of a death being laid to
their door. With such dangerous enemies to combat, the
old pawang has no light task, for on him falls all the
responsibility for any accident or mischance, unless he

---

[1] One who has performed the pilgrimage to Mecca.

can shift the blame on to the injured party. This, however, let it be said to his credit, he can generally do satisfactorily.

The old man is working out with lines and crosses a calculation, based principally upon the day of the month, which will show from which direction danger may be expected. Beside him lies a *sidin*, known as "the head of the *sidins*." It is supposed to have a peculiar efficacy, and may be distinguished from the others by its being ornamented with the skull of some such bird as a kingfisher or a woodpecker, and with a bit of some curiously twisted root or creeper.

By the time that the sun is above the horizon two men, who had been told off overnight to examine the rice-fields for fresh deer tracks, return and report that the deer have fed again in the crops, and that, as on the preceding days, they have entered the patch of secondary forest. where they almost certainly now are. The headman comes down from his house, and there is a general discussion as to the direction of the intended drive. The arguments show that the ground in which the deer are supposed to be is of considerable extent, and that it is bounded on one side by the rice-fields and on the opposite side by a deep swamp. On the south it runs into a narrow neck, which connects it with a limitless expanse of virgin forest. The ground can be driven in two ways, either directly away from the rice-fields and towards a row of *sidins* erected alongside the swamp, or the line of the drive may be parallel to the rice-fields, in which case the *sidins* would be set up at the "neck."

The pawang takes everything into consideration,—his experience of former drives in the same place, the direction of the wind, and his own forecast regarding the side from which danger may come,—and decides to have the line of *sidins* at the neck.

The word to start is given, each man shoulders his heavy coil of nooses, the headman leads the way, and in irregular single file the party follows him. The village

through which their path leads at first is not what we
mean by a village in English. Our interpretation of the
word is a collection of houses. The Malay village is a
collection of holdings. Each man owns his two or three
acres of land, in the middle of which his house stands;
and as the holdings generally extend in a narrow strip
along a river bank, a village containing only a hundred
houses is perhaps two miles long. Each man's holding is
more or less thickly planted with coconut-trees and with
a somewhat miscellaneous assortment of fruit-trees, round
the roots of which grows a neglected crop of grass where
goats and an occasional sheep find pasturage. The only
public buildings in the village are the *musjid*, which is
the property of the community, and the school, which is
the property of the Government. The nearest police-
station is thirty miles away.

When the path leaves the village it emerges upon the
level and scientifically irrigated rice-fields, and continues,
a foot or so above the level of the liquid mud, along one
of the innumerable little embankments that criss-cross in
every direction, and serve the double purpose of retaining
the vivifying water and of forming boundaries between
one man's crop and another.

There are no houses in the rice-fields, but here and
there are rude shelters consisting of a few bamboos and
palm leaves strung together, which afford a certain
amount of protection to workers during the heat of the
day, and which are useful when it is necessary to protect
the ripe crops from the depredations of wild pig and
occasional deer.

The two men who had found the fresh deer tracks
earlier in the morning point out silently and from afar
where the deer had entered the rice-fields, where they had
fed, and where they had re-entered the forest. The path
now skirts along the edge of the forest, and as the deer
may be lying up within a stone's throw of the party, no
one talks above a whisper. The men soon arrive at the
neck between the secondary forest and the virgin forest,

and here the strictest silence is enjoined. The pawang points out the line in which he wishes the *sidins* to be erected, and as quietly as possible some men clear a track a foot wide along this line. They have to take care that, while cutting away as many branches, creepers, and rattans as will allow the *sidins* to hang freely, they do not cut away so much as to make the nooses conspicuous. This is soon done, and all stand aside. The pawang picks up "the head of the *sidins*," slings it over his right shoulder, and looks round for a suitable tree to which to tie it. Selecting one on the line that has just been cut, he chips off a small piece of the bark with his knife. The bark falls to the ground on its face—that is, with the inner side downwards — and the tree is a lucky one. (Were the bark to fall on its back another tree would be chipped until a lucky one is found.) Taking care, then, not to stand on the roots of the tree or in its shadow, he graps it with his left hand at about the height of his head, and in a rapid mutter, with here and there a word thrown in in a louder tone, he makes this petition. The words cannot be distinguished by the listener, but the following is a literal translation: —

> "Hail! all hail!
>   Mother to the earth!
>   Father to the sky!
>   Brother to the water!
> I crave permission to enter on your domain,
> And to tie my nooses to this tree."

This preliminary invocation is over in a few seconds. The pawang then opens the strings that bind the still coiled-up nooses, takes hold of the rope at the end of the main line of the *sidin*, and brings this rope round the tree at about five feet from the ground, so that it will be ready to be tied when he has finished the next invocation. Then in the same guttural tones he begins the charm against untoward influences. It is of four lines and in rude verse, being the only one of this collection that is so. As is always the case in Malay verses, the

first two lines mean little, and are only there to rhyme
with the last two. In such manner does the artless
Malay evade a difficulty that poets of more civilised
countries struggle to surmount.

> "Sirih unta pinang unta
> Mari tanam tepi blukar
> Hantu buta malang buta
> Jerat aku katakan akar."

The lines may be thus translated:—

> Betel leaf, Camel, Betel nut, Camel.
> Come, let us plant at the edge of the young forest.
> Evil spirit be blind! Evil influence be blind!
> Say that my nooses are but forest creepers!

The pawang then ties the rope round the tree, and leaves
the indefinite to address the *jinggi, bahdi,* and *genaling,*
who are more particularly interested in the work that is
toward.

> "O evil spirits!

> Down with your powers, may my power defeat them!
> Down with your charms, may my charms defeat them!
> One hundred and ninety charms!
> Move ye from hence!
> Go to birdless forests,
> To fishless seas,
> To rockless mountains,
> To grassless plains!
> Go in the name of Allah."

The pawang now opens the first three nooses of the *sidin,*
and moves back a pace or two from the tree. He calls
on the deer—

> "Hail! all hail!
> Ye that trample the earth!
> Ye that pass like lightning-flash!
> If ye pass the nooses' farthest end,
> Ye fall into the deepest seas;
> And if ye pass the nearer end
> Ye reach the great volcano's fire.
> Take ye the broad road by the high land!
> Here is the way for ye to follow
> To return to the fold of *Nabi Sleman.*"

IN MALAY FORESTS

This last line is illustrative of the Malays' belief in an animal's sanctuary, the fold of their master *Nabi Sleman* (King Solomon, who is one of the prophets of the Muhammadan religion). Within this sanctuary only animals that have obeyed the laws of their kind are admitted. It is imagined that the deer which live close to the habitations of human beings, and which feed on the crops of man, are trespassers, and have done wrong by wandering too far from their proper home. By so doing wrong they have forfeited in part, but only in part, the protection of forest spirits. It follows, therefore, that the deer which frequent the haunts of men are an easier quarry than the purely forest-dwelling deer; and it is the former, for obvious reasons connected with the accessibility and nature of the ground, that are more often caught. A further development of this idea of wrong-doing is seen in the case of man-eating tigers and crocodiles, which are imagined, by their unnatural appetites, to have put themselves outside the pale of God's creatures, and to be surrendered by the spirits to traps and snares that animals which have not so transgressed would detect.

But to return to our deer. They are warned of the perils of fire and flood that lie to right and left of the only way back to the fold of Nabi Sleman. Across this way lies the long line of nooses, and they are to return—if they can.

When this invocation to the deer is concluded, the strength of the knot and rope is tested by a strong pull, and lastly the *sidins* are addressed—

> "Hail! all hail!
> Thou long and trembling line!
> If two deer pass, hold thou two;
> If only one pass, hold thou him;
> Be he big or small, hold him!
> And I will speak good, not ill, of thee.
> If thou breakest, I will not mend thee;
> If thou art lost, I will not seek thee".

Ptu—ptu—ptu. The pawang spits three times on the
knot, and rapidly unrolls the rest of the *sidin*. Every
one gives a long breath, for the ceremony, which has
lasted two or three minutes, is over. The extremity of
the *sidin* is tied to a convenient tree on the line that has
been cut through the forest, and another bundle of nooses
is brought up to the pawang, who unrolls it and ties one
end of it to the tree where the first *sidin* stops, and continues his way along the line. Where the second ends
the third begins, and in a few minutes the *sidins* are
transformed from a number of circular bundles of rattans
into a continuous line of nooses some hundreds of yards
long, and stretching right across the narrow "neck" that
lies between the ground to be driven and the virgin
forest. The series of *sidins* which form this line of
nooses are independent of one another, for each is
supported by the trees to which it is tied at either extremity, and in no way by the adjacent *sidins*. Thus, if
any one is torn down by a deer, the displacement does
not affect the others. To prevent any sagging, the long
line of nooses is propped up between the supporting trees
by forked saplings. The main line is about five feet
from the ground, and the bottom of the nooses is at the
height of one's knee, or about eighteen inches above the
ground. While tying to a tree the end of the last *sidin*,
the pawang makes the following petition: —

> "O Tejah-tree at the head of my *sidin!*
> O Casuarina-tree at its foot!
> Remain ye here, I go to hunt
> The deer, the raiats [1] of Nabi Sleman".

The preparations for the drive are now complete, and the
men are divided into three groups—one to drive, another

---

[1] The derivation of this word shows how apt its use is in
this connection. Yule and Burnell's 'Glossary of Anglo-Indian
Words' has the following: "Ryot. Arabic *ra'iyat* (from *ra'a*, to
pasture), meaning originally, according to its etymology, 'a herd
at pasture', but then 'subjects' collectively. It is by natives used
for a 'subject' in India".

lot to "stop" along the edge of the swamp to turn the
deer in the unlikely event of its attempting to break away
in that direction, and the third lot to watch the *sidins*.

The men told off to drive reach their places and as
soon as the line has been formed they advance upon the
sidins with shouts and yells. When the pawang hits
upon the fresh deer tracks, he lets loose the dogs that
have hitherto been in leash, muttering as he slips them—

> "Go, my dogs! Si Panji Lela! Si Panji Ladang!
> Go hunt ye the raiats of Nabi Sleman,
> Who trample the earth, who pass like lightning-flash,
> Wearing earrings of gold and waistlets of gold,
> Who wait outside the fold of Nabi Sleman".

When the dogs give tongue, the owner shouts a long
tu-u-u-u to encourage them, adding under his breath the
mystic words—

> *Telekul lam telekul*,
> This is in the hands of Raja Una.

(Raja Una is the Nimrod of Malay mythology.) Soon
the dogs are in full cry, and after a few minutes of tremendous excitement, during which the deer attempts to
break out, but is judiciously turned by one of the stops,
the hunted animal, with the dogs close upon its heels,
dashes into one of the nooses. The *sidin* for some yards
at either side is torn from the slender saplings that support it, and gives to the impetus until the strain is felt at
the two extremities where it is tied to the trees. It then
suddenly tautens and throws the deer down. The nearest
of the ambushed watchers runs out, hamstrings the deer,
and, if he happens to be a *haji*, cuts its throat, repeating
as he does so a verse of the Koran; but if not, with that
callous indifference to pain in animals so marked in all
Asiatics, he allows the animals to live until a *haji* comes
up. But in the meanwhile he hastily and roughly replaces the *sidin*, which has been disarranged in the
struggle, calls off the dogs, and quickly goes back to his
hiding-place, in the hope that there may be another deer
in the ground. The stricken animal is not released from

the fatal noose that holds it; but it rarely struggles after being hamstrung, apparently giving itself up to death.

While this is going on at the *sidin*, a shot is heard from the beaters' side, and before long they come up, and the drive is over. Questions and answers are shouted on every side. The success that has attended the nooses is equalled by that of Che Mamud, the headman's son, who was with the beaters, and who has shot a deer that was concealing itself in a thicket in the hope of breaking back through the line. It is lucky that he succeeded in so doing, for his neighbour would probably otherwise have got the bullet, the *jinggi* the blame, and the poor pawang the reproaches. Nothing, however, goes wrong to-day, and the second deer is brought up by four men and deposited close by the still living animal. The throat of the latter is then cut with all ceremony. The throat of the other deer was cut as soon as it was shot, for fear of its dying of the wound, in which case it would not have been lawful food for Muhammadans. It is interesting, as showing the distinction between the Malays' present religion and their pre-Muhammadan superstition, that this ceremony is not performed by the pawang.

There is now an interval for rest and refreshment, and while the cigarettes and betel-leaf pass round, the incidents of the day and the weight of the deer are discussed. The man who turned the first deer and the man who hamstrung it tell their story with many details and some improvements, and Che Mamud shows them all how he saw and aimed at and shot his deer. Every one congratulates the pawang, to whom the credit of the success is considered to be entirely due; and the enthusiastic or ingenious compare the present success, with obvious deductions, to the failure that attended the efforts of his rival in the neighbouring village on the occasion of the last deer-drive undertaken there. The congratulations generally take the characteristic Malay form of an address to the speaker's nearest neighbour, in a tone of voice that is most obviously meant for the

general ear, and especially for the ear of the subject of
the eulogy. It is a somewhat artificial method, but none
the less sweet; and really to-day the pawang is to be
congratulated, for mishaps are far from rare. Often the
deer breaks back or escapes at the side. Sometimes the
noose is old and rotten, and snaps; and even when
caught, a hind will, if not quickly hamstrung, extricate
itself by getting its fore-feet into and loosening the catch
round its neck. A stag can rarely get free because of its
antlers.

But to-day everything has gone well, and when all
are sufficiently rested the pawang rises to complete the
ceremonies. He first goes up to Che Mamud and takes
his gun from him; then, going to the deer which Che
Mamud had shot, he stands between its fore-legs and
hind-legs. Holding the gun with his left hand near the
lock and his right hand some way up the stock, he points
the muzzle at the head of the animal. He then slowly
passes the muzzle of the gun over the deer from the
head over the neck, along the back, and down to the
extremity of the hind-legs. When he gets to the end
he carries the gun smartly off from the body, with the
action of one sweeping something away. Going through
this performance three times, he repeats the following
words—

"O   bahdi!
I know whence ye got your powers.
With the fall of Adam your powers began.
I have the means to destroy your powers.

O Malik Zabaniah!

Keeper of the gate of the end of the world,
Open a secret door for me;
I wish to throw away all the powers of *bahdi.*
Open a place from which there is no return;
I wish to throw away all the powers of *genaling.*

Let no claim be made against me,
Against my house and family,
Against my friends and companions,
Or against my hounds. If claim is made,
Thou shalt be doomed to Hell by Allah."

He then, in the low muttering tone he has used throughout, counts one—two—three—up to ten, and then shouts "Lepas!"—"Be free!" Every one echoes the cry, and the deer is now freed from evil influences.

This performance is called *sapu bahdi*, or sweeping away the evil influences, which are supposed to follow the direction of the gun, and be thus expelled from the body of the deer. Until this is done every one takes great care to avoid standing behind the deer, for soon after death the bristles on the back move, and stand on end with the contraction or relaxation of the muscles; and to come within the range of the aim of these bristles, which have the position they assume when the living animal is enraged, is to invite the attacks of the *bahdi*. It is thought that they are waiting to avenge the death of the deer, and that the movement of the bristles is caused by their preparation to leave the body of their protégé: until driven out by the pawang, they will dart out upon any one who passes, and inflict upon him such ill as is in their power. No one, of course, is absolutely safe from them, for they can move freely anywhere, but a position at which the bristles point is one of supreme danger. The pawang then hands the gun back to the owner, proceeds to cut a leafy branch from some tree close by, and lops a second branch, of which he makes a small stake. He goes up to the deer, which still lies with the noose round its neck, and drives the stake into the ground close to its heels. Then standing in the same position to the deer as in the last case, he passes the branch three times over its body in the same way that he had done with the gun before, and using the same words. The ceremony is not, however, complete when he has done this, for he next works the noose from the neck of the deer down over the body and along to the heels of the hind-legs. Here he draws the noose tight again, and then suddenly slips it from the heels on to the stake placed in readiness, upon which he tightens it, and shouts "Lepas!"

The shout is again echoed, and the ceremony complete. The idea is the same as that already mentioned, and the evil influences are imagined to be transferred with the noose to the stake, and there to be localised. The two deer are then cut up, the pawang taking a quarter of each animal, and the rest of the meat being divided among the men: the antlers go to the village headman. Cigarettes and betel-leaf are again produced. After a short rest the fatal noose is slipped from the stake, which is not again touched, the *sidins* are rolled up, and the men return to the village contented.

CROCODILE CATCHING.

We were in the back verandah of my bungalow, and in front of me a Malay squatted on the floor, and beside him were weird implements—some gigantic hooks, four or five coils of rattan, a basket full of odds and ends, and four dead fowls.

Manap was his name,—Abdulmanap bin Muhammad Arsad, to give him his full ceremonial name, and Manap Rimau or Tiger Manap, to give him his distinguishing name. He was a professional crocodile catcher, making his living out of the reward offered by the Government for the extermination of these animals. His skill and extraordinary daring in shooting tigers, also of course for the Government reward, had earned him his *sobriquet*. He lived near the sea, close to the mangrove swamps where his work lay, and had come up to Taiping in answer to a letter from me. As he sat on the floor amid his paraphernalia we talked of indifferent subjects for the period prescribed by etiquette, and then I asked him to show me the lines he had brought with him.

"It is cooler in the house than by the lake," he said, picking up the basket; "shall I bait the hooks here?" He pulled out a knife, with a cutting edge some twenty inches long, and carefully thumbed the blade. "And the Tuan wants to know not only how to catch crocodiles but learn the charms and lore in connection with it? Well, whatever it be that one intends to learn, one must start from the beginning. The boys at school begin with Alif, the first letter of the alphabet, and to catch crocodiles one must know the beginning of crocodiles. The first

crocodile had its origin in the following manner. Siti
Fatimah was the daughter of the Prophet Muhammad,
and Petri Padang Gerinsing was the name of her nurse.
One day the nurse took the sheath of a betel-nut palm-
leaf, and on it moulded some clay into the shape of what
is now a crocodile; and the palm-leaf sheath formed the
belly of the animal. Of the joints of some sugar-cane
she made its ribs. On its head she placed a pointed
stone, and bits of turmeric formed its eyes; its tail was
a leaf of the betel-nut palm. She then tried to give life
to it, but at once it fell to pieces. Twice this happened,
but the third time she prayed to the Almighty God for
life for it, and at once the animal breathed and moved.
For many years it was the plaything of the prophet's
daughter, but at last, with increasing size, it became dis-
obedient, and, Petri Padang Gerinsing being by this time
old and feeble, Siti Fatimah cursed the animal, saying,
'Thou shalt become the crocodile of the sea, nothing
that thou shalt eat shall have taste for thee, and pleasure
and desire shall not be known to thee.' She forthwith
drew out all its teeth and pulled the tonsils from its
mouth, and then to close its mouth drove nails through
from the upper to the lower jaw and from the lower to
the upper jaw. The crocodile was allowed to escape, but
soon found a way to open its jaws, and the nails driven
in by Siti Fatimah have become the teeth that it now
has."

Manap knew the folk-story off by heart, and probably
repeated it in the identical words in which he had first
heard it.

"Now," he continued, "we must remember this: the
eyes of the first crocodile were made of turmeric, and
to this day a crocodile cannot struggle successfully
against a man who knows the properties of turmeric. A
piece of it rubbed on the line weakens the crocodile's
resistance, and if we sprinkle the boat with water in
which it has been soaked the crocodile will not attack

it. Turmeric, if rubbed on a crocodile's head, when the proper charms are repeated, will quickly kill it."

"And this is the way to bait the hooks."

From the coil of rattans he produced one about twenty yards long; a piece of stout native-made rope about three yards long was attached to one end of it, and at the end of the rope was a hook. The fine standards of which the rope was composed were separate from one another, and when the hook was taken by a crocodile they would slip into the interstices of its teeth and afford nothing on to which the animal could bite.

The hook was some seven inches long, and three and a half inches across from point to shank. It was of native-wrought iron, and half-way up the shank on the side towards the point of the hook was a loop. The rope was attached to the hook at this loop; that is to say, it was attached to the hook half-way up the shank, instead of at the end of the shank, as is the case in the ordinary hook. The point of the hook was not barbed, and the end of the shank was sharpened.

The effect of this curious attachment is obvious: supposing the bait to be swallowed, a strain on the line would tend to pull the hook transversely across the gullet of the crocodile; the point of the hook would catch in some part of the throat, and, as soon as this happened, the sharpened shank-point would catch in the opposite side of the throat. An animal thus hooked could only escape by breaking the line.

"I brought fowls for bait because I was hurried. White fowls are the best, for the crocodile can see them farther, but if I had time I would have shot a monkey. There is nothing that a crocodile likes better than one of the grey long-tailed kind. He sees them playing and leaping in the mangrove-trees at high tide, and trooping over the mud flats at low tide: at all times they scream and scold and chatter at him, for between the crocodile and the monkey there is an old standing feud. It is seldom that a crocodile catches a monkey, but when he does it is very sweet to him."

Manap then took a fowl, which he had previously gutted and half-plucked, and eyed it carefully, and, after looking at it and at the hook from every point of view, split it open down the breast. He then buried the length of the hook in the incision he had made. The bend of the hook fitted closely to the curve of the fowl's rump, and the hook's point was hidden under the wing, while the sharpened point of the shank could be felt near the fowl's neck. With some native fibre he then bound the bait as tightly as possible to the hook near the loop, taking great care not to impede the pivotal action of the loop. At the two extremities of the hook he tied the bait on with a much finer fibre, and tied it so that, while the meat could not slip and uncover the hook, yet at a sudden jerk on the main line the slender bands would snap, and the hook-point and shank-point would start from the protecting covering and stand ready to pierce any part of the crocodile's gullet that they might touch.

It did not take him long to bait the four hooks he had brought, and he was then ready to make a start. In the meantime I had explained the reason of my having sent for him. Taiping, the town in which we were, is the capital of the leading native state of the Malay Peninsula, and is happy in the possession of a beautiful public garden and an ornamental lake. Until they were made, their site had been a wilderness of abandoned mine-holes and spoil-banks. The Chinese method of winning alluvial tin ore (the mineral on which the source of the wealth of Perak at present depends) is to open an enormous pit and to bodily remove the earth from it until the substratum that carries the tin ore is exposed. When the mine is worked out and abandoned, there is left a hole which may vary from twenty to sixty feet in depth, and which, in exceptional cases, may extend for half a mile in length and a hundred yards or more in breadth; and beside this gigantic excavation, which

in the rainy climate of the Peninsula quickly fills to the
brim with water, there are mounds of corresponding
extent where the over-burden has been taken out and
deposited. To form the Taiping lake a series of such
abandoned mines were connected, a dam erected at their
lower end, and a small mountain-stream deviated into
the enclosure. Many of the old spoil-banks were left to
form islands in the lake, some of them covered with
closely-mown turf and dotted with palms, while others,
by way of contrast, were allowed to remain under the
wild, rank, luxuriant growth of nature. A circular road,
some two miles long, runs through the gardens and
round the lake, and here the European community rides
and drives in the afternoon; the golf-links are on one
side, and on the other is the race-course. It is not the
sort of place where one would expect to find crocodiles:
one looks for them in tidal rivers or backwaters, but not
in an artificial lake in a public garden. Crocodiles have,
however, the most extraordinary roving propensities, and
often leave their native river to make journeys of many
miles overland. In the interior of Perak they have been
found in abandoned mine-holes so far from any stream
that it is difficult even to guess from which direction
they have wandered, or to tell whether it was by an
accident or design that they have discovered an isolated
pool in a limitless extent of tropical forest. It made it
none the less extraordinary, but it was easy to see how
the crocodiles had got into the Taiping lake: the Squirrel
River, though a small, shallow, gravelly stream, incapable
of affording food or shelter to a crocodile, runs close
by, and lower down joins a tidal river. A crocodile could
make its way either up the channel of the Squirrel or
through the forest on its bank for a distance of some
three miles and it would then be opposite the lake. After
that to travel some two or three hundred yards overland
and to cross a metalled cart-road would afford but little
difficulty. It is easy to see how it is done, but who can
say why it is done? Why should a crocodile leave a

river stocked with food, and explore an utterly unsuit-
able tributary for miles and then wander inland until it
strikes a pool? All that one can say is, that it does; and
it was said that three of these brutes had found their
way into the lake. So long as they confined their attention to the fish, and perhaps an occasional duck, no one
objected to their presence; but when one of them began
to take the sheep off the bank as they came down to
drink, and had even gone so far as to make an attempt
on a cow, it was felt that the brutes ought to be exter-
minated. When children and ayahs were playing at the
water's edge anything might happen. The crocodiles
never came up to sleep on the bank in the heat of the
day, for they had not yet so far made themselves at
home as to dare to expose themselves to the public gaze.
There was therefore no chance of shooting them, and
so I sent for Manap.

When the baits were all ready Manap and I went
down to the lake and pushed off in a Malay dug-out to
reconnoitre. The lake was fairly shallow toward the
sides, but in the centre there were some very deep old
mine-holes, and to approach these pools, which were
almost certainly where the crocodiles were to be found,
one had to pass by one or another of the islands. We
decided to leave a baited line at each entrance between
the islands, and Manap proceeded to unwind one of the
coils of rattan, and straightened out the curves in it until
it followed the canoe, floating on the top of the water
like a yellow snake. Out of his basket he produced a
piece of wood large enough to carry the hook and bait,
and buoyant enough to support its weight above the
level of the water. To this wood he fastened the bait
with some bamboo pegs, and then gently stopped the
canoe at a narrow entrance that led between two islands
to a deep secluded pool. Carefully placing the bait and
its wooden support in the water, so that it floated true
and upright, he muttered the following invocation: —

"Sang Raga, Sang Ragai,
Receive this gift from Siti Fatimah.
If thou receive it not,
The water will choke thee,
The bones of animals will choke thee,
The skin of animals will choke thee,
The blood of animals will choke thee!"

He then picked up the paddle and struck the water three resounding blows with the flat blade. "The crocodile will hear that," he turned to say, "and will come the sooner." He then pushed the bait about two or three yards away from the land so that it floated in open water, and carefully disposed the rattan-line along the bushes that fringed the island in such manner that none of it lay in the water. The end of the rattan was not fastened to anything, and the crocodile was free to carry off hook, line, and bait whither it chose, but withersoever it might go the rattan would float on the water's surface and betray the presence of the crocodile. We placed the three other baits in suitable localities, and then had done all that we could do for the present. The sun was setting, and as he paddled back Manap explained that a gorge-bait is necessary and a snap-bait impossible; even if, as sometimes happens, a crocodile seizes the bait the moment that it is put in the water it must be given time to swallow it, for the hook will find no hold in the bony cartilage of its mouth. What surprised me more than anything was the smallness of the bait; it seemed surprising that any animal addicted to carrying off cattle should deign to notice so insignificant a morsel as a chicken. "They will eat anything," Manap said—"frogs or rats, if they can get nothing bigger."

We were back at the lake a little after sunrise the next morning, and as soon as we got near the place where we had set the first line we saw that the bait had disappeared. Manap's eyes glistened. He put everything in order in the canoe, pushed the boat-pole, his enormous knife, and compendious basket into the bows of the canoe, and paddled gently towards the spot. Suddenly his face fell. "Misbegotten child of Satan!" he muttered. Then he turned to me, "See, it was not a crocodile, but a scoundrelly iguana that has taken the bait. There is the rattan still hanging on the bushes. A crocodile would have swum away to its retreat with line and all before it swallowed the bait." We paddled up and found that the "scoundrelly iguana" had taken the bait out of the water, dragged it a few yards on to the land, and had then stripped the hook clear, leaving nothing but the bare metal. There was nothing to be done but to coil up the rattan and take it away. Most loathsome animals are these iguanas, to call them by their popular name, though "monitor lizard" is their more proper name. They have wonderful powers of scent, and are always to be found near carrion. When sitting up for a tiger over a "kill," one often sees them; they come shambling awkwardly through the undergrowth, and after a careful scrutiny on every side tear huge mouthfuls of flesh out of the carcass.

We found that the three other baits had not been touched. and all that we could do therefore was to objurgate the iguana and go home to hope that a crocodile would soon feel hungry.

On the way back Manap told me the story of the feud between the crocodile and the monkey, to which he had alluded the day before.

"Once the crocodile's wife was very sick, and it seemed as if she would die. The doctors and sorcerers who were attending her declared that the only chance of her recovery was that she should eat a monkey's heart. So the crocodile set off in search of a monkey. He left the sea, and ascended a river until he met a monkey playing on the banks. The crocodile called to him — 'Oh, Sir Monkey! who is the wisest and cleverest doctor in this land?'

"And the monkey of course said 'I am'.

"The crocodile then explained that his wife was very ill, and that he would be for ever grateful if the monkey would prescribe for her. An enormous fee was demanded and agreed to, and the monkey stepped on to the back of the crocodile, who at once swam away down the river.

"When they got out to sea, the crocodile was so pleased with his skill and address in having duped the monkey that he could no longer keep the joke to himself. So he explained to the monkey that he was going to give his wife the monkey's heart to eat.

"The monkey, though he nearly died of fright, showed no outward signs of alarm. On the contrary, he said that his heart was entirely at the disposal of the crocodile's wife, but declared that it was a thousand pities that the crocodile had not explained his purpose earlier, for he had left his heart hanging on a tree on the bank where he had been playing when the crocodile had met him.

"He suggested that they should return to get the heart, and to this the crocodile, who realised that the monkey without its heart was of no use to him, agreed.

"Back they went, therefore, and at the bank where they had first met the monkey pointed out a tree and was allowed to land. He sprang ashore, and climbed to the top of the nearest tree, whence he screamed and chattered his wrath and defiance at the astonished crocodile.

"Ever since then the crocodiles and the monkeys have been enemies, and whenever a family of monkeys see a crocodile, they gather round him and ask him rude questions about his wife, and inquire whether he has lately met many monkeys' hearts hanging on the trees".

The same afternoon, when the heat of the day was over, we went out again and found another bait gone. Rattan-line and all had disappeared, and there was no doubt that it was a crocodile this time. We carefully examined a deep pool that lay close by, and then a second pool, and afterwards a third inner pool from which the others led, and here we found a piece of wood on which the bait had floated. There were marks of crocodile's teeth on it. At the farthest end of the pool we saw the end of the rattan-line floating on the water, and knew that the crocodile was at the other end of it. Decks were cleared for action: Manap was of course barefooted, and I took off my shoes and stockings so that my bare feet might have as good a hold as possible on the smooth bottom of the dug-out. Everything was pushed up into the bows except the barbed spear which was to play an important part in the proceedings. This spear was made on the same principle as a harpoon: a rope is attached to an iron spear-head, into a socket of which a shaft loosely fits; as soon as a blow has been driven home with the spear the shaft detaches from the head, and the striken animal is held by the rope and the barb.

I stood up in the middle of the canoe, and the spear with its coil of rope lay at my feet. Manap sat in the stern paddling gently. As we approached the rattan-line glided away mysteriously. The crocodile had seen us coming, and, unconscious of the fatal rattan that marked its course, had moved into deeper water. I seized the line and pulled in the slack rapidly; in an instant I felt the crocodile on the line, and jerked the line hard so as to snap the slender fibre bands round the bait and to set the hook free to catch in the crocodile's gullet.

Then I held on and drove the hook well home. The curious electric sensation that thrills a line when a fish is on it told that the crocodile was well hooked. At once it moved off into the deep water at the centre of the pool, dragging the canoe after it. The sensation of blind terror that the brute felt at the pain of the hook, and of the force that bound it to it knew not what, was plainly transmitted along the tautened line. For some few yards it sullenly resisted, as I slowly hauled in the line hand by hand. It was numb and sick with fright; but only for a few yards, and then it burst into a wild fury. For years it had been the tyrant of the lake, and, since it had left its native river, had never come into contact with anything stronger and more powerful than itself, and it would not yield the supremacy, much less its life, without a struggle. Wildly lashing the water, it turned to dive to the bottom and to break the rattan-line. I was brought almost to my knees, and had to pay out the line I had pulled in; and it was all that I could do to hold on to the end of the line while the crocodile towed us, canoe and all, towards the second pool. Again I hauled in the line with all my might, and Manap skilfully kept the canoe head on to the crocodile. In the contest I had the great factor in my favour that I had not so much to pull the crocodile up to the canoe as to pull the canoe up to the crocodile; but, on the other hand, my foothold in the unstable cockleshell of a canoe was not always as sure as might be desired. After a lengthy struggle I managed to get the crocodile within three or four yards of the canoe, and in the clear blue water of the pool we could see its yellow length under the canoe fighting and snapping at the line, and turning and twisting as it fought. But the sight of the canoe was too much for it, and with a desperate effort it tore the line out of my grasp until again only the end of it remained in my hands, and continued the struggle in the depths of the pool. Again I pulled in the line, and yard by yard it yielded. This time I saw that I could get it within reach of the canoe, and when it was within three or four yards of us, I handed the line to Manap, in accordance with a preconcerted arrangement, and picked up the spear.

"Stab it in the soft part of the throat, Tuan, or under the stomach, not in the back or sides; and stab quickly, for the line may be partly bitten through." With straining muscles Manap hauled on the line, and, swirling like "Ugudwash, the Sun-Fish," the crocodile came up fighting through the water. As it came to the surface, the water that heaved and rocked to our exertions burst into a fury of foam. In the middle of the turmoil one could see four outspread claws with every nail outstretched, a swinging, lashing tail, and a long flat head with open jaws; all were mixed into a horrid inextricable knot like the drawing of a Chinese dragon on a plate. For a second it straightened, and as it did so Manap hauled its head above the level of the water, and I had a clear view of a whitey-yellow throat, at which I stabbed with all my strength. Who is responsible for the traveller's tale that the crocodile's skin is impervious to steel weapons, and even to bullets? Under my thrust I felt the spear slice its way, parting the soft yielding flesh before it. The spearhead entered up to its hilt, and then I wrenched the shaft free from the socket and seized the coil of rope at my feet. Thus we now had a double hold on the crocodile—Manap holding by the rattanline and hook, and I by the barbed spear and rope. If there had been a storm before, there was a tornado now. At one moment the open jaws would surge out of the broken water, and snap together in unpleasant proximity to our legs; the next moment the heavy tail would swing free of the water, and, lashing through the air with the cut of a flicking whip and the weighted swing of a falling tree, would hit the side of the canoe a blow that made it shiver.

More than once the taloned claws got on the gunwale of the canoe, and it seemed as if in the blind turmoil the brute would get on board. We were both drenched from head to foot in the water that flew in every direction, and the little canoe rocked so violently in the waves of the commotion that there was no small risk of losing one's balance and falling in on top of the raging brute.

"We have him too close to the boat", Manap shouted. "Let out more line!" We slowly paid out the two lines, with the result that not only was the struggle continued at a safer distance. but that the crocodile entangled itself in the lines. As it writhed and twisted and turned on every side and in every direction, the rope caught an outstretched leg on one side, made a loop round it, and then caught in a leg on the other side. As each limb was caught we let out more line, so that, while of course the line was always taut, there was sufficient length of it between the crocodile and ourselves to enable it to entangle itself still further. In a few minutes all four legs were caught, and the animal's struggles became less violent; for though most of its power lay in its tail, yet the legs were needed to balance the body in the water, and without this balance its muscular efforts became ill-directed and uncertain. Twice in its contortions the crocodile slipped the ropes from its legs, and the struggle began anew until they were again entangled. In the restraint of the entangling ropes the crocodile's efforts, though they increased rather than otherwise, had only a diminishing effect, and a few more minutes were all that was necessary. "I think that we can manage now", Manap said. We both pulled our lines in until the crocodile was a few feet from the canoe. "Will you take both lines—one in each hand?" Manap handed his line over to me, and picked up a piece of stout box-cord some three or four yards long with a running noose at one end of it. "Now hold steady with the line on the spear-head and pull hard on the hook-line, so as to bring his head as far as possible above the water". I followed the directions, and as the open mouth appeared above the water Manap dexterously slipped the noose over the animal's upper jaw and pulled it tight, some six inches behind the point of its nostrils. Then, snatching his opportunity, with a quick turn of his wrist he slipped the slack of the cord round and under the lower jaw. By pulling on the cord he could now bring upper and lower jaw together and close the animal's mouth. He then asked me to pull the crocodile closer into the boat. I did so, and for a part of a second the animal lay quiescent, with its mouth bound by the single turn of the cord. Like lightning, Manap in that time had twisted his wrist, and a second circle of the cord lay round the closed jaws. He drew the cord tight, and the teeth of each jaw pressed home into the sockets of the other. "Now pull his head over the gunwale of the canoe". As the long pointed head appeared over the side of the canoe Manap firmly seized it by the nostril. It seemed the maddest thing possible. Here was a brute that a few seconds before had been raging like a devil incarnate. We were still half blinded by the spray it had flung in our faces, and the dug-out still rocked in the waves its wild struggles had raised. For a moment it was still, and a cord was round its mouth; but the cord might so easily slip with any sudden movement either of the crocodile or of ourselves, and there was nothing to show that the struggle was over — far from it. One shuddered to think of what would have happened had the cord slipped. The hand that pressed so confidently on the brute's nostrils would be snapped and seized in a second, Manap would be taken overboard and worried and shaken like a rat by a terrier, and would drown before my eyes in the crocodile's embrace. But no such thing happened. Manap grasped the point of the head with one hand, and with the other rapidly wound the cord round the clenched mouth, ending it off with a half-hitch knot. The extraordinary thing was that while Manap did this, though the time as a matter of fact was only three or four seconds, the crocodile remained comparatively still. The front feet, it is true, clawed wildly at the canoe's side, but they could not reach Manap's hands. The surging, swirling turmoil ceased, and from the moment that the cord had just been slipped round its jaws the crocodile appeared to give up all heart. No sooner was the knot tied round the crocodile's mouth than Manap produced another cord and slipped it over a fore-leg. Pulling the leg up to the animal's side, he then slipped the line over its back and caught up the other fore-leg with it. He pulled the two fore-legs together over the crocodile's back as far as he could, and, passing the cord round them once or twice, tied

it in a knot. With a third cord he noosed and tied together the two hind-legs.

"Sudah", he said. "That is finished".

What he had effected was perfectly marvellous. In
two minutes he had transformed a ravening water-devil
into a trussed-up monstrosity, and his only weapon had
been three pieces of box-cord. The furious monster
that, all open mouth, whirling tail, and outspread claws,
had bent itself into strenuous coils like the Dragon of
China, now lay long and limp beside the canoe. The
tightly closed mouth and the legs tied awkwardly over
its back made it look almost ridiculous. The fight was
over. I held the rattan-line, and Manap paddled the
canoe ashore. The crocodile did not make another effort.
A deep groan burst from its clenched mouth twice or
three times, and it allowed itself to be towed alongside
the canoe like a dead thing. When we reached the edge
of the lake Manap dragged it ashore by the golf-links
and killed it with a few blows of a heavy wooden bar.
It was between nine and ten feet long, and the clear
water of the lake had given it a most beautiful bright
yellow colour. The girth of its body and its weight showed that it had been feeding well, and as it had taken
to attacking cattle it was time that it was caught. A
man seized by it would have had no possible chance of
escape.

Such was the taking of the first crocodile that Manap
and I caught together. Though we often set baits for
the other two crocodiles that were said to inhabit the
lake, we never caught them. But in the old mine-holes
round Taiping I caught many afterwards, sometimes with
Manap and sometimes without him. The second time
that I went out I took the cord myself to tie up the
crocodile's mouth. It was one of the most exciting
moments I have ever experienced. As in other hazardous
enterprises that require some nerve, such as playing with
poisonous snakes or making parachute descents, what

one most needs in the first essay is the confidence that can only come from practice.

On another occasion B. and I set some lines in an abandoned mine-hole near a big mine where some twelve or fourteen hundred Chinese coolies were working. A crocodile was hooked, and when the coolies saw us playing it at the water's edge, they flocked round us to satisfy their curiosity, and so thickly and so closely did they press upon us that we were nearly pushed into the water on top of the struggling animal. It was only by threatening them with the spear that I was able to keep the barest space around us. Another time S. and I set two lines in an abandoned mine at Kamunting, and when we returned the next morning could find no sign of them. We paddled round the water's edge and examined every inch most carefully; then we inspected a little creek that flowed into the hole, and followed it for half a mile or so. Not a sign of any rattan. We followed the creek where it led out of the pool, and went down it for about a mile. Again not a sign anywhere, and coming to the conclusion that some rascal of a Chinaman had seen the rattans and had stolen them, we returned home in disgust. About a week later a note was brought to me from the police-station to say that a Malay had come there with a crocodile, which he said he thought belonged to me. I went over at once to the police-station, and there saw one of my missing lines, and attached to it a young crocodile. The Malay's story was that he was cutting firewood in the forest about a mile from the pool in which I had set my lines, and had seen the rattan lying on the ground. He naturally picked it up, and was considerably surprised to find a crocodile at the end of it. It was a small one, and with assistance he killed it. Having heard of my lost lines, he naturally concluded that this was one of them, and brought it to the police-station. To his delight I told the police to pay over to him the Government reward for killing a crocodile. Nothing was ever

heard of the other missing line. I imagine that both
lines were taken by crocodiles, and that the animals,
after swallowing the baits, had felt suspicious of the
rattan-lines which followed them wherever they went,
and had left the pool in the hope of getting rid of them.
That the animal which the Malay came across should
have been resting so far from water is remarkable; and
that the two animals should have taken the baits on the
same day, and that both should have abandoned the
pool to wander overland, is extraordinary.

Sometimes one hooks a crocodile that is too big to
be tackled. A crocodile more than twelve feet long has
such weight and bulk and strength that it cannot be
played from a boat without an undue amount of danger.
"Have a rifle handy", was Manap's advice, "if you think
that you have hooked a big crocodile, and play it from
the bank if possible, for sometimes it will 'amok' and
attack a boat. If the crocodile floats up to the top and
looks over the water to see what it is that pesters him,
then do one of two things at once: shoot him if you
have a rifle, or else drop the line and go home. For
the next thing that he will do when he feels the line again
will be to dash at the boat and board it. And then what
is one to do?"

In the Taiping Museum hangs a crocodile twenty-
four feet eight inches long, and when one stands in
front of it and pictures the scene suggested by Manap,
one cannot but echo his question—

"And *then* what is one to do?"

SLADANG.

THE Indian bison, known to the world at large as
the gaur, is called by the Malays sladang [1]. It is only
found in India, Burmah. and the Malay Peninsula. There
is a tradition in Ceylon that it formerly existed in the
island but has become extinct, and this would seem to
be true, for Robert Knox. who nearly two and a half
centuries ago was a prisoner amongst the Cingalese for
twenty years, gives in his "historical relation of the
island" the following account of the "Creatures Rare
in their kind"—

*Here are also wild Buffalo's; also a sort of beast they
call Gauvera, so much resembling a Bull that I think it
one of that kind. His back stands up with a sharp ridg;
all his four feet white up half his legs. I never saw but
one, which was kept among the Kings Creatures.*

This description, though excellent so far as it goes,
will bear a little amplification. A big bull sladang, the
largest and noblest of all the splendid creatures of which
the tribe of oxen and bisons is composed, stands eighteen
hands, or six feet, at the shoulder. But it is the animal's
massive bulk rather than its height that is impressive.
The forelegs are short, and the body comes down to
within two feet of the ground; at the shoulder, therefore,
the sladang presents an expanse whose breadth and
depth are most imposing, and suggestive of enormous
weight and power. A big bull will weigh nearly a ton.
The "*ridg*", to which Knox refers, runs from the point

---

[1] Pronounce slâ-dàng.

of the shoulder half-way down its back, where, with a
sudden drop of about three or four inches, it disappears:
it is caused by the elongation of the vertebræ above the
spine, and, unless the eye can take in the noble girth
of the animal, is apt to give it a somewhat "humped-up"
appearance. Except on its forehead and below its knees,
the colour of a bull sladang is a rich black, the hair
being fine and sleek, and so short that the hide shows
through it. The legs have cream-coloured stockings,
which well set off the prevailing black. The hooves are
fine and neatly shaped, and very small in proportion to
the size of the heavy animal they have to carry—much
smaller than the splayed-out hooves of the buffalo, which
is a far smaller animal. The head is very broad, the
distance between the eyes being exceptionally wide, and
the muzzle is very square. The forehead rises between
the horns into a high arched ridge, that gives the animal
a peculiar look of lofty dignity, and this frontlet is
covered with short, crisp curls of ash-grey hair. Lower
on the forehead the hair gets shorter, and at the level
of the eyes gradually shades into the glossy black of
the rest of the body.

But it is in the massive girth and shapely curve of
the horns that the great beauty of the sladang lies. At
their base, the base of an old bull's horns are deeply
annulated and indentated, and covered with many scars
and rugged pits that would seem to tell of much batter-
ing. The horns sweep out boldly from the brow, curving
in again at their extremities; and in a most beautiful
head, belonging to the first sladang that I shot, the distance between the points is exactly the same as the
distance between the eyes—thirteen inches. These horns
measure six feet and a few inches from tip to tip along
the outer curve and across the forehead, and their circumference at the base is nineteen inches. But on the
living animal the head looks small in proportion to the
gigantic bulk of the body. It is the relatively small
head and extraordinarily small hooves that give the

sladang an appearance of high breeding, which goes far
to make it so noble-looking a creature. The dispropor-
tion between the size of the head and the bulk of the
body is so marked, that my disappointment at the head
of the first sladang that I shot is still fresh in my memory. It was a splendid animal, exactly eighteen hands
at the shoulder, and of enormous girth; but I had not
seen a sladang before, and the head looked very small.
T. and I were in the wilds of the forest of the Semantan
district, and when we returned to the boat we sent his
five boatmen to get the head and as much of the meat
as they required. I was surprised to find on their return
that it was as much as they could do to carry the head
alone, and still more astonished to discover later that,
with the luck of a beginner, I had obtained one of the
finest heads ever seen in Pahang.

T.'s head boatman, whose visions of preparing a vast
supply of sun-dried meat were dispelled, was seriously
annoyed. "The meat is left in the forest while the
bones are preserved in the house", was his scathing
comment.

The Malays have, I think, an exaggerated opinion
of the savage disposition of the sladang. They believe
that it will often charge unprovoked, and they always
take great care to avoid any place where fresh tracks
are to be seen. But I have not heard of an authenticated
case of an unprovoked attack, and in the instances where
men have been charged unawares, the cause may
perhaps be reasonably ascribed either to their stum-
bling upon an animal that was nursing a wound inflicted
by some one else, or to their meeting the mother of a
newly-born calf.

A wounded sladang is probably the most dangerous
of all big game. Not only will it charge, but it will
hunt down a man with the utmost vindictiveness and
tenacity of purpose. Of this, a striking instance came
under my notice in an inquiry regarding the death of
a Malay in the Tembeling district. Two men had gone

out to shoot sladang, and the survivor, who told the story, had wounded a bull. It charged him, and he tried to seek refuge behind a gigantic *merbau* tree, that, luckily for him, stood in a little open spot, unencumbered by undergrowth or creepers. But the sladang saw him, and came round the tree after him, like a terrier after a rat. Round the tree dashed the Malay, keeping an outspread finger on its trunk, and round after him came the sladang. He could not gain on it, and it could not catch him; but, as he ran, its jaws slobbered blood and saliva upon his back.

While the animal followed him with outstretched muzzle, its horns, of course, lay innocuous upon its shoulders; and the moment that it tried to get its head down to throw its horns forward into action, the circle in which the two ran was so small that the man gained ground. The other man watched this performance from behind another tree, and after a while rashly shouted to his friend to make a rush to another tree. The sladang heard the call, stopped, saw the man, and charged him straightway, goring him so that he died a few minutes later.

To corroborate his story, the survivor produced his coat, the back of which was drenched and clotted with blood and saliva.

Of the supreme courage of a sladang I once saw a striking instance when a bull, so badly wounded that it could only manage a shuffling hobble, preferred to charge me at this slow and painful pace rather than to die with its back to a foe.

When I was in charge of Ulu Pahang some years ago, sladang were comparatively common in the down river districts, but my official duties kept me so busy in the mining area up river that it was only rarely that I was able to visit that part of the country. I had no regular tracker, and when I could get away took with me as gun-carrier one of my boatmen, or a local Malay.

On one occasion I was able to take advantage of some

Government holidays, and as the long, hot, lazy hours of the afternoon were wearing away my house-boat gently drifted alongside a landing-stage at the village of Pulau Tawar.

There we tied up, and as soon as we had made fast my old friend the district chief came on board to hear my news and tell me his. I had intended to go on farther to Padang Tunggal, a plain some distance farther down the river, but he suggested that instead of that, the next morning I should go to a plain, some three miles inland on the opposite bank, which was periodically visited by a herd of sladang. As soon as I had decided to act upon his recommendation, he sent for his two local Malays, brothers named Saleh and Yusuf, who had some reputation for tracking and shooting deer, to go with me as guides. The discussion which followed their arrival abundantly proved two things—first, that we ought to arrive upon the plain at the first dawn; and secondly, that in order to do so we ought to start about two hours before daylight. This being the case, the two men, after some expostulations and promises, acquiesced in my demand that they should sleep the night upon my house-boat.

At three o'clock the next morning the alarum went off just as I was striking a match to see what the time was. I tumbled the blanket off me—for, though we were little above sea-level, and only three or four degrees north of the equator, the nights in the Malay Peninsula are cool all the year round—and pulled on my clothes while the crew and the servants bestirred themselves lighting lamps and setting a fire. Breakfast was soon prepared, and at about a quarter to four we were ready to start. The night was pitchy black, the sky weighted with heavy clouds, and the air full of the smell of rain. By the light of a lamp we lowered ourselves from the house-boat into a little dug-out that lay alongside. It was an unstable little craft at any time, but the darkness seemed to make it more perilously sensitive than ever to the slightest motion of an occupant. Hurricane lamp and rifle were placed in front of me, the Malays took the bow and stern, and then, with barely an inch of free-board, we pushed out into the full current of the broad, black, swifty-flowing river. The stream swept us away, and the darkness swallowed up the house-boat. The Malays kept the dug-out in a diagonal line across the river, ever aiming at unseen points, below which we were ever drifting, and at last, after hard and long paddling, we made the farther bank. We landed safely, and then by the light of the lamp had to make our way along a path through the forest. Everything was very still in the darkness. Occasionally we disturbed some small bird that broke into frightened twitterings, and then after a sleepy chirp or two fell asleep again. Sometimes a cicada awoke to utter one sudden piercing shrill, to be followed by as sudden a silence; and now and again some brown thing would scuttle from under-foot. After half a mile, made long and slow by the difficulties of the darkness, we emerged upon an open plain. It was covered with a strong rank growth of lalang grass that reached up to our waists. It dripped with dew. On every blade hung beads so full and so weighted that they could scarce hold to their support. As we forced our way through the long grass, the swathes bent themselves to the pressure of our bodies, clung closely and heavily to every curve and movement of the limbs, and, as it were in an agony of self-abnegation, rubbed off on us all the moisture that they carried.

In a minute we were wet through, and I had to transfer my cartridge-belt from my waist to my neck, and to hold my rifle above my head. And in the darkness of the night how cold the clammy wetness was. Long dead, fallen trees lay across the path at intervals, and over their trunks, covered sometimes with loose treacherous bark that slipped under our feet, we had to clamber. Smaller trees and unexpected branches formed every now and again painful traps to the shins of one or another

of us. After a time we came to a little stream. This
in its normal state was not more than knee-deep, but
a local rain-storm at its source a few miles away had
swollen it into flood, and now in petty vehemence it
swirled almost breast-high.

The wet lalang grass had thoroughly chilled us, but
this forest torrent was icy cold. As we lowered ourselves
carefully from the bank into its black depths, toeing to
find the bottom, it took our breath away. Holding lamp,
rifles, and cartridges high above our heads, we had then
to stem the rushing water, while step by step we felt for
foothold among the loose boulders that strewed its bed.
Though the stream was not more than a few yards wide,
the passage was—in the darkness that our lamp but feeb-
ly pierced—far from easy or even safe. At last we stood
upon the farther bank, dripping and miserably shivering.
Our path continued through the plain for some little
way, and then we re-entered the forest. A short walk
took us to another plain, which was the place where
we might expect to find the sladang. We were slightly
before our time. There was a grey light in the east,
but it was still so dark that an object at a distance of
more than a few yards was invisible. The light increased
momentarily, and as it spread higher and wider through
the sky the grey grew clear and pure and ivory-like in
a seeming transparency. The birds awoke to shake themselves and to utter their first morning twitterings, and
among the tree-tops a family of gibbons called to one
another in melancholy piercing cries. The nightjars,
that had sat silent for the hours since midnight, bestirred
themselves to swoop and circle, uttering their plaintive
call, for a few minutes before they sought a shady shelter
for the day. We could soon discern the line of forest
that surrounded and shut in the plain. The ivory grey
of the sky quickly turned to saffron, and the saffron to
yellow. The yellow turned to gold, and then we could
see the extent of the plain that lay before us. A light
mist rose from the open expanse. It broke up into curl-

ing flocks, which blew lightly away with the first gentle breeze of morning, fading as they rolled over the tree-tops into thin steam-like streaks.

Far away in the corner of the plain to our right I could see, in the still uncertain light, a brown mass like an ant-hill: then it moved a few paces, and we knew that it was a sladang. The first thing to be done was to test the wind. The direction taken by the mist showed that the little wind that moved was in our favour. We decided that our best chance was to cross the open plain at the point where we were, and then to skirt along the forest on the farther side. Crouching low in the tall lalang grass, we made our way with little difficulty through the plain, and noiselessly crept through the forest undergrowth to make for a point whence I wished to get another view of the sladang.

We reached the spot in safety, and saw, some 300 yards away, two magnificent animals grazing in the open plain. Now that it was daylight, they were seeking the cover of the forest, but, as it was yet early dawn, they walked quite leisurely, browsing as they went, moving forward a step or two at a time and stopping again to feed. Towards our left, some quarter of a mile away, the plain ran into the forest in a little secluded bay, and the sladang had their heads turned in this direction. We crept back into the forest to intercept the sladang. There was no time to lose, for the animals would certainly not remain in the open much longer, and any sudden alarm—a squirrel's chatter or a sudden meeting with a wild pig—might send them trotting into the safety and cover of the forest. On the other hand, we had to move in perfect silence, for every animal knows the risks to which the exposure of the open plain subjects it, and is doubly watchful.

Even when one hacks a path, it is not easy to make a way through the wild profusion and tangled thorny growth of a Malay forest. But when one is tracking one dares not use a knife, for the sound of the first chop

would give the alarm. It is bad enough to have to
crawl and creep and wriggle and struggle with every
obstacle that thorn and spike can offer, but that is not
all. Far from it. You see a bough barring your way.
In its present position it is too low to be crawled under,
too high to be stept over: you must raise it slightly with
your left hand and then insinuate yourself underneath it.
Your right hand holds your heavy rifle. While you are
in this strained attitude, looking for a place where you
can noiselessly set down your right foot, you see that
the bough is covered with red ants, which ran down to
it from their nest on the parent tree the moment that
your touch communicated the alarm. Their little black
beady eyes gleam with fury, and their red mandibles
are open to their widest extent. They carry the after
part of their bodies high in the air, so that the slim
waist is strained almost into a right angle, and they seem
to writhe in a frenzied anticipation of the moment when
the time to bite will come. You cannot draw back: you
must go on, and you cannot afford to wait. An ant or
two runs up your wrist, while others bide their time,
waiting until you are under the bough to drop on to you.
One bites at your coat, but missing the responsive twinge
of sentient flesh, races over you until it finds the nape
of your neck. Here it stops, and gives you a bite so
full of formic venom that it feels more like a sting than
a bite; and though you have been expecting it, you cannot help wincing. The ant holds on in fury, the mandibles, legs, and fore-part of the body so tightly clenched
to your skin that they are almost motionless, while the
after part of the body wriggles convulsively to put more
force into the bite. Other ants bite your face, or dive
into your hair to bite your scalp. Suddenly you find that
an ant has found its way down your neck under your
vest, and has run on until it has reached the small of
your back. There, when retreat is impossible and death
certain, it bites and bites and bites until you kill it. And
then, when you attempt to pluck it away, often you pull

it in two, and leave the head hanging on to the skin in
which the mandibles are embedded.

But the ants are not as bad as the leeches. Walk
you never so lightly, the weight of your footsteps gives
the news of your approach, and upon the leaves and
grass-stalks and the decaying vegetation that lies everywhere underfoot, the brown forest leeches stand up in
eager anticipation. They are of all sizes, from the baby
that is scarcely thicker than a thread to the full grown
one of an inch and a half long. They stand on their
tails, swaying their bodies and bowing their heads on
every side to discover the direction from which the
sound comes. They have a quaintly fantastic, mincing
appearance, from which the Malays borrow a simile
to express the affected walk of the damsels of their
country.

But when a leech sees the object of its search there
is no further delay—no more bowing and curtseying;
it races towards its goal. The head is thrust out as far
as it will reach, and the mouth seizes hold of whatever
it may touch, a leaf or blade or the bare soil. The body
is bent into a great loop that brings the tail up to the
head. Then the long body straightens again, and the
head is thrust forward once more. Each step is the
full length of the body, and the leech covers the ground
in graceful sinuosities that remind one of galloping
greyhounds.

And when the leech gets on to you it wastes no time.
Should there be no opening at the top of your boot,
and should the folds of your putties afford no entrance,
it climbs until it reaches the place where your knicker-
bockers button at the knee. This is the place where it
generally finds access. But it is immaterial to the leech
where it gets at you: get at you it will. If every other
opening is unavailable, it will, if not picked off sooner,
climb until it reaches your neck. The sense of smell seems
to be strongly developed in these pests, for when your
blood begins to flow after a leech has dropped off you,

gorged and pear-shaped, all the leeches that get upon you subsequently make their way to the one place. Sometimes you may pick off a handful of leeches that hang in a cluster, all clotted with gore and slime, round the side of your knee, and find that you have only three or four other leeches on the whole of the rest of your body.

It adds to the difficulties of attempting to pick a way over a carpet of fallen twigs and crackling leaves, when you see that a leech is racing to catch your boot. In another two or three strides it will reach you. To move your foot before you can seize hold of it may mean that you may snap a dry branch underfoot, and alarm the animal you are stalking; to let the leech get on to you, means that unless you stop to pick it off it will leave a punctured wound upon you that will cause you some days of considerable irritation; and to stop to pick it off may mean that another leech, or perhaps two, will take advantage of the delay to climb upon you unawares. Among your winged worries are mosquitoes, horse-flies, and an occasional skirmisher from a wasp's nest.

I well remember the leeches in this patch of forest, for one of the bites ulcerated, and some months elapsed before it was cured. When we got to the forest edge I got on my hands and knees, and crawled until I could peer over the plain. What a sight it was! Instead of the two sladang that I had seen, a herd of eleven of these magnificent animals was quietly grazing in the open plain in front of me. Not thirty yards away, and just opposite to me, were a couple of bulls. A huge gaunt cow was a little distance behind them, and beyond her—the farthest of all—but not more than seventy yards away, was the big bull of the herd. A smaller bull and some cows with calves were feeding a little way apart, and somewhat to my right. The little bay or inlet, where the plain ran into the forest, was slightly to my left. The wind blew from them to us, bringing a faint odour of the sweet rich fragrance of cattle. Only once have

I had a sight of animal life that could compare with this herd of sladang; and that was when a Malay and I were alone in the depths of the wildest forest—far from any human habitation—and at midnight saw a great solitary wild elephant taking a bath at a sulphur spring, peacefully drinking and besprinkling himself, while the moonlight poured down through the silent trees and shone upon its black glistening body and long gleaming tusks.

But I had little time to watch this herd of sladang. The big bull had his head in the air, and was staring in my direction over the ridge of the gaunt cow's back. As he seemed suspicious, I was afraid that he had seen us move, and made haste to fire before he should give the alarm. How clearly I see it all—the great noble head, the grey hair upon the brow, the glossy jet black of the rest of the head, the massive size and shapely curve of the horns.

I only saw his head, for the gaunt cow covered the rest of him, and, aiming to shoot clear of the cow, I aimed too high, and—missed.

The whole herd dashed away to my right, leaving in the first alarm the little bay for the open plain. The four animals in front of me presented their broadsides, but the big bull was hidden by the cow, and I was unable to get a second shot at him. With my left barrel I fired at one of the other bulls. Then suddenly the sense of the dangers of the open plain overcame the first panic, and the whole herd turned sharply and, with the big bull leading it, galloped back again over the open plain, making for the nearest cover, which was the opposite point of the little bay. They were not more than a hundred yards away, and broadside on.

I turned for my second rifle to Saleh, who had been standing close behind me when I fired. But to my horror I saw that he had slipped away a yard or two to one side of me; and, even as I turned, I saw him fire both barrels into the air high over the backs of the galloping animals. I reloaded my own rifle as quickly as possible,

but before I could get the stock to my shoulder the
animals had reached the cover of the forest. It was all
over. I turned again to Saleh, who was reloading the
rifle, and, now that the madness of the moment had left
him, was looking somewhat sheepish in anticipation of
my displeasure.

But I could not trust myself to speak. It was bad
enough to have missed such a shot at seventy yards,
and to know that the chance of a lifetime had presented
itself only to be thrown away; but it was far worse to
feel that there had been such an extraordinary opportunity of retrieving a failure, when the big bull's great
shoulders had offered so easy a shot as he galloped by
at the head of his herd, and that this wretched man had
spoilt everything by his miserable imbecility. It was
not as if I had not told him what to do, I said to myself
miserably. It was not as if he had not known perfectly
what he had to do. If there had been any possible good
in what he had done, one could have stood it; but to
think that he had senselessly, uselessly, loosed off both
barrels into the sky! It was excruciating. I realised
helplessly that the big bull and the herd that had been
so close to me were still galloping madly, scattered in
several directions, through the forest. Though they had
passed out of earshot, I knew that they were still crashing their way through every obstacle, and that it would
be hours before they recovered from even the first shock
of the firing. It was out of the question to follow them.

But as the herd had wheeled about in its gallop
through the plain, I had seen the bull, at which I had
fired with my second barrel, leave the others and turn
away to the right, alone. I told Yusuf to take the gun
from Saleh and to give him the lantern and luncheon
case instead; and then the two men followed me into the
plain. We soon found marks of blood. When the rest
of the herd had turned, the instinct of the wounded
animal had led it to leave its fellows, and to nurse its
pain and wound in seclusion. We followed the tracks

in gloomy silence. As we left the plain to enter the forest again, the unhappy, disgraced Saleh spoke to me for the first time.

"Pardon, but there is something that we should do before we follow farther".

I stopped, and he explained what he wanted to do. Plucking a couple of leaves from the nearest tree, he folded each leaf in two, and slipped one into the other, so that the fold of the top leaf enclosed one half of the lower leaf, and the fold of the lower leaf enclosed a half of the top leaf. Then with a small twig he pegged the leaves into a footprint of the wounded animal, and muttered over them a charm to prevent the sladang from turning to charge us. The folding of the leaves is symbolical, and is the expression of an idea that is common to many countries. An insect that crawled along the folded leaf from its stem to its tip would find itself, at the end of the journey, no farther than it had been at the beginning. In the same way the animal against which the charm is directed is supposed to be unable to advance, and to be forced to retire by the way that it had come. The shape of a horse-shoe conveys the same idea. The shoe that is so often nailed to the stable or the dairy door in English farmyards is placed there to turn back any fairies and spirites that might cause mischief among the horses or cows. The superstructure of a Chinese grave is built in the shape of a contracted crescent, in order to repel any evil spirits that may attempt to enter the tomb. And the folded leaves are supposed to prevent the big game of the Malay forests from charging its pursuers. We followed the tracks for some little distance, going slowly and carefully through the thick undergrowth, for we knew that we should probably be charged. On every side, where the thickets spread a leafy covering over the darkness that they enclosed, and the tree-trunks massed closely one behind the other to intercept the line of vision, we tried to make out, pausing between each step, the form of the

great animal we sought. At last I heard its heavy labour-
ed breathing. I crept up cautiously and saw it lying
down. As it leapt to its feet I fired, and it fell, struggling
in the convulsions of death. The Malays saw that it
was helpless, and rushed upon it to cut its throat before
the breath of life should have departed.

When this was done, and the sting of the "might-
have-been" somewhat deadened in the comparative success of the day, Saleh found a fit time to make his apo-
logies and excuses.

"I could not help it", he explained; "when your gun
said *rap*, my gun had to say *rap* too. It would not be
resisted. I was wrong, and any punishment that is inflicted I will undergo. But—but I did it because I could
not help it".

After a short rest we finished our cigarettes and returned to the river to get men to cut up the carcass. It
was nearly midday, and the open lalang plain through
which we had so painfully stumbled in the darkness was
baking in the sun. The dew had long since evaporated,
and the grass blades stood stiff, hard, and dry. Long
wavy lines of heat rose from the plain and quivered
against the background of a cloudless sky. Dragonflies,
iridescent and bejewelled, poised themselves over the
grass, or, darting with crisp, crackly noises, hawked for
wasps and flies. Rosy-breasted swallows circled overhead, and bee-eaters, with gorgeous plumage of purple
and green, were making short flights with sudden upward
swoops to catch the dragon-flies.

On the topmost branch of a small shrub, conspicuous
by its isolation in the middle of the plain, an extraordinary bird called a crow-pheasant seemed to be drying
itself in the sun. Its tail and wings were spread out
to their fullest extent, and every feather seemed either
to be awry or on the point of dropping out. One felt
sorry for the ungainly and awkward appearance of the
poor thing, which looked like a very dilapidated and
badly stuffed pheasant; but any sympathy was misplaced,

for, in reality, it was showing itself off for the benefit
of a mate which lay hidden on its nest in a lalang tussock
close by.

When we reached the bank, the great Pahang river,
so dark and fiercely flowing when we had crossed it in
the little dug-out not many hours before, lay at our feet,
a broad, smooth, untroubled sheet of silver.

THE LIGHTS OF CHANGKAT ASAH.

On the west coast of the Malay Peninsula, between the Perak and the Selangor rivers, lies the great Bernam river. At its mouth a fishing village, evil-looking and evil-smelling, huddles on either bank: then the great river sweeps inland; it is navigable to steamers for a greater length than any other river in the peninsula, but an occasional Government launch is the only vessel that disturbs its waters. About a hundred miles inland it opens into a vast, dreary, dismal morass, named Simpang Kadangsa, and loses itself in a wide spread of floating vegetation through which the Malays with trouble hack a way for their boats. Above this horrible pathless expanse it is a clear mountain stream flowing through magnificent forest, inhabited only by herds of elephants and numbers of rhinoceroses. Near the hills from which it takes its source, at a place where the stream is little more than knee-deep, one suddenly comes upon a Malay village of considerable size. It is a lovely spot, and its beauty is intensified by its contrast with the sombre forest from which one emerges: a wide plain of crisp springy turf, grazed short by buffaloes and cattle, with coconut palms waving over the brown thatched houses that fringe the riverbank, and padi-fields covered with the rich and tender green of the young rice-plants.

Tin-ore was found in small quantities in the hills behind this village, and the consequent immigration necessitated a magistrate being stationed there. I was sent there in 1895, and Tanjong Malim as I knew it was a purely Malay village.

My quarters were placed on the river-bank, and facing the house, a little more than a mile away, a hill named Changkat Asah rose abruptly from the level plain that stretched out on all sides around it. The cultivated area extended to its base, but thence to its summit, some 700 feet high, it was clad in virgin forest. The huge dark mass dominated the beautiful village at its base. It was of course the feature of the place, and an object of superstitious dread to the Malays. Many were the stories told of the spirits that dwelt there, and no searcher of rattans or gutta dared to remain on its slopes after dark. Every Jin and Efrit known to the Eastern mind; the malignant demons that change their form at will; the familiar spirits of sorcerers; heads of women that roam the forest to suck the blood of men; the Voice-Folk whom all can hear and none may see—every kind of spirit lived on Changkat Asah. The mass of stone that forms its highest point was said to be a *bilek hantu,* "a spirit's room". The Malays believed that this formless mass took shape at night; and men have told me that the lights in this meeting-room of the spirits might occasionally be seen from the plain below.

Some years ago the Trigonometrical Survey Department had wished to have the summit of the hill cleared for an observation station, and, as might be expected, had experienced the greatest difficulty in getting any Malay to take up the contract. Finally a foreigner from Sumatra—a man named Baginda Sutan—was induced by the high price offered to undertake the work. He persuaded some other foreigners from the states of Kedah and Kelantan to join him, and at first they climbed the hill every morning to their work and returned before dusk. But they thus lost half their day's work, and after a while Baginda Sutan asked them if they were prepared to sleep on the hill. This, though he made light of the local reputation of the hill, and pointed out that hitherto they had met with no supernatural obstacles, they absolutely refused to do. As no promises of higher pay would move them, Baginda Sutan decided to shame them into compliance, and announced his intention of staying on the hill the next night by himself. He felt confident that after a night or two, when nothing had happened, his men would be encouraged by his example, and that they would all sleep on the hill, and be able to put in a full day's work. The next day, therefore, when the Malays returned down the hill in the afternoon, Baginda Sutan chaffed them cheerily for a lot of cowards, and remained behind hard at work felling a tree. When the men returned next morning they found only a raving lunatic.

The contract not unnaturally terminated abruptly, and when I came to Tanjong Malim, the Trigonometrical Survey Department was still without a station on Changkat Asah. I saw Baginda Sutan once by chance in a Malay house, and thus heard the story of his fate. The poor man, who had once been a flourishing energetic petty contractor, was in a state of absolute idiocy; and never since the day that his terrified men had conducted him down the hill, had he been able to give any account of what he had experienced.

Soon after my arrival an officer named B. was sent by the Survey Department to put up a station on Changkat Asah. He employed Javanese coolies, and at first lived with me, climbing the hill daily with his men until they had put up a shanty for him and another for themselves. He then went to live on the hill while superintending the clearing of the site and the erection of the station, and the fact of his being a white man gave his men sufficient confidence to follow him. Two or three days later he tottered into my house. Never have I seen a man in such a state of absolute collapse. Ghastly white, as if all the blood had been drained from him, with shaking hands and trembling mouth, he told me his story. I hasten to say that it had nothing to do with the supernatural inhabitants of Changkat Asah; his adventure had been with a tiger. On Changkat Asah his apology for a house consisted of palm-leaf walls, a split palm floor-

ing, and a palm-leaf roof. It was built on the side of
the hill close to the summit, and the slope of the ground
was such that, while on one side the flooring was on
the level of the ground, on the other it was some two
feet above it. His Chinese servant occupied a small lean-
to, which was built a few feet lower down the hill, and
his Javanese coolies lived nearly two hunderd yards away
by the source of a small stream whence they got their
water-supply. The second night that he had slept on
the hill he had been awakened by some animal breathing
and moving outside his shanty, but, imagining the sound
to be that of wild pigs, had turned over and gone to
sleep again. The next morning his coolies pointed out
to him the tracks of a tiger that had walked round and
round him during the night. He had no weapons with
him, and very foolishly did not think of sending down
the hill for any. He went to his day's work forgetting
all about the matter, and at night went to bed without
a thought of any danger. Soon after he had gone to
sleep he awoke with a start and heard the tiger close
beside him outside the house.

His mattress lay on the floor close to the wall, on
the side near the summit, and here, as I have said, the
floor was on a level with the ground outside. The tiger
was on this side of the house, on the rising ground above
him, and only a few feet separated them—a few feet and
some palm-leaves loosely strung together. His first idea
was to make a rush for the door on the other side of the
house, but this he did not dare to do, for fear that the
tiger hearing him attempt to decamp might forget its
caution and jump in upon him. He therefore lay motionless and shouted for his Chinese boy to bring a lamp—
but then, getting a sleepy answer from the boy, unluckily
told him to hurry up, as there was a tiger outside. After
that the boy not unnaturally refused to move, and so B.
lay there on his mattress absolutely defenceless and in
the dark. When he had shouted to the boy the tiger had
kept quiet, but as soon as he stopped shouting he heard

it again. He heard the tiger smelling at him, and the sniff-sniffing of its nostrils as it tried to take in all that there was to be smelt, in the same way that a hound snuffs up a state scent or tries to make out what some strange food may be. The heavy fetid breath of the animal was over him, and the deep body sound that is half purr half growl vibrated in his ear.

Again B. shouted until he had to stop for want of breath, and again the tiger kept perfectly quiet. When B. stopped shouting, and lay with gasping lungs and throbbing heart, hoping that he might have frightened the animal away, he would hear after a minute or two a gentle sniff outside which told that the tiger was still there. Again he would yell as long and as loud as he was able, but all in vain; when his voice ceased, he would hear the quiet sound outside, within perhaps two, perhaps three, feet of him—not more—patient as the mouse within the wainscoting, imminent and awful as death incarnate. The wretched man soon despaired of making himself heard by the coolies in their shed below: they were a considerable distance away, and as they were on a lower elevation, B.'s voice did not reach down to them through the heavy forest. There was nothing to be hoped for from the Chinese boy, who had seen that his best chance of safety lay in perfect silence—though, poor wretch, he too would probably have been glad to have been able to relieve his feelings by yelling. Let those who, under like circumstances, would have carried unarmed a lamp from one house to another accuse him of cowardice.

B., though he had no hopes of obtaining assistance, had no option but to continue shouting as long and as often as he could, for the brute outside seemed to gain encouragement, as evidenced by deeper and louder sounds from anything longer than a momentary silence. Twice he tried to rise stealthily from his mattress to make a rush from the door, but, though he attempted to cover the sound of his movements by his shouts, the creaking of the light flooring betrayed any movement, and a savage growl warned him to desist. Though in this agony of mind and utter physical exhaustion, B. was, he said, beset by a curious difficulty: he was at a loss for words to shout. He had to shout to keep the tiger from leaping in upon him, and he could not shout unless he could think of something to articulate. He had ceased to call for his men, and for hours yelled furious orders to the tiger. Finally, as hour after hour passed by in the alternations of the paroxysms of the man and the subdued contented sounds of the tiger that held him at its mercy, he was so wrought that, without hope of any chance of life, he shouted out at the top of his voice the prayers he had learned as a child. Every time he ceased for want of breath it seemed as if the strength to begin again would fail him. More than once he was tempted to hasten the end he felt could not be far off by getting up from his bed and thus bringing the tiger upon him. But this he could not bring himself to do. In this way the poor man passed the night. He first heard the tiger at about nine o'clock, and it was not until the day began to break that it left him.

After hearing B.'s story, I decided to go up the hill with him and to wait for the tiger that night. In the afternoon two Malays came up with us and tied up a goat outside the house in which B. had slept, making a seat for us on the trigonometrical station that was being erected a few yards away. I was surprised at the tracks outside the little palm-leaf house: the tiger had walked up and down, up and down, beside the house, and deep prints showed where it had lain facing the place on the bed where B.'s head had been. The two front paws were within two feet of the bed, and the impression showed that the tiger had been there for many hours. The palm-leaf wall was so flimsy (any cat could have jumped through it) that the only human reason for B.'s marvellous escape must be that the tiger had imagined the house and its inhabitant to be a trap like those often set by the natives, and, though obviously hungry, had lacked the courage to put it to the test. Our men returned down the hill, and after an examination of the paths leading to the place we climbed into our seats. It was about five o'clock, and the sun was dipping to the western forest. The cultivation and clearing that formed Tanjong Malim lay all open at our feet. On every side it was shut in by forest: to the east it ran up to the great densely timbered mountains that form the main range of the peninsula; to the south it continued miles upon miles towards Selangor; to the north the same featureless expanse of heavy-leafed trees extended to Perak; and to the west it swept away past the hill on which we were to the low-lying hills of the Wild Dogs, and beyond them to the wide pathless swamps of Simpang Kadangsa. In the midst of this sombre dark-green sea of eternal forest, like a jewel fixed in some plain setting, lay the beautiful clearing of Tanjong Malim. Several bends and stretches of the Bernam river lay clear and cool in an atmosphere permeated by the setting sun, and in the far background gradations of light and shadow showed its valley and its source in the distant mountains. The village seemed to be almost at our feet. Every house stood distinct, and we could clearly hear the "moo-ah" of the buffaloes, and the barking of the dogs. Beyond the small row of shops was the police-station, beyond it my quarters, and a path from the village led past my house to the mines farther up the valley. As the sun sank over the mountains a little breeze sprang up and alleviated the heavy heat of the day-time, and then, as the Malays say, "the day turned to become night". As evening approaches a little breeze, wandering imprisoned among the tree-trunks, like a disembodied creature, blows chill upon one's cheek, and there is an eerie feeling of expectancy that will not be dispelled from the mind of any one who is alone at this time in the forest. The darkness increases rapidly. It seems to settle down among the tree-tops in layers, and to sink thence slowly to the ground, falling like black, impalpable snow and shutting out the light above. Even at sunset I doubt not that Baginda Sutan felt thåt he had been over daring. One knows that at nightfall the animals whose tracks may be seen on every side but which themselves are rarely seen in the daytime, will be moving in search of food. The great tree-trunks stand like enchanted giants, and seem only to await some signal to escape from the charm that binds them. Again the little damp breeze puffs upon the belated Malay, and this time it seems to have been blown by some unseen mouth. The animals that have slept all day are stirring now, and he cannot but doubt that so too are the spirits. A shadow seems to move from one tree-trunk to behind another, and as he turns his head suddenly towards it, he sees at the side of his eye other shadows move at the spot from which he has just turned. Then, as it gets darker, everything around him alters its appearance; where stood a bush now looms the shadowy form of a rhinoceros, and something with the outline of a tiger crouches at the foot of a black tree-stump. The more his eyesight strains, the less real does the object on which he gazes become, and lights and spots dance and flicker beside his eyes. Curious squeaking, chirping noises become more frequent as the darkness increases, and as they cannot be definitely assigned to bird, frog, mammal, or insect, suggest a supernatural origin; and if by chance any of the awful eagle-owls scream—uttering an ear-piercing yell, like that of a woman suddenly seized and tortured—the nerves of the man are strong who can repress a shudder, and the Malay would be rare who would not think that it was connected in some way with the forest spirits. When night had closed in, and the darkness prevented any possibility of retreat, it cannot but be that Baginda Sutan bitterly repented him of his foolhardiness.

The lights of the valley below us twinkled brightly. We could see the outline of the village streets, the police-station, and my quarters, while little specks of light

marked the scattered houses up and down the river-
banks. The unhappy goat, after a few plaintive bleats,
followed at intervals by heart-rending and consumptive
coughs which seemed to be directed at us, settled itself
to sleep and silence. The moon was in its last quarter,
and would not rise until past midnight. So we sat lonely
on our peak waiting for the hours to pass. Suddenly I
saw two lights far up the Bernam valley hurrying down
towards the village. "Fight among the Chinese in the
mines", was my comment; "and here are two men coming down to the police-station to make a report". We
watched the progress of the two lights down the valley,
seeing them pass the miniature blaze that marked my
quarters and go on towards the police-station on the
river-bank. Then in an instant the two lights flew up
into the air, and rushed straight at us. So fast did they
fly, and so directly did they aim at us, that before we
could realise that they were not the lamps of Chinese
miners clamouring far below us outside the distant
police-station, two great balls of light sped by within
fifty feet of us. To say that we were frightened is to
put it lightly. I gave a gasp, and but for the support
at my shoulders would have fallen backwards out of
my seat. The suddenness of the assault was overwhelm-
ing. From our lonely eminence we had watched the
lights making their way down the valley, my interest
tempted with thoughts of the court case they might
portend for the next morning; and in a second, even
as we watched them, the tiny lights had turned to fiery
globes of the size of a man's head, and their speed had
become terrifying. However, as our visitors passed us,
we saw that they were natural phenomena, and either
chemical gases or electric fluids—that is to say, they
were either of the nature of a Will-o'-the-wisp or of a
St. Elmo's light.

These two lights seemed to us to have arisen from
the marshes above the village. Thence they were gently
borne by currents of air down to the river-bank, where

they were caught by the night breeze and carried up to where we sat. Soon after several more came drifting down from both sides of the valley towards the river-bank, and all, as they reached it, were seized and whirled by the wind in all directions. Before long there were over a hundred to be seen. The wind was fickle and variable, and sometimes a dozen of these balls of light, which were now all round us, would fly down the river together and meet others floating lazily by: they would play round one another as though in doubt which way to take, and then a current of air would come eddying round the hill and catch them up and hurry them out of sight. When the wind dropped and there was perfect calm, six or eight would rise, moving in and out among one another as if in some game, and mount up through the air, playing and dancing until they became small bright specks, then slowly sink, revolving and interlacing, until again a breeze would spring up and send them flying helter-skelter up or down the river. We noticed that the lights, as they moved upwards, downwards or sideways, were always sound in front and tapered away slightly so as to become somewhat pear-shaped. I imagine that this shape is caused by the pressure of the air upon the moving body. Thinking of this curious shape, I realised what we were watching. The dancing and flying lights were the spooks known as *penanggal.* The Malays believe that sometimes when a woman dies in childbirth she becomes a *Penanggal,* and that at night her head, with a short part of an entrail, breaks from the grave and flies through the country, flame-coloured and with open mouth, to suck the blood and life of any man who may fall within its power. "That which is detached", is the literal meaning of the word. The head with its gruesome appendage can only detach itself at night-time, and must return to the grave before day-break; and if it should lose its way, or become caught in any thicket so that it is overtaken by the light of day, there is an end of it. It falls to the ground or remains held by the thorns, and the passer-by sees it there—no longer luminous and nebulous as at night-time, but in the materialised form of the head of the woman that had been. It was, I have said, the peculiar shape of these balls of fire that made it flash upon me that they were *penanggal,* and we could then understand the terrors of Baginda Sutan when he found himself alone on the hill—known and feared by all as the home of spooks and devils—and saw himself surrounded by numbers of these unholy phantoms. What was really a wonderful and beautiful sight meant to him a diabolical orgie at the meeting-house of the spirits; and he must have looked upon himself as lost and doomed to a lingering death amongst these horrible graveyard ghouls.

All night long the lights beguiled the tedium of our vigil, for they did not disappear until a saffron light over the eastern mountains heralded the coming day. Damp with dew, and chill and stiff, we clambered down from our seats. The wretched goat awoke and bleated at us reproachfully. We had not seen nor heard anything of the tiger; and the goat had thus been luckier than it knew of, while we had seen something far more interesting than any tiger, and therefore did not take it much to heart. When we emerged from the forest path at the foot of the hill, and were making our way through the padi-fields, we happened to meet the district headman, Haji Mustapha, who was, under me, the chief Government official of Tanjong Malim. I told him of what we had seen, explaining how we had first observed the two lights come running down the path above my house. "By the Mercy and Grace of Allah", he exclaimed, "you have been marvellously preserved! *Penanggal* in truth were they; for know that the direction from which those lights came is that of our old disused burial-ground".

The question is, What were these lights? They certainly seemed to us to come up from the swamps of the valley, and this would point to their being of the nature of a Will-o'-the-wisp, which is only marsh-gas,

CH_4, a chemical compound of carbon and hydrogen. But in England, at all events, a Will-o'-the-wisp is a small, feeble, flickering light hovering only a few feet (if so much) above the level of the marshes. These lights, on the other hand, were the size of a man's head, shone with a phosphorescent glow, and, as they passed over the summit of Changkat Asah, were at least 700 feet above the level of the plain. Perhaps they were St. Elmo's lights. The objection to this is that St. Elmo's lights are supposed to be caused by an electric disturbance of the atmosphere, and are generally stationary, attaching themselves to a fixed point like the masthead of a steamer; whereas the night on which we saw these lights was clear and bright, and, as I have said, the lights flew upon the wings of the wind. I cannot say what they were. If they were composants—the sailor's name for St. Elmo's lights, and his corrupted form of the words *corpo santo* (holy body)—there is a curious parallel between the superstition of the British sailor and the Malay.

I never saw the lights again; and neither did B., though he spent some weeks on the hill. The tiger roared close to his camp a few nights later, and he and another officer in the Survey Department sat up for it several times without success.

No other European that I know has seen these *penanggal*, but Malays have told me that they have seen them; and the people of Tanjong Malim agreed that these must be the lights that were occasionally seen on Changkat Asah from the village.

I wish I knew what those flaming balls were. But of one thing I am certain: when we watched those flying and dancing lights, we looked upon that which had robbed Baginda Sutan of his mind*

---

* See Appendix II.

TAPIR

There is fascination in stalking a tapir. To anyone with a little imagination, what can be more interesting than to follow through vast gloomy forests the tracks of an animal that is one of the oldest mammalian forms— an animal that once existed in England, where fossil bones, practically undistinguishable from those of the living species of to-day, are found in the Miocene deposits of Suffolk; and an animal of a date so much earlier than that of the hippopotami, elephants, and rhinoceroses that once roamed through the valley of the Thames, that in the days of the Pleistocene period, when they played and fought on the river-banks, it had already become in England as extinct as they are to-day.

When one follows its tracks one can see imprinted upon the ground the history of its incalculable antiquity, for the front foot has four toes, and the hind-foot has only three. That is to say, the tapir, in its efforts to leave the primitive five-toed type, has only succeeded in discarding one toe of the fore-foot and two toes of the hind-foot. It is, therefore, a stage behind the rhinoceros, which has three toes to each foot; and both are far behind the horse, which has arrived at the irreducible minimum of a single toe. Long before the days of the hipparion, the three-toed ancestor of the horse, the tapir existed in its present form; and while the three-toed horse evolved through countless generations, species after species passing away to be replaced by a form more nearly approaching the one-toed ideal, the tapir has remained unchanged. A rhinoceros-like animal, with the awe-inspiring name of titanotherium, a contemporary of the tapir in the Miocene period, also reached the stage of having four toes to the fore-foot and three toes to the hind-foot. The titanotherium has passed away, but the tapir is still with us.

Then, too, the tapir's little proboscis, a mere elongation of the upper lip and snout, with the nostrils at its extremities, seems to be only an early rudimentary effort to attain a feature which has reached such high development in the elephant. It is true that it is useful to pluck a bunch of leaves or a tuft of grass, but it gives the animal the ridiculous appearance of wearing a false nose. Weirdly primitive, too, is the coloration of the Malay species. The head, shoulders, and fore-feet are a jet glossy black, the body is pure white, and the hind-legs are jet black. The two colours do not in any way melt into one another where they meet; on the contrary, the line of demarcation between the white and the black is most boldly and vividly drawn.

At its birth the baby tapir, a most laughable little caricature of its ungainly parents, is striped from head to foot with narrow bands of yellow and brown.[1] After a few months the young tapir loses its stripes and assumes a marbled mottled coat, which later becomes covered with irregular spots of black and white. Gradually some of the black spots turn white, and some of the white spots turn black, until eventually the adult animal assumes the fantastic particoloured coat which I have described, and which can best be imagined by picturing to oneself a gigantic black pig with a white

---

[1] In this respect the young tapir resembles the young of the wild pig, an animal with which, inasmuch as the one is an odd-toed and the other an even-toed animal, it is in no way connected. The stripes are particularly interesting, for the theory of recapitulation —namely, that in the embryo and young of an animal is recapitulated the history of that animal's evolution—would lead us to believe that the adult tapir was once striped, and therein resembled other members of the odd-toed group, such as the zebras and, perhaps, the primitive horses.

sheet pinned round its body. Yet the extraordinary thing is that, despite this weird marking and strong contrast of colour, the tapir in its native haunts is not a conspicuous animal. In the heavy forest which it inhabits, where the chequered light and shade fall irregularly, it seems as though the shade darkened the whiteness of the skin, while the light mitigated its blackness, and when the animal is alarmed and seeks safety in flight, black and white melt into one another to form a strangely invisible grey—the grey of a fleeting mist. It takes the two strong colours to produce this effect, for if the animal were really the grey that it appears to be, it would, in its surroundings, be almost as conspicuous as if it were white.

Malias, my tracker, was anxious that I should shoot a tapir. Though they are very shy, they are far from rare. Not many miles away from his house, he said, there was a sulphur spring which was often visited by a solitary tapir. Early one morning, I called at his house on the fringe of the forest. Following a native track for a mile or two through secondary forest, we came to the Pari river. This we crossed by a primitive bridge, consisting of a series of shaky poles resting upon insecure posts. A mile farther on we came to a little opening in the forest, where some enterprising Chinaman had boldly ventured to find alluvial tin, and had lost his capital. In the middle of a few acres of felled timber, which was fast being covered and smothered by a dense growth of entangling vegetation, was the pit, some fifteen yards square, in which his money had been sunk. It was now full of water, to which the clayey soil lent a colour of a weirdly unnatural blue, a dull dead turquoise. Like a glassy eye, it directed an unresponsive stare at the brilliant sky above it. Beside this chill pool stood the abandoned coolie-house, a tottering ruin. In the high grass that grew beside it, we found some old tracks of the tapir, which had found something palatable in the alkaline taste of the refuse-soiled earth around the kitchen. From this point we proceeded slowly, for we were not far from the sulphur spring, and it was possible that the tapir, after wallowing and drinking there, might turn its steps in our direction, in which case we might, if unawares, stumble upon it, or might pass its tracks unwittingly, and later suffer one of the most annoying experiences of a tracker, to find the tracks some miles farther on, to follow them patiently, cautiously, warily, and then, after an infinity of ungrudging toil, to find one-self at a place where, gaily tramping down a path in the gladness of the early morning, with eyes full of what the day might bring forth, and heedless of the signs upon the ground, one had passed, and overlooked, these self-same tracks. We found no fresh signs, however, and after a while left the little path. Malias pointed out the general direction that we were to take, and I gently opened a way for ourselves through the tangle of the forest undergrowth. Soon we came upon a path made by the tapir, and, following this cautiously, found the ground open suddenly into a narrow, swampy valley. Through a marsh, in which thick reeds and heavy grasses grew, a little stream wound a tortuous way. At our feet, under an overhanging rock, it ran through an unsavoury, inky-looking sludge. This was the sulphur spring of Jenali. It seemed a fetid little pool. The leaves that had fallen in it were heavy with a black, slimy deposit, and a sulphuretted odour clung to the soil, and even to the surrounding trees.

Here we found fresh tapir tracks. The animal had come down in the early evening, and then, after drinking and wallowing, had fed through the swamp grass in circles, returning three or four times in the night to seek in the strong mineral deposit a corrective to the rich lush vegetable diet. The tracks were like a tangled string: loops of various sizes were drawn into a tight knot at the sulphur spring, and we had to find the end of the skein—that is, the route by which the tapir had left the place. We spent some time in following tracks

that appeared to be taking us directly away, only to find
that the tapir, unable to resist the temptation of the sulphur spring, had turned once more to its fascinations.
At last we found the end of the ravelled skein, and then
for half a mile followed the tracks along a wood-cutter's
path. The animal, having once made up its mind to go,
had walked steadily along the path without stopping to
feed. After a while it turned aside to ascend some rising
ground. For some time we followed the path that it
made for itself through the thick forest undergrowth,
and then, after we had left the sulphur spring some two
or three miles behind us, saw that the tapir had begun to
dawdle and to pluck such young shoots and leaves as
had tempted it. The distance that we had travelled had
been covered very slowly; for, apart from the necessity
of making our way as silently as possible through all
the obstacles that the dense undergrowth of a tropical
forest can offer, the hard, dry ground had made tracking
difficult. By this time it was between ten and eleven
o'clock. Before long we came to a place where the tapir
had lain down, but not finding itself comfortable, perhaps, had moved on again. We were almost certain,
therefore, that it was asleep somewhere close by, and
the greatest care and silence became trebly necessary.
In tracking a herd of animals that are feeding one may
move fairly freely, for the noise that they themselves
are making will generally prevent them from hearing
the sound of any snapping twig or crackling leaf: even
a single animal, if walking or feeding, may miss an
accidental sound, but a solitary animal lying down will
take alarm at the slightest thing. We moved with the
most elaborate caution, therefore—every step being carefully considered and thought out. And at every yard we
peered through the dense foliage to discover anything
that might be the black and white of the tapir.

But before we had gone much farther we suddenly
heard the sound of an animal in flight crashing through
the forest some forty or fifty yards in front of us. We

could see nothing, of course, for the forest was so thick that even at half the distance we should have barely caught more than the most fleeting glimpse. There was nothing that we could do. We stood in silence until the sound died away in the distance, and then, somewhat disheartened, followed up the tracks.

The great, wide-splayed marks where each outspread toe had cut deep into the ground showed the frantic haste of the first panic. Gradually, as the pace slackened, the spread of the toes and the depth of the impression decreased, and before we had covered half a mile the tracks regained the normal appearance of the animal's usual walking pace. We traversed some gently falling ground, and then came to a swamp. At its edge the water was knee-deep, and as we waded in we found a treacherous bottom of rotten soil and tangled roots that cheated the feet and turned the ankles. Gaunt, starveling trees grew at intervals, and from the water's edge to a height far above a man's head the swamp was covered with a dense mass of mengkuang palms, whose leaves, shaped like clay-mores, but eight or nine feet long, are covered with double rows of saw-like teeth. Through this we painfully made our way, and emerged upon the farther side, where we found ourselves faced by a small hill. We reached its summit, and continued along it for some distance. We had no idea how far in front of us the animal was, and had to set our pace as best we could, avoiding impatience on the one hand and over-caution on the other, mindful of the Scylla of carelessly disturbing the game and the Charybdis of progressing at a slower rate than it. After some time we heard the alarm again, the sound of the headlong flight through the forest undergrowth, but again no call or cry of alarm. Then suddenly there was a heavy crash, then another, then another, a series of crashes, and then the sound of a tremendous bump. The direction and nature of the sounds told us what had happened. Somewhere in front of us there was a ravine, and the tapir's blind flight had taken it headlong down it.

"Quick! quick! he has fallen", urged Malias, pushing past me as, in my haste to follow, I caught in a tangle of rattans. But I could not move. I had fallen into the clutches of an enemy as beautiful as it is vicious. A delicate-looking tendril, light as the air upon which, far flung from the parent stem, it bent in a graceful curve; bare for half its length, and all along the lower half lovely with a wealth of slender drooping leaves; strong as wire, and armed throughout with rows upon rows of hawk-like talons—had seized me by the shoulder. As I stooped to free myself, two other airy tendrils, agitated by the pull upon their stem and vindictive as hornets, leant forward to dig a row of claws into my topi and my bare neck. My topi was plucked from my head and flung into a thicket, but the hold upon my neck was fast. It was useless to struggle: to have done so would only have meant being caught by other fronds that, with all the beauty of kittens at play, swayed towards me with every movement that I made. Keeping as still as I could, I had to lop off with my knife such tendrils as I could reach, and then endeavour to unhook myself from the grip of the bands upon my neck and shoulder. And all the time Malias, who did not see my plight, maddened me with a senseless reiterated "Quick! oh, be quick!" After a movement of desperate calm I freed myself, and having paid toll in the form of a long tear in the cloth covering of my topi and a row of little jagged punctures on my neck, ran quickly forward.

We soon saw what had happened. The tapir, when startled by us, had run for some twenty yards, and then a steep ravine had interrupted the way. Down this it had gone headlong. Saplings, rattans, creepers, everything had given way before it; for, luckily for itself, it had not run into a tree of any size, and it was only a thick tangled clump of rattans that, by receiving the

impact of the fall and by acting as a buffer, had saved
it from a broken neck. We got to the bottom of the
ravine as best we could, and heard the tapir moving
slowly, and apparently painfully, in front of us not more
than a hundred yards away. It was quite hidden from
sight. That ravine contained as murderous-looking a
mass of twisted trees and knotted creepers as one could
wish to see. Every inch of stem and branch and twig
of every growing thing seemed to be studded with spikes
and hooks. I think the very roots had thorns. And
every gnarled and knubbly tree had interlocked its
branches with those of every other tree; while sinuous
coils of rattans, enwrapped in thorny sheaths, bound
altogether into a compact and solid whole, which offered
a resistance as unyielding as that of a barbed-wire entanglement. To move forward even a step was a matter
not only of difficulty but one that called for considerable
ingenuity: ten or perhaps fifteen separate branches,
creepers, or rattans would bar the way, and it was necessary to decide which one would pull down, which press
down, which shove upwards or sidewards, and which,
in such silence as was possible, one would slice through
with the heavy knives we both carried. Sometimes the
opening would look clear to right or to left, and hope
would lead us thither; but generally we found that, after
a comparatively open space of a yard or two, we were
confronted by a thicket so impenetrable that it seemed
better to retrace our steps and try to find some other
way.

Although the tapir was so close to us, we found it
impossible to catch it up, and within half an hour it
was obvious that it had been moving faster than we
were. We also saw by the impression of the feet that
it was not even going lame, and that our expectations
of its having broken a limb had not been realised. After
following the tracks for some distance farther, we reluc-
tantly came to the conclusion that there was no chance

of seeing it again that day, and therefore decided to return home.

From time to time, we went to the sulphur spring of Jenali. Starting at daybreak, we reached the place at about half past seven; and then, if there were fresh tracks, between eleven and one o'clock we came upon the sleeping tapir. We were never able to get up to it before it had lain down for its siesta, and we invariably disturbed it before we came within sight of it. Sometimes a nodding tree or waving branch showed the line of its flight, but that would be all. Once we were close behind it when it plunged into the Pari river and crossed to the farther bank. It would have been especially interesting to have seen it then, for we might have learned whether it swam or whether, as the South American species is said to do, it walked upon the bottom of the river-bed. How far we followed the tapir after we had first disturbed it would depend upon many things—the time, the distance, the heat or the rain, and, more than all else, the degree of our patience.

Our knowledge, derived from the tapir's tracks, of its habits was that it left the sulphur spring a little before daybreak, moved away through the forest for an hour or two, then fed, and afterwards lay down to sleep from ten to three o'clock. The length of the midday slumber depended very considerably upon the weather and the season, and it was sometimes broken up into two siestas, with a short interval between them. At three o'clock it moved away in the direction of the place it had chosen as the site of its evening meal and drink.

We knew that we could not come up with the tapir before it lay down for its siesta, and admitted that it was hopeless to attempt to surprise it in its sleep: the only solution of the problem was, therefore, to arrange our start so as to come up with it after it had awakened again in the afternoon. But when I suggested this to Malias, he pointed out some obvious objections. Even if we arrived at the place where the tapir had slept a few minutes after it had left it, we should only have three hours of daylight for tracking, and might easily be benighted. Of this, however, I decided that we must run the risk: we could take torches, and by this time we knew the lay of the forest fairly well. Malias' next objection was that even if we did get a shot and merely wounded the animal, we should not have time to follow up the tracks. His greatest objection, however, was one of which he said least, and that was that it was not the custom to begin tracking in the afternoon. In a land where they have a proverb, "Custom encompasseth all", innovations are not welcomed.

The next time we did not start until midday. At about three o'clock the tracks brought us to a little gravelly stream not more than knee-deep. We crossed this, and followed up a well-beaten path that the tapir had used whenever it visited the sulphur spring. On the hard ground it was very difficult to track; there was a number of footprints, leading in both directions, and of every age—days old, weeks old, months old. And from these we had to distinguish the lightly superimposed fresh prints that we were following. Before long we both suspected that we had lost the fresh tracks, and were following up a stale trail. We accordingly went back to the little stream, and cast round to discover where the tapir had left its usual path. We could discover no other tracks, however, and therefore returned to the beaten path. Soon we saw that we had undoubtedly lost the fresh tracks, and again went back to the stream. We walked in its bed down-stream for some little distance, and then discovered that we were doing exactly what the tapir had done.

Lower down we found the tracks where it had left the water, and hurried up the bank to follow on, for we had lost some little time on the stale trail. We had not gone more than a hundred yards when we heard the well-known sound of the tapir crashing through the forest.

We stood still to listen.

Then Malias gasped. "He is coming this way!"

A grey form burst through the undergrowth not more than twenty yards away, running, it seemed, blindly. Its pace was a lumbering gallop, the head being held low between the two fore-legs that were flung high up and far out in front of the body. It passed by us broadside on. The first bullet from my rifle hit it too high in the shoulder, but the second dropped it dead.

And our long quest of many months was over. We examined the tapir's weird features, its ridiculous little proboscis, its bizarre colouring, the strangely numbered toes, whose tracks we knew so well—and then we fell to discussing the extraordinary chance that had led the tapir's flight in our direction. An inspection of the ground showed that a curious thing had happened. The tapir had been returning to the sulphur spring along the beaten path, which we had followed when we had gone astray on the stale trail, and had there come upon our fresh tracks. This it was that had alarmed it. It was from the danger presented by our tracks that it was running, and its blind flight had led it up to us.

A FISH-DRIVE.

Schools, railways, and foreign immigration are making the Perak Malays of the present generation a class of men very different from their fathers; and old Alang Abdullah was one of a type that is fast disappearing.

He and the men of his age saw the younger men hurry in to the towns and mining centres to pit their brains and energies against those of the immigrant Chinese and Indians; but they themselves stood back from the press and turmoil, and watching the fever of the money-getting around them with uncomprehending eyes, explained their want of understanding by saying that they were *Orang Hutan*—"forest men".

Alang Abdullah had been born within a few miles of the spot where his present house stood, and all his life long he had never been any greater distance from it than he could cover easily on foot within two days. The year for him was one uneventful circle, marked only by the padi time, the fruit time, the rainy season, and the dry season. He was a Muhammadan, of course —"there is no God but Allah, and Muhammad is His Prophet"; and he would have died rather than renounce a syllable of the profession of his belief. He fasted most strictly throughout the month of Ramthan; and every Friday he attended the village mosque, where he heard the imaum read extracts of the Koran in the original Arabic—a language of which neither the reader nor the audience understood a single word. He would have been horrified to hear that any person should say of him that a belief in the Spirits of the Forest and the

Water had more meaning for him than had any teaching of Muhammad, but such was nevertheless the case. Among the Malays who live, remote from the civilisation of the ports and towns, in the up-river districts, where the villages are sparse and few and the forest vast and all-encompassing, the veneer of Islam is as thin as the pre-Muhammadan belief in spirits is deep: Allah and Muhammad are far from this life, and six heavens in six layers lie between their heaven and this world; but the Jins, the Dewas, and other demons and spirits, actually walk the earth.

To Alang Abdullah, Batara Kala and Hana Taskun, the great Water Jins, were very real, very terrible, and very present. He had recognised them riding by his house on the roaring December floods, and in the silence of the night he had heard the Earth Jins hunting and holloaing through the forest. Less than three miles from his house was a hill where one might chance upon the Voice-Folk, the spirits whom all may hear but none may see; and not many miles down the Perak river was a district named after the Demon Bota, where to this day the spirit deludes men into the forest with sights of gorgeous palaces and lovely female forms, and promises of feasts and delights, and leaves them when morn appears fainting or dying in some gloomy thicket close by the scene of the night's phantom pleasures.

The river ran by the door of Alang Abdullah's small house, and at the back of his holding lay the great forest; and the Jins were no farther away than either the forest or the river.

The old man was a pawang, and was skilled both in the casting out of devils when a sick person had to be treated for some malady, and in the propitiation of spirits when any enterprise or excursion had to be undertaken.

But the old order was changing; the hajis and the immigrant Arab sheikhs looked with disfavour upon his incantations, and they instructed the boys who attended the Koran classes to have nothing to do with his heathen superstitions.

In every way the country was not now as it had been. In his youth footpaths and elephant-tracks had (other than the rivers) been the only means of communication between village and village. Then the British had come into the country, and bridle-paths and agricultural roads had soon taken the place of the native tracks. Later came the "great-roads" with their metalled surfaces and iron bridges, and now there was a "way of the fire carriages". All had been change and progress. It had affected even his river, the great Perak river. He well remembered the institution of the Government ferry, when the first bridle-path had reached the river's banks on either side. Then the great trunk road was made, and hundreds of yards of pontoon bridging connected the two banks; and now, on huge frames of iron-work, the fire carriages screamed as they crossed the river safe above the highest flood level.

But all this progress had passed by Alang Abdullah and had left him on one side. He did not understand the white men, and he knew that they did not understand him. He was afraid of the Government offices with the punkahs, the peons, and the police, the Court-house where they shouted "silence", and the Land Office, where even the officials were hot and hurried.

He knew that his lot was far better than it had been. The days of slavery, of forced labour and forced contribution, were over: he recognised that the ways of the Government were good, but he did not in the slightest degree comprehend them.

In his mind (so far as he thought of it), he recognised the Government as a fact in exactly the same way in which he recognised the existence of telegraphic communication. But the ways of the Government were as much beyond his understanding as was the working of the telegraph.

His second son was a forest guard in the Forest Department, and his youngest son was learning English and qualifying for an appointment in the clerical service. Only Alang Abdullah was himself too old to learn the ways of the new regime. "A new custom and an old man", he would say, shaking his head.

The scene he looked upon called forth reminiscences of the "old custom", for among the throng on the sandy bank of the Perak river below him, where in his youth no white man had dared to venture, some dozen Englishmen mingled with the crowd of Malays.

The occasion of the gathering was the great fish-drive which was to take place the next morning. Every year during the dry season, when the river was at its lowest, the datoh, the native chief of the district, organised a drive, and Alang Abdullah, ever since his father's death, had been in charge of the operations; for whatever the hajis and sheikhs might say, things had not yet come to such a pass that any one would think of attending a fish-drive unless the spirits of the wood and of the river were duly propitiated. To Alang Abdullah the fish-drive was by far the most important event of the year.

It was an animated scene down by the river. Some of the Englishmen had returned from shooting, others had been spinning with a minnow for the Malay perch, and some were swimming in mid-stream. The shelving bank was fringed with boats. There were craft of every size, from the tiny dug-out which carried a single occupant, and made its way through the press like a darting needle, to the huge be-flagged house-boat which lay anchored bow and stern. On the bare sandy stretch little clusters of Malays gathered round rice-pots and improvised fireplaces: others were hurrying on various errands between the boats and the datoh's house, and some were overhauling the casting-nets which were to be used the next morning. From a young raja's boat came the booming notes of the assembly call of the war-gong. Every one was wearing his gayest and brightest sarong—pink, and green, and yellow, and purple; every one was excited, and every one was happy.

Only old Alang Abdullah, standing on a bluff behind the river-bank and looking up to the range of mountains at the river's source, was uneasy. Until three days ago the whole month had been rainless, and the river had been so low that a man might wade dry above the hips from bank to bank, and so clear that the water flowing over its sandy bed seemed, but for its ripples, to be of molten glass. This was the condition of water requisite for a really successful drive. But in the last two days there had been heavy rain in the hills, and the river was now charged with mud and silt, and was running more than a foot above its former level. His disappointment was the more bitter because he had originally selected a day in the preceding week as a propitious one, and it was to suit the datoh's European guests that the day had been postponed. Ever since the day when the datoh had decided to have a drive, Alang Abdullah had made every offering that he knew to be acceptable, and had used every incantation and observed every mystic rite to keep the rain from falling until after the appointed day. But despite it all the rain had fallen: and if it rained again that night it would be impossible for the drive to take place. It was with a sinking heart that he eyed the lowering clouds which wrapped the mountains at the river's source, and from time to time muttered to himself, "It is not right; it is not right at all".

On an island in mid-stream thirty or forty men were busy putting the finishing touches to the enclosure into which the fish were to be driven. The drive was to begin some seven or eight miles up-stream, and a rope through which glittering strips of palm-leaf were threaded would be dragged through the water between two boats to scare the fish and send them down-stream. This rope is known as a *relap*, and when it reached the door of the enclosure the gate would be shut, and the imprisoned fish be caught by means of the ordinary casting-net.

Alang Abdullah had staked the river on one side of the island and thus prevented any fish from passing that way, and had decided to make his enclosure on the other side.

His original intention had been that the island and the river-bank should form the two sides of his enclosure, and then all that would have been necessary would have been a barrier at the lower end, and a barrier and an entrance-way at the upper end. But the swollen river had made him alter his plan. The water by the river-bank was now so deep that the barriers would barely show above water, and if the river were to rise another six inches the fish would escape over their tops. He had therefore been compelled to stake off this deeper water, and his enclosure now hugged the shallower waters beside the island, alongside of which it ran in a narrow strip.

The enclosure was simply made: into the sandy bottom of the river stakes were driven a foot or two apart, and were firmly bound together with lengths of bamboo. From these hung "chicks" (blinds of fine split bamboo laced together with rattans), which men had been making for the past month under the datoh's house. The top of the chicks appeared a few inches above the surface of the water, and the bottom was firmly pegged into the sand of the river-bed; the chicks overlapped, affording no means of escape, for the fish rarely if ever attempted to leap over them.

At the lower end of the enclosure was a purse, known as a *magun*, which was built on the same principle as the ordinary crab-trap. The fish could find their way into it from the enclosure, but could not get out again, and round it the palisading was carried to some height above the level of the water, and was made of double strength.

The men worked with a will, and by midday the enclosure was finished, and in the early afternoon all the boats that were to join in the drive were poled upstream.

By four o'clock they reached an island with a beautiful sandy bank, and here all the house-boats tied up for the night.

In the cool of the afternoon the majority of the Englishmen set about practising the use of the casting-net, for few of them had realised that it was the only weapon that would be used on the morrow, and fewer still had ever thrown one. Other men went in search of jungle-fowl, and some took out their rods again.

Alang Abdullah went up-stream another mile or two to a spot which he had selected. Here he and the men who were to drive spent the night. His men disposed themselves to sleep as soon as they had finished their evening meal; but he spent most of the night in burning censers full of fragrant resin, and in making small offerings to the Jins of the Water and of the Forest. He promised them further offerings of rice, and eggs, and limes should the drive yield a good catch of fish, and implored that they would assist him, and save him and his party from harm and mischief.

The next morning the men were astir early, and when they had had their morning meal Alang Abdullah drew the *relap* out from his boat. It was merely a long line of native rope; at intervals of about a foot strips of thin yellow palm-leaf were threaded into the line at right angles to it — and that was all. When the line was dragged through the water the palm-leaves whirled madly round, like windmill arms, and the unnatural appearance and weird glitter that were due to the sparkle of the river and the rapid revolution, were well calculated to strike panic into any fish.

With his final invocations, Alang Abdullah gave one end of the *relap* to his eldest son, and sent him with it to the opposite bank of the river.

He himself remained with the other end under the nearer bank. The line with its bright streamers thus stretched from bank to bank, a distance of some two or three hundred yards. Special men were then told off in boats to take poles and splash and thrust under the river-banks where the trees overhung the water, and where the line could not therefore be dragged.

Then a row of boats carrying men with casting nets was arranged in front of the drag-line. Their main object was to add to the splashing, and the odd chance of catching some fish that might be breaking back was only a secondary consideration.

Soon the array was set in order, and amid the shouting of men and the booming of gongs the drive started away down-stream.

By eight o'clock the line of boats came in sight of the island where the house-boats were tied up. Every one on the island bestirred himself, and in a few minutes the palm-leaf awnings, under which the Malays had been sleeping on the sand, were pulled from their supports and rolled up; boat poles were brought out, cooking-pots were shoved away somewhere out of sight, and by the time the drivers approached, the island, on which a large party of men had encamped, was abandoned. The drag-line was cut in two at the head of the island, and the drive continued in duplicate on either side of it. The house-boats naturally followed the wider stream, and as they swung out into mid-stream, each sounding the assembly call on its war-gong to take up their places in the drive, they were greeted with the Malay *sorak* or battle-yell. "Sorak", shouted old Alang Abdullah, "Whoo! Whoo! Whoo!" and a series of whoos, terminating in a final screaming "Whooi!" issued from his throat. Every man in the boats that were drifting down with the drag-line joined in the yell. "Reply! Reply! Sorak! Sorak!" shouted the datoh; and the men in the house-boats roared back a mock defiance, every man shouting the final "Whooi!" at the utmost pitch of his voice, and prolonging the sound until he strained his throat nearly to cracking.

At the bow of every house-boat stood an Englishman with a casting-net over his shoulder, and such as could not get the firm footing of these heavy craft betook themselves to those of the dug-outs which looked most stable.

There was really no necessity for them to commence operations at this stage of the proceedings, for, as I have said, the present object of the casting was only to scare the fish from the deeper pools, where they might not be affected by the glitter of the revolving palm-leaves on the drag-line and the surface splashing of the poles. Of course some fish might by chance be caught, but it would only be a few that might be trying to break back up-stream. The Englishmen's initial display was not edifying, for even those who could give the net some little spread when standing on dry land found it a very different thing on the unstable support of a dug-out. However, no one thought of the figure he was cutting, for every one was simply "at play". The whole party, from their point of view, was a schoolboy's game, and they entered into it just as they would enter into any other game that was going on, without caring whether they were good at it or not, so long as there was fun to be got out of it.

In contrast with the efforts of the Englishmen, watch the Malay. He uses the ordinary bell-shaped casting-net which a few years ago might be seen on any English river, and with which I presume most people are acquainted. His net is sixteen feet high from the summit of the bell to its foot, and the leaden ring of chains at its base has a circumference when at its full spread of nearly forty feet. He collects the whole of the upper part of the net into his right hand, holding it about two and a half feet above the leaden chains. He then raises it, shakes out any dead leaves it may have caught, and straightens the lines of the net until they all hang true. He disposes one-third on his right arm so that it covers his forearm and extends a little over the crook of the elbow which keeps it in position; one-third he takes in his right hand, and the remaining third he holds in the left hand.

As he stands ready and poised in act to cast, he is a magnificent subject for a sculptor. And now watch him cast. The curve of the movement starts from the waist, and a sweeping line of action rises to the right shoulder; then simultaneously there is a swing of the right arm, a turn of the left hand, and a swooping lateral movement of the right shoulder; straightway the part of the net that had been held in the right hand flies out horizontally over the water, followed by the part that had hung on the right forearm and elbow. As they fly out the left hand moves forward, and when held out in front of the body gives a fan-wise lateral motion to the meshes and checks them as they slip over the fingers, and thus gives the net its full spread. The sweeping curve of the right side of the net is given by the swing of the right hand and the right wrist; the full curve of the left side is given by the restraining action of the fingers of the left hand. As the net reaches its full spread it falls in a level ring upon the surface of the water. In a level ring it sinks at once to the river-bed. The thrower then slowly draws it in by a string attached to its summit: as he draws, the ring in which the net fell contracts, until, finally, when he is about to raise it from the river-bed, a solid mass of lead hangs together. Any fish that was inside the outspread ring when it fell in the water is now somewhere enmeshed in the net. The net is carefully brought to the surface and the fish taken out.

The flotilla drifted slowly down the stream. In the front line was the row of boats carrying the men with casting-nets and the men who were splashing with poles. Alang Abdullah, holding one end of the drag-line close under one bank and his eldest son holding the other end under the opposite bank, formed the second line. Behind them came the rest of the people, happy and careless and holiday-making, watching the work of the men in front, excited by the sunshine and the water-borne boom of the gongs, by the laughter, the shouts, and the throng. Alang Abdullah never for one moment relaxed his anxious care: where the stream was deep he let the drag-line sink lower in the water, using all his skill and science to prevent any skulking fish from dashing up-stream under or over it. The pools were well known, and the nets explored them thoroughly; under the banks on either side, where the forest-trees came down and bent over the stream, the men with poles were beating and prodding and splashing. Suddenly a cry arises, "Sangkut! Sangkut!" The line has caught. Then there is a yelling and a shouting. The line has caught in midstream. Immediately the men who imagine themselves to be nearest the obstacle plunge overboard, and swim and dive to find the submerged line. Keep back the boats; back water; splash with your poles, every man of you; the line has caught, and the fish will turn back and escape up-stream. Overboard with you, sluggard; jump in and splash with your arms. Who is that sitting idly in his boat? Overboard with him!

Every one yells to every one, while two or three boats, deserted by every man that they had held, drift idly down-stream. Then amid the shouting and the splashing a little old man, with thin grey wisps of hair hanging over his streaming face, emerges from under the surface, and we see that he holds on to the end of the line. He pulls himself along it hand over hand up-stream, until he reaches the snag on which it is caught. Three or four men, swimming, leaping, and diving, reach the snag almost as soon as he. They lift the line clear. "All right; no harm done; it is clear; go on". And on we go again.

Then a young raja uplifts his voice as he hauls in his net, and, carolling cheerily, holds it up for the inspection of the throng, with a silvery two-inch fish struggling in its fold. "Lu-lu-lu, I've caught the first fish", and every boat shouts congratulation and applause. But even as he turns the net round for all to see his prize, the little fish with a despairing wriggle slips through the meshes and falls back into the river. "Adohi! [alas!] adohi!" he cries in genuine dismay; and up and down the line condolence follows fast on compliment.

And so we went on. There was but little incident. Now and again the line got hung up on a snag or rock; occasionally a man caught his net on some submerged obstacle, and had to extricate it amid volleys of chaff; more than once a man fell or was pushed overboard. And after some time a few fish were caught at rare intervals in the casting-nets. By eleven o'clock the sun was very hot; the mists and rain-clouds that had brought the cool of the early morning had melted away, and a blazing sun striking on to an expanse of glittering water through a cloudless sky of purest blue set our skins a-tingle. But just as the faint-hearted began to weary, a whisper went round of rice and curry. Soon dug-outs with steaming bowls were seen to leave the datoh's boat for the men with the drag-line, and then of a sudden the house-boats converged with one accord. Alang Abdullah only let go his hold of the line for a few minutes, and as soon as he had finished his bowl resumed his careful handling of the glittering line. The Englishmen put their nets aside, and, all dripping with water, devoted themselves to huge platters of piled up rice and innumerable little saucers and bowls of sambal and curry.

By the time that the meal was finished the flotilla turned a bend of the river, and we found ourselves within a mile of the enclosure. We saw that the head of the island was thronged with Malays, and their gongs rang back a challenge to ours. "Who is for the water?" shouted our host the datoh. As he called he plunged in, and before he had wiped the water from his eyes the river was full of Malays. A long line of men, leaping, yelling, splashing, extended from bank to bank. In the

deeper places they had to swim, but for the most part
the stream was not more than breast-high.

By this time Alang Abdullah saw that the drive would
not be a success. Had it been in proper condition, we
should have been able by now to see the masses of fish
that we were driving in front of us. We should have
seen them racing through the clear water just before us,
or else leaping in mad fright in the distance. The Jin
of the Water has not been appeased, and the efforts of
the men who are now driving, the work of the men who
have toiled at the bamboo frame of the enclosure, and
his own long strivings, have all been of no avail. And
the meaning of it all is that the water is too deep and
too much discoloured, that the fish have not therefore
seen the drag-line sufficiently clearly, and that at the
splashing of the nets and poles they have scattered almost
as much up-stream as down.

But we who were at play shouted and splashed none
the less cheerily. Shame on him who would make the
little less. We worked our way steadily through the
water to the head of the island; the drag-line was brought
up to the gate of the enclosure (which was an opening
some thirty yards wide), and then a number of men ran
out with a bamboo "chick" frame and closed the entrance. Dug-outs were allowed into the enclosure by a
shallow spot at the edge of the island. Every one rushed
forward with his casting-net. Those who would not wait
their time in the press of craft struggling through the
narrow entrance ran down the island, and rushed waist
deep into the water to get their haul of the fish. For
although the drive was held to have failed, there was a
very considerable quantity of fish in the enclosure. At
first the nets took them three and four at a time, but
these were mostly fish of not more than half-a-pound.
Every one was furiously at work. We cast our nets,
drew them in again, extricated our fish from its meshes,
strung the catch on the rattan-line we carried at our
waists; and before we had breathing-time we hurriedly

disposed the nets on our shoulders, and dashed on to make another cast. Some magnificent fish were caught. The heaviest turned the scale at fifty pounds, but any fish over three pounds were rare. The man who caught the fifty-pounder fell on to it as soon as he saw it gleaming in his net, wrapped the folds of his net round it — fighting it spider-wise—and then, hugging the encircling meshes to his breast, struggled to the island with his capture.

But soon the yield of fish diminished and the nets more and more often drew nothing, and at last we wandered up and down the enclosure drawing blank at every cast. Then we shook the water from our heads and faces, and said that it was over, and making for the welcome shade of the house-boats wondered to what extent the sun had taken toll of our skins. The men's "work" was now over, and we collected round the *magun* to see the "play" of the women begin. It will be remembered that the *magun* is the trap into which the fish could find a way from the enclosure but from which there was no escape. This had not yet been touched, and we could see that it held a very fair supply of fish. Malay chivalry leaves the *magun* to the womenfolk. Soon the Malay ladies, headed by our host's wife, all gay in wonderful silks, emerged from their boats and stepped into the water. The entrance to the trap was sufficiently opened to let them enter, and one by one they filed in. They were armed with things like short-handled shrimping-nets, and began to scoop about in the water. At once there was a tremendous leaping and splashing. Little fish jumped high into the air, spluttering and squattering and trying to work their way up the bamboo paling that hemmed them in; large fish, with their broad backs surging high out of the water, dashed vainly round the fatal enclosure.

The women scooped wildly in every direction, missing the fish and banging one another, and screaming wildly the while with expectation and annoyance, excitement

and despair. Then, amid cheers from the throngs of
men on the boats which surrounded the enclosure, one
woman got a fine seven-pound fish in her net. "What
am I to do with it?" she screamed, as she held the fish
high above the water. The roar of contradictory instructions she received from the boats, and the vain efforts
of her friends to assist her—efforts which she insisted
to be meant to rob her of her prize—so confused her
that, when another fish leapt up close beside she scooped
at it wildly with her net, and of course released the fish
she already had. At this she all but wept, and was about
to retire to one side to compose her shattered nerves
when luckily another fish was caught, and she immediately dashed forward to claim it as the one she had released.

Suddenly a splendid forty-pound fish launched itself
out of the water, fair between the arms of a buxom dame.
She gave a piercing yell of agony, but by some reflex
action of the mind flung both arms round it and clasped
it to her breast. When she realised what she had done,
she screamed again with pure fright; but the power failed her to open her arms and let it go. The heavy massive body of the fish writhed and struggled in her arms,
its broad tail splashed the water on every side, and its
great fleshy lips gasped into her face. But though she
was half dead with fright, her terror only made her
clutch the tighter. The other women rushed to help her,
and the first, not knowing what she was doing, put her
hand into the fish's mouth.

Luckily it was a toothless carp-like creature, but she
was so surprised to find her hand there that she could
only stand still and scream. Another lady seized the
first round the waist, and with some frenzied idea of
rendering assistance wrestled with her and nearly pulled
her under water. It really looked as if the fish was more
than a match for them all, when a man passed a rattan
over the top of the palisade, and a cool-headed lady
slipped it through the fish's gills, and it was eventually
hauled out by the men outside.

A few of the ladies were however quite dexterous, and set to work in the most business-like way, strung each fish to their rattan-line as soon as they caught it, and without a moment's delay scooped about for another.

The fish that gave the most play were the half-pounders. One of them would leap high into the air, at least three women would scream, and two or three nets would be swept like butterfly-nets near the place where it had been, and would wildly clash in mid-air.

By this time the fish would have fallen back into the water, and a *melee* of nets would wheel and dash madly into the water after it. It was the wildest sight imaginable, but eventually the last fish was caught and the whole drive was over.

The datoh gave the order for the bamboo "chicks" to be detached from their supports and to be put into boats for removal to his house, and then every one turned to estimating the weight of the catch. There were perhaps a dozen fish between ten and fifty pounds each, two or three dozen between three and ten pounds each, a considerable number of fish over a pound, and some hundreds of fish averaging half a pound.

But this was very little when the size of the river and the distance the drive had covered is considered, and it was obvious that the drive had passed over a very large percentage of the fish. In other words, the drag-line had had few terrors for the fish, and Alang Abdullah could not but feel that this meant that the fault was his.

He knew that he was not really to blame, and that the failure was entirely due to the postponement of the date he had selected. But it meant that he had done his best to keep back the rain, and yet the rain had fallen; that he had invoked the help of the Jins of the earth and of the water, and that they had not heard him; that he had used all his charms to make his drag-line a blinding, driving terror, and that a large proportion of the fish had disregarded it—it meant, in short, in spite of all excuses that could be made, that he had failed.

The Englishmen were using their towels in the house-
boats or lying down on their mattresses. They had en-
joyed themselves thoroughly. It had been capital fun,
and there had been enough fish for everybody. "A pity,
though", said one of them, "that rain on Wednesday and
Thursday".

But it was far otherwise that old Alang Abdullah
thought of the rain on those two days. He thought of
the successes and huge catches of bygone years, and
thought of the fish that he might have caught on this
occasion; he thought of Batara Kala and Hana Taskun,
and the assistance vouchsafed by them in former drives
and denied this year: and he turned away from the
river with tired back and weary steps. He saw the
gathered rain-clouds settling lower on the mountains, and
deep in his heart he murmured, "It was not right! It
was not right at all!"

THE WILD GOAT

"The unicorn, a very curious animal, is found in the vicinity of this lake". The lake is Atdza, and the author of this grave statement is the editor of the Chinese Official Itinerary of the road between Lhassa and Peking. M. Huc, the French missionary who more than two hunderd and fifty years ago travelled from Peking to Lhassa and back, quotes the Itinerary and writes as follows: —

"The unicorn, which has long been regarded as a fabulous creature, really exists in Thibet. You find it frequently represented in sculptures and paintings of the Buddhic temples. Even in China you often see it in the landscapes that ornament the inns of the northern provinces. The inhabitants of Atdza spoke of it without attaching to it any greater importance than to the other species of antelope which abound in their mountains. We have not been fortunate enough to see the unicorn during our travels in Upper Asia".

M. Huc then gives the following extract from M. Klaproth's translation of the Itinerary of Lon-Hoa-Tchon: —

"The unicorn of Thibet is called in the language of this country *serou*, in Mongol *kere*, and in Chinese *ton-kio-cheou*, which means the one-horned animal, or *kio-touan*, the straight horn. The Mongols sometimes confound the unicorn with the rhinoceros, called in Mantchou *bodi-gourgou* and in Sanscrit *khadga*, calling the latter also *kere*".

The Thibetan tradition of how a unicorn saved India from the Tartar hordes that overran the rest of Asia is not as widely known as it deserves in a land where a lion and a unicorn are the supporters of the Crown. M. Huc continued: —

"When Jengis Khan had subdued Thibet in A.D. 1224, he set out to conquer India. As he was ascending Mount Djadanaring he perceived a wild beast approaching him. It was one of the species called *serou*, which has but one horn on the top of the head. This beast knelt thrice before the monarch, as if to show him respect. Every one being astonished at this event, the monarch exclaimed: 'The Empire of Hindustan is, they say, the birthplace of the majestic Buddhas and Buddhistavas, and also of the powerful Bogdas or princes of antiquity. What, then, can be the meaning of this dumb animal saluting me like a human being?'

"Having thus spoken, he returned to his country".

This "curious animal" is the one known to Indian sportsmen as the *serow*, and to zoologists as Nemerhedus or the "goat-antelope". It is not, of course, one-horned; and the only foundation for this belief that I can imagine is, firstly, its rarity, and secondly, perhaps, an artistic cult of drawing the animal in profile, and thus only showing one horn.

Nemerhedus has a range from Cashmere along the Himalayas to Thibet, from Thibet to the Burmo-Chinese frontier, and from Burmah down to the Malay Peninsula. It is also found in Sumatra.

Bubalinus, thibetanus, and sumatrensis are the names with which scientific men have thought fit to afflict the three species of an animal already burdened with the name of Nemerhedus and branded with the designation of "goat-antelope". *Kambing Grun* is the Malay name for this poly-syllabic animal.

It is the only goat-like creature found in the Malay Peninsula, and I content myself with calling it a goat. Its distribution is as scanty as its range is wide, and its extremely shy and retiring habits, even in the parts of Asia where it is least scarce, make it one of the animals that fall most rarely to the rifle.

In the Malay Peninsula, Sir Frank Swettenham, the late High Commissioner for the Federated Malay States, is, so far as I know, the only European who has shot one. Very few white men have ever set eyes on a living specimen, or even come across the animal's tracks, and a considerable proportion of the European community is unaware of the animal's existence in the country.

The limestone hills that are studded over the alluvial plain of Kinta, in the state of Perak, are the home of a considerable number of these goats. The sides of these hills are sheer precipices, and one gets a good idea of their general appearance when one learns that, in some period of geological pressure and upheaval, the limestone was forced up in a liquid state through the granite in the same way that oils in a painter's tube are squeezed out: the hills stand up above the plains in exactly the same way that the oil stands up above the mouth of the tube. The trees and plants that cover them, wherever seed can find root, do not differ greatly from those of the forest that covers the surrounding plains, but so precipitous are the hills that in the landscape each of them looks as solitary as any crag that thrusts its head above the level of the waves in the wide sea. When one is close, the first general impression is that of an expanse of chill grey limestone, so sheer or overhanging that not even a fern can find root-hold on its bare side, and of a line of forest trees growing upon the summit in bold outline against the sky, and completely cut off by the precipice from the forest of the plains. A second glance, however, generally shows that the precipice is broken in places where the stone appears to have crumbled away, and that here the trees of the hilltop come down to meet the trees of the plain. The hills vary in size, some being little more than gigantic isolated boulders, whilst others are two thousand feet high and many miles in circumference. The slopes of the granite mountain-ranges that run down from the Burmo-Siamese frontier, and form the backbone of the peninsula, are infested by tigers and panthers, and it is probably from a fear of these animals that the goats have betaken themselves to the isolated and precipitous limestone hills, where they live in perfect safety from molestation. One of these island-like crags is called Gunong Kroh. I first came upon it by accident, and spent a night in a Malay house at its base, whilst in search of the tracks of a rhinoceros. The hill rose, like a wall, out of the level plain, within a few hundred yards of the house. Its highest point was some seven hundred feet above the plain. It was perhaps a mile long, and half a mile in width—a great roughly rectangular mass of limestone that lay upon the plain like a brick upon a smooth floor. There were places where the precipice was broken, and there, though the fall appeared to be only a few degrees less than perpendicular, trees and bushes grew so closely and so directly under one another that the tops of the lower trees seemed to brush against the trunks of the trees that sprang from the rocks above them.

Hussein, my host, described the hill as not difficult of ascent, its precipices being easily avoided, and said that it was the home of a number of wild goats. He told me that from the house, where we sat, he often heard them bleating; and that whenever men climbed the hill in search of the rare and valuable *Kamuning* wood they generally saw fresh tracks. It was seldom, however, that any one saw the animals.

"Shoot them?" he said, in answer to a question. "No, no one ever tries to shoot them. Why should a man climb a rock as high and as steep as that to shoot a goat when, with half the trouble, he could shoot a deer twice its size on the plain below?"

It was certainly an alluring prospect. There were some goats, perhaps even a considerable number, living upon this isolated rock, whose area was comparatively small and most strictly circumscribed. Even if they wanted to do so, the goats could not get away, and from the moment that one set foot on the hill one was within a mile of them. Viewed from below, the summit of the hill appeared to be fairly level, and it seemed to me that there was less undergrowth on it than there was on the plains, and that the trees were less closely packed together. I hoped, therefore, that when we reached the top we might have a fairly open view, and, if we moved quietly, perhaps have a chance view from one crag of a goat standing upon another crag.

I decided to return at the earliest opportunity to climb Gunong Kroh, and went on the next morning after the rhinoceros, which I was lucky enough to shoot. A few weeks later W. and I slept in Hussein's house, and early next morning, accompanied by our host, began the ascent of Gunong Kroh. A nearly perpendicular climb of a few hundred feet, which was much easier than it looked, brought us to a ledge, and then we saw that the hill was not the solid mass of rock that I had imagined it to be, but really basin-shaped, and that a considerable area of ground on the same level as the plain of the Kinta Valley was enclosed within its lime-stone walls. Hussein, who had often climbed the hill before in search of forest produce, was of course aware of this formation, but had omitted to tell us. We clambered down to explore the extent of this secret hollow, and found goat tracks all over it. In the side of the hill there was a cave which seemed to be used as a place of shelter, for inside it and round its mouth the ground was trampled deep with hoof-prints.

After a careful examination of the ground we came to the conclusion that it was only at night that the goats came down to the level ground in the basin. The highest points of the hill were at its western and eastern extremities, and the sides of the basin on the north and south dipped considerably below the level of the two highest peaks. To reach our present position in the hollow we had climbed over the rim of the basin at one of its lowest points. We decided to climb up the opposite side of the basin, and to make our way round its rim to the western higher-most point, and thence back, also along the rim, to the place where we had made the ascent. The lower part of the climb up from the cave was not difficult, and we were able to carry our rifles in one hand. But after the first hundred feet or so we found

that both hands were required for climbing, and had
to improvise rifle-slings out of the stems of forest creepers. Wherever the face of the limestone was not absolutely perpendicular—wherever, that is to say, seed could
lodge or root could cling—there grew some plant or
bush or tree. They seemed in some way to receive a
sustenance from the bare rock, for there was no soil.
Great snaky roots clambered for yards upon yards over
the barren limestone, dropping a little bunch of rootlets
into any crevice that offered a hope of moisture or of
support. Often the trees grew out of the rock horizontally, and the trunks did not turn skywards until a few
feet from their base. But, so far from affording the
assistance in climbing that one would have expected,
both tree trunks and roots always seemed to block
the way. The surface of the limestone had, through
long subjection to alternate heat and rain, become rotten,
and the roots insinuating themselves into every crack
and interstice had loosened great masses of rock. Not
only were there places where a rock that jutted forth to
offer a tempting foot-hold was really ready to drop the
moment that the least weight was laid upon it, but often
we found ourselves underneath a boulder that had been
broken off, and that hung, supported by a cat's-cradle
of creepers, ready to fall at the slightest oscillation.

We reached the rim of the basin, with nothing worse
than cut hands. The amount of vegetation on the top
of the hill was surprising, and leaf-mould, which was
practically the only soil, had accumulated to a considerable depth where the rock was level enough to prevent
it being washed away. Some of the trees were of considerable girth, and rattans, with their thorny covering,
writhed over the rocks and blocked the path in every
direction. Between every tree hung festoons of creepers.
There was a profusion of begonias, with coarse, quaintly shaped leaves and little bunches of white flowers; and
hanging ferns of every variety grew wherever there was

moisture, and dwarf spiky palms wherever there was
shade.

The luxuriance of the undergrowth completely upset
our calculations, for, as I have said, we expected to have
a moderately open view among the larger trees of the
hilltop. We found, on the other hand, a vegetation no
less dense than that of the plain below growing out of
gigantic masses of rugged rock. At places the ridge nar-
rowed to a ledge not more than a few feet wide and then a
little distance farther on it widened to an irregular broken
surface of rock that was perhaps a hundred yards across.
Sometimes we had a sheer fall of some hundreds of feet
below us, on one side or the other, towards the open
forest plains or towards the central basin; and sometimes we could see the way of a more or less practicable
descent through tumbled masses of boulders and forest
growth.

At one spot I had a narrow escape. We had left
the top of the ridge, and were making our way along
the side, when we came to a sheer precipice. It rose
above us in an almost straight unbroken line, and its
base was hidden from view underneath us. Where we
were it was not, however, more than a few feet wide,
and irregularities afforded hand and foot hold.

W., clinging like a star-fish, worked his way across
it in safety, and I followed. I had to reach out with
one leg, as far as I could, to the foothold of a crevice, and,
thus supported, to lean out until I could seize hold of a
bush that grew out of the sheer face of the precipice.
Holding on to this, I had to stretch forward again to
get foothold on a little knob of rock that jutted out a few
inches, and thence reach a sapling which grew out of
more practicable ground. Holding on to the bush, with
two or three hundred feet of sheer fall below me, I was
putting my foot on the projecting rock when it gently
gave way under my weight. The little knob and part
of the rock behind detached itself from the cliff and
dropped in silence out of sight, and it was some seconds

before we heard the crash in the depths below. All my weight was thrown on the bush, which stood the strain for a moment; but as I turned to make my way back to my starting-point, my support began to give way. The roots came slowly out of the bare rock, first brown, then browny-white, then white. I was only a few feet from W. on the one side and from Hussein on the other, but it was almost impossible to move towards either of them. Luckily W., holding a tree-root with one hand, was able to reach over to seize my outstretched hand and pull me into safety. It was only just in time; and we left the poor little bush, with all but its last white roots torn out, hanging head downwards over the precipice. Hussein had to go back and make a detour to reach us.

We were making our way over and round, up and down, gigantic masses of boulders covered with vegetation, when we heard a tremendous crashing through the trees not many yards in front of us, and then the sound of an animal going sheer down the rock to our left. Thud —thud—thud. It sounded like the fall of a leaping rock, and we could hardly believe that a living animal could be charging down such a break-neck spot at so headlong a pace. In a few seconds we heard it wildly galloping through the undergrowth of the central basin below us. Then the sound died away, and that was all. We saw nothing, of course.

We found the place where the goat had been sleeping, and picked up some long coarse hairs. We kept on our way, and soon the rock began to rise towards the western peak. The central basin, which we had on our left-hand side, now came to an end, and we turned our backs upon it to climb the peak. It was a great dome-shaped mass of rock covering a great many acres, and, like the rest of the hill, was broken, rugged, and densely covered with forest growth. We found several marks of goats on it, and on our way down put up, and did not see, another goat, which, like the first one, dashed away in the direction of the central basin.

Our only other adventure was W.'s narrow escape from falling down a natural pit. All the limestone hills are riddled with caves and pits, which are the immemorial home of colonies of bats, and of curious white sightless snakes that feed upon the bats. A crack or crevice in the rock, covered with a fibrous matting of root, leaves, and moss, often connects with great caverns that extend into the centre of the hill; and one has therefore to be careful where one treads, for a man who disappears down one of these pits has little hope of being rescued. W. stepped straight into one trap, and plunged in until his outstretched elbows saved him. We quickly extricated him, but he was lucky to get off with nothing worse than a shaking.

By the time that we had made our way back to the point where we had first ascended the hill, we saw that the combination of dense vegetation and broken precipitous rock prevented any chance of our coming upon the goats by surprise. We decided, therefore, to try to drive them, and returned to Hussein's house to make the necessary arrangements for the following week.

In the course of the conversation Hussein gave us an interesting piece of information regarding the cave in the secret hollow of the hill. I had noticed that he seemed rather afraid of the cave: it was, he said, because he was afraid that he did not tell us at the time that the cave was supposed to be the home of *Orang Bunyi,* or Voice Folk. These are invisible supernatural people who inhabit the forest, and who may sometimes be heard but never seen. Stories are told of Malays who have wandered in the forest depths until they reached the outskirts of villages inhabited by the Voice Folk, and heard the cooing of the tame pigeons round their dwellings. The Malays say they occasionally hear the Voice Folk calling to each other in the forest, and that their voice is exactly like that of human people. He who hears them generally

finds that the voice is calling him by name. "Awang!
Oh, Awang!" it will cry, if Awang be his name; "come
here, some one is calling you. Come quickly". When
one hears the voice, the only thing to do is to seek safety
in flight; but sometimes a man, either mistaking the
tones for those of some fellow-mortal, or fascinated into
wilfully seeking his doom, answers the call. If he does
so, his fate is sealed. He cannot turn back: an irresisti-
ble force compels him to follow the voice farther and
farther into the forest depths, where finally the Voice
Folk make themselves visible to him. He then becomes
one of them, and, like them, invisible to mankind. Once,
the Malays relate, a man returned to his village after
having married a Voice Woman. But he, they say, is
the only man who has ever returned, and he died nearly
twenty years ago.

Upon the day appointed for the drive, W., my brother
Eric, and I met Hussein and some dozen Malays at the
foot of Gunong Kroh. Our plan was that these men
should take up stations at regular intervals round the
eastern end of the hill, and that each man should then
climb to make his way as best he could towards the
highest western peak. We thought that any goats that
there might be on the eastern end of the hill would
naturally, upon the first alarm, make their way to the
further end, and that to do this they would either pass
through the central basin or along the rim on either
side of it. We told the men not to shout or yell; they
were merely to rap the trees and to make such reasonable
amount of noise as a wood-cutter or rattan-collector
would make in pursuing his vocation. As soon as the
Malays had moved off to take up their stations round
the hill we drew lots for places. The central basin fell
to my brother, the northern rim to W., and the southern
rim to myself; and we betook ourselves to our positions.

I made my way along my side of the hill until I
reached the place where, at the end of the central basin,
the southern rim began to rise up into the western peak,

which was the point for which the beaters were to make. I found a goat track, and selected a hiding-place from which I could watch it. In front of me the limestone rose abruptly in great jagged crags and broken boulders, through and among which tree-stems fought their way and tree-roots crept. To my right a steep descent led down through tumbled masses of stone and tangled vegetation towards the central basin, and on my left was some broken rock ending in sheer precipice. Near the base of the precipice was Hussein's house. The sensation of having another scene at one's feet was extraordinary. It was quite different from the feeling one has when from a mountain top one sees a valley spread out beneath one; for there, though one says that it is as though the plain were at one's feet, yet the sense of atmosphere and of perspective dispel the illusion even as one gives utterance to it. But in this case the expression was literally true: underneath me I could see Hussein's wife winnowing rice at her door-step amid a number of hens that clucked and cackled at her feet. In the little stream beside the house her children were shouting and splashing. All were very small and far away, though in a horizontal distance they were not very much farther away than one can throw a ball; and, looking down upon them from the height of the precipitous limestone hill, I felt as though I looked down upon them from such land as grew on Jack's Beanstalk.

I had a long time to wait before the drive would begin, and screening myself behind a tree I made myself as comfortable as possible. By good fortune a pair of tiny long-billed birds were making a nest in a branch within a few yards of my head, and they would have kept me interested for many hours longer than I had to wait. The joy of these beautiful little creatures in their building was so intense that no one could fail to be affected by it. Their nest was a hanging one of delicate woven fibre, and it looked as if they had robbed the spiders' webs to make it. As each of the pair flew up with its tiny contribution, it called to its mate to see what a beautiful thing it was bringing; and as each flew away it called again as if to say that it would find something yet better next time.

When I had been in my place a little over an hour, a magnificent python, some twenty feet long, moved past me within its own length's distance of me. It had probably been disturbed by a beater when basking on the rocks; but it was in no way alarmed, for it moved slowly and deliberately. A truly splendid creature: it had recently shed its skin, and its new coat shone and glowed in the bright sunshine, and all the shades of purple and yellow in the mottled reticulated pattern of its colouring alternately reflected and retained the light. Its broad massive head and round bright eyes, its royal length and girth, all told of a dignity and majesty even among the beasts that creep upon their belly.

A few minutes later, and then came a tremendous crash among the trees on the heights in front of and above me. Instinctively my hands gripped the rifle tight, and for a second or two there was a wild pit-pat at my heart. Most people's hearts go wrong for a second or two in a drive, I think, when they first hear the game afoot. It is perhaps the sudden change from passive inaction to active expectation; and that is the reason, perhaps, why one does not have the same sensation in tracking big game, for there the exercise keeps one's pulse steady, and it is generally only a matter of the change of the degree of expectation.

Crash! again, and then a heavy thud on a rock; silence for a moment. and then another thud, followed by a crash. The noise was coming straight towards me, and I shook my elbows free of the coat-sleeves. Then came a crash within twenty yards of me, and then—oh, horror and disgust!—a big, black, long-tailed monkey hurled itself into sight. It landed with a tremendous thud on a bare rock within a few yards of me, and then nearly collapsed with fright on finding my solemn eyes returning its stare. It flung itself on to the nearest rock, and thence, with a wild leap through space, swung into a tree. The moment that it caught its breath it uttered a series of piercing, hysterical whoops, and, screaming and crashing through the trees, it passed out of earshot.

There was some time to wait after this, and then on the heights in front of me I heard a sound as if some one had dropped a pebble. Tpp! that was all. A few seconds later there was the same sound again—tpp! After a few moments again the same sound—nothing more; each time the sound seemed to come closer. I could not imagine what the cause might be, but had a vague idea that it might be a small monkey. Then I saw something on the higher elevation to my front left drop a distance of some six or eight feet and land lightly on a rock. Tpp! It was too far for me to see what it was, and the bushes and tree-trunks hid it almost entirely. Again it leapt down a sheer fall of rock and landed among some boulders about thirty yards away from me. And then I saw that it was a goat. It was only a young one—not more than a third grown, I imagine. From the glimpse I had of it, it seemed to be covered almost to its heels with tremendously shaggy brown hair. That and its immature appearance was all that I had time to take in. It saw me as soon as I saw it, and though I instinctively raised my rifle before I realised that it was too small for me to shoot, it gave a wild bound and disappeared behind a rock before my rifle had reached my shoulder. A second later I heard it dashing headlong down the precipitous descent to the central basin, where my brother was stationed.

It was worth all the toil and trouble that we had gone through to catch merely the one glimpse that I had had of the animal. It would have been worth many days' journeys to have been able to see, and not merely imagine from the hearing, the dainty way in which the animal leapt down the sheer limestone from crag to crag, and to have seen and not merely heard the mad flight through the blind undergrowth and murderous limestone pitfalls. That was the only glimpse that I have ever had of a *Kambing Grun*, but I would not have missed it for a good deal. I am glad it was a young animal, for had it been some patriarch of the herd my recollection of the encounter might have been embittered by my inability to get a shot, whereas now I can hug to myself the thought that even if I could I would not have fired.

Not long after some of the beaters came up, and the drive, so far as my side of the hill was concerned, was over. I sent the men down the hill to the central basin, in which my brother was stationed, for as this was the direction the kid had taken I thought that other goats had probably collected there, and I made my own way to the point where we had ascended the hill. After a considerable interval my brother and W. came up, and the beaters straggled in close behind them. Neither of the other guns had seen or heard a goat, and both heartily condemned the proceedings as a failure. One of the beaters, a brother of Hussein, had, however, come upon a goat which had refused to give way to him. His story, which is quite worthy of belief, was that he was making his way up the steep side of the hill when this goat stood in his path and refused to let him come any farther. It stood still in one place facing him, shaking its head at him as if about to charge, and stamping the ground with its hoofs. Discretion was the Malay's only policy, and he wisely retreated and sought another path.

The beaters all spoke of fresh goat tracks on all sides, and their explanation of the ill-success of the drive was that paths made by the goats led in every direction. There was no means of driving them in any particular direction, and that a goat should pass any given point was purely a matter of chance.

After a thorough discussion, during which various plans and theories were suggested, we finished our cigarettes and made our way back down the hill to Hussein's house.

On several subsequent occasions we tried our luck on Gunong Kroh, but never did any of us see another goat.

It is now some years since I was stationed in Kinta, and I am prepared to tell the world the locality of Gunong Kroh. On those limestone heights, isolated in a little world of their own, far apart from the animals and life of the wild plain below, the goats are still to be found. The little goat I saw is now, if it is still alive, a patriarch of the herd, but in my thoughts it always remains the kid that once I saw. Mine are the only eyes that have ever seen it—for no one, except an occasional wood-cutter, has climbed the hill since our last drive, and, for all that the rest of the world knows, it and its brethren may be some of Monsieur Huc's unicorns.

To seek it, go out from Ipoh seven miles on the Sungei Raja Road, and you will see the sheer sides and timbered crest of Gunong Kroh standing up in the forest on your right-hand side. The animals are there, and when you have once scaled the hill you are within a mile of them: all that remains to be done is to decrease that distance. And when you go there, may the best of luck attend you!

THE BLAT ELEPHANT

Ahman, my head boatman, came into the verandah by the front stairs, and I knew that he had important news. The old man had his own way of doing everything, and whenever he came to see me about the Government boats, or any other matter of pure business, he came in through the servants' entrance. If he came on an errand connected with shooting or fishing, he felt that the relationship between us justified him in using a side entrance to the bungalow. But when he came with *khabar* of big game, he always presented himself at the front door. When I looked up from my official correspondence I saw him in the doorway. A smile beamed upon his face, and with an air of appreciation he scratched his left shin-bone with the gaunt big-toe of his right foot. He stood in silence, waiting till my expectancy should reach that happy moment when it is fully ripe, and is as yet untouched by the canker of irritation. His smile grew and broadened until he showed every ragged tooth or empty socket in his old head.

"The Blat Elephant is feeding near Kuala Sol". He paused to let me take in the news to its full extent, and then continued: "The tide will be running up this afternoon. If we start at five o'clock in the big house-boat we shall reach Kuala Sol by eight o'clock, and can start tracking the first thing to-morrow morning. May I give orders accordingly?" A few questions and a little consideration showed that Ahman had thought the whole matter out, and that nothing was left for me to do but to acquiesce.

He went away to make the necessary arrangements, and a few minutes later Sleman, another of my boatmen, came up to put my 10-bore rifle in its case. He was the youngest of my crew, and always accompanied Ahman and myself upon our shooting expeditions. An exceedingly nice youngster of about nineteen, he came from one of the northern unprotected states of the Malay Peninsula, and being new to the ways of the white men was, when he first joined my service, somewhat shy and awkward. He was very keen, however, to learn all that he could about every form of sport, and under Ahman's tuition was going through a regular course to "obtain courage". Abstinence from certain kinds of food, *ghee* in particular, seemed to be the most important condition, but there were many charms and invocations to *jins* and legendary heroes to be learnt, and there were some rather extraordinary observances to be kept. Both men looked upon the course as a very serious matter.

Punctually at five o'clock everything was ready; the house-boat pushed off from the landing-stage at the bottom of my garden, and the incoming tide bore us smoothly up the Kuantan river. Ahman kept the boat in midstream, and the four boatmen, who sat in the bows, gently and rhythmically rapping the boat's side with their paddles at each stroke, had little more to do than to maintain sufficient steering way.

Both banks of the broad river were covered with a dense forest of mangroves, and trees with dark, glossy, fleshy leaves and quaint-shaped fruit pushed one another actually into the river. A couple of miles above my house we entered a tributary of the Kuantan, the Blat, which gave its name to the elephant we were seeking.

At the next bend of the river Ahman pointed to the bank, and asked me if I remembered it. I remembered it well. Some months before, when the Blat Elephant had last made one of its periodical visits, Ahman and I had tracked it into this mangrove forest. It was not easy to forget the horrible, slimy, stinking mud, punched by the elephant's feet into great oozy holes, between which we had to pick our way; the dense entanglement of branches and leaves all thickly besmeared with heavy slavers of the same mud wiped off the elephant's body; and the almost unimaginable myriads of the mosquitoes. Every separate nipah-palm leaf, every single mangrove branch, was the resting-place, not of dozens, but literally, I believe, of hundreds of the most venomous little brutes. From each leaf, each branch, there darted forth at our touch a crowd of mosquitoes that can only be compared to a swarm of bees at an overturned hive. Our faces, necks, and hands were black with mosquitoes. They bit with extraordinary viciousness, and the agony, as of an incessant beating with stinging nettles, was almost intolerable. The myriads that hung in clouds round our heads made it difficult to see, and almost impossible to hear. And it was in great part due to the mosquitoes that when we got up to the elephant, which had by wallowing protected itself with a thick coating of mud, we were unable to get close enough for a shot. I managed to see some branches moving, but that was all. At last, when the elephant either scented or heard us and made off, we were so tortured as to be glad of any excuse to return to our boat.

The banks that hid this most unpleasant spot were sliding quickly by us, and soon after sunset the houseboat entered the Sol, a tributary of the Blat. A short way up this river the mangroves were replaced by ordinary forest, and before long a bend in the river disclosed the cheerful light of a small house in an isolated clearing on the bank. We tied up at the landing-stage, and in answer to our hail the owner of the house, a man named Brahim, came down to the boat.

He was able to give us all the information that we required. The great solitary elephant, which for years out of memory had appeared at intervals in the valley of the Blat, played no small part in his life and in that of the agricultural population of the district. On every visit it did an enormous amount of damage in the plantations and gardens, destroying coco-nut and plantain trees and knocking down houses, and Brahim and the Malays of the district looked upon it as one of the ills to which their life was subject. They regard as they would regard a flood, a harvest failure, or an outbreak of smallpox. All of these things were alike in this respect, that of none of them could the occurrence be prevented by any human power, and that forethought was therefore merely an unnecessary and unintelligent anticipation of a possible future evil. A calm acceptance of the fate that placed him within the area influenced by the elephant thus gave a curiously impersonal tone to the manner in which Brahim thought and spoke of it. He told us that the elephant had fed the night before in an abandoned clearing about a mile farther up the river, and that he expected it to invade his plantation this night or the next, but talked in a voice so unconcerned that one could hardly realise that he was speaking of the imminent depredation of what was practically the only property that he had in the world. I was struck, too, by the way in which he appeared to regard the elephant as a tool in the hand of some maleficent demon rather than as a voluntary harm-doer, or as a manifestation of evil rather than as the evil itself. Against the elephant itself, therefore, he appeared to have no ill-feeling. He seemed not to have the inclination, which would have been natural to many people, to curse it. He did not even call it a beast or a brute. He only spoke of "it". This did not, of course, in any way prevent him from having a hearty desire to see it killed.

He told us that he had vowed to slay a goat when the elephant was killed, and mentioned the names of some of the richer Malays in the Blat district, each of whom had vowed to slaughter a buffalo upon the same auspicious occasion. Almost every man in the watershed of the Blat and Sol appeared to have made some vow to be fulfilled upon "its" death.

While we were thus talking, voices hailed us out of the darkness that lay upon the river. A couple of Malays passing down-stream in a dug-out, recognising my house-boat and guessing our errand, called out to let us know that they had just heard the elephant feeding on the opposite bank of the river, about half a mile up-stream. Brahim told us that the ford by which the elephant generally crossed the river was at this place, and we decided that, if we waited there in a boat, we might possibly surprise the animal at the shallows. Ahman, Sleman, and I therefore took a dug-out and started without further delay.

Before we had gone far, we heard the elephant feeding, about a quarter of a mile inland from the river bank. It is not easy to say how impressive the sound was in the stillness of the night as it came from the darkness of the forest, which stood up wall-like above the river bank. There was the peaceful sound of the elephant's slow, contented feeding, mixed with occasional sounds of the flapping of an ear, rumbling and squelching noises in its stomach, and an intermittent thwacking of its tail upon its sides. Now we could hear a bough being snapped off and now a bunch of grass being torn up by the roots. It seemed a shame to think of killing an animal so huge and so unseemingly inoffensive; and it was necessary to harden my heart with the memory of the mischief that it wrought. The wind was blowing from it to us, and we waited in silence beside the ford. It fed slowly towards us until only a couple of hundred yards separated us, and then stopped a long time under a tree to pull down a hanging creeper. The whole operation was marvellously distinct. We could hear the branches shake, and bend, and creak, as the animal tugged at the creeper's stem, and then the creeper's hold would give a little—its tendrils would release some part of their clutch of the leaves and twigs of the tree, and the tearing and rending of the severance was followed by the elephant's slow munching of the lower part of the creeper until it had eaten up as far as it could reach and began again to pull down more. While this was going on, a couple of bears passed by "woofing" to one another as they shambled hurriedly through the forest in search of food. Soon afterwards the elephant stopped feeding, and moved away. I do not know whether a treacherous slant of air gave it our wind, whether the smell of the bears offended it, or whether it wished to seek a fresh pasture. At all events, we heard it no more, and after a while returned through the darkness to the house-boat.

Before sunrise the next morning we were back at the ford, and picked up the elephant's tracks at the place where we had heard it feeding the night before. There was nothing to show that it had been alarmed in any way: it had walked slowly away, feeding as it went. I had often seen the Blat Elephant's tracks before, but the fresh deep prints with the clean cut impress of the toes always struck me with an ever new feeling of the hugeness of the animal. We followed the tracks through fairly open forest, passing a place where it had slept, and then heard it feeding some two hundred yards away. The wind was in our favour, and I moved towards it as noiselessly as I could. I got within fifty yards, and could hear with the most tantalising plainness the flapping of its great ears against its neck, and the swishing of a branch that it held in its trunk to fan its sides. I could also hear the gurgling noises attendant on digestion. But I could see nothing. I crept stealthily closer, and saw a branch move. It swung gently to and fro as the elephant slowly rubbed itself against a tree. Then there was a sudden silence. This continued for a few seconds, and then I heard the elephant move rapidly away. To have hastened after it in the hope of catching it up would have been worse than useless. The only thing to do was to keep quiet for a few minutes until the elephant had left the scene of its alarm. We were surprised to find it so wide-awake and suspicious, and Ahman expressed the feelings of us all by saying that even a deer would not have shown such a lamentable excess of caution.

We followed up the tracks for many miles after this without seeing or hearing anything more of the elephant. When the afternoon was wearing on, we decided to give up for the day, and cut a line through the forest to return to the house-boat. It was nearly dark when we got back. As we were of opinion that the elephant was making for a point some few miles higher up the Blat river, I had the house-boat poled up there in the hope of finding fresh tracks the next day.

After dinner, while I lay upon my mattress in the house-boat, I heard old Ahman telling Sleman and the other boatmen stories that deserve to be recorded. This is one way to kill a rhinoceros.

Take a piece of hard wood (*lengapus* for choice), eight inches long and two inches thick, and sharpen the two ends to as fine a point as possible. Armed with this, follow the rhinoceros. When you come upon it, shout and boldly advance. The rhinoceros will thereupon rush at you. As is the custom of the animal, it will charge at you with its eyes shut and its mouth open. When it approaches, step aside, and taking the stick between your thumb and first finger—so—hold it out perpendicularly, and put it in the animal's open mouth. The rhinoceros will snap upon it, and the pointed ends entering the upper and lower jaws will close the mouth for ever. As it cannot eat it will starve, and all that you have to do is to follow it until it drops down dead.

The system employed by a friend of Ahman's for killing elephants also has much to recommend it. Elephants, it is well known, move on from one feeding-ground to another in a regular rotation and at fixed times. Ahman's friend could go to any place where elephants had been feeding and tell from the appearance

of the trampled ground and the condition of the new
grass and leafage how long it would be before the herd
would return. When the elephants were due at any place
he would arm himself with a long iron spike and a
mallet, and climb up into a convenient tree. When the
elephants came—of course they came—he waited until
a tusker passed under the tree, and then let himself drop
upon its back. He then scrambled his way to its neck,
seated himself firmly there, and proceeded to hammer
the spike as quickly as he could into the animal's brain.
The elephant, of course, would not stand still while this
was being done: it would crash away through the forest,
but no branches could sweep Ahman's friend from its
back. Where it could go, he could pass, and the elephant seldom went far before the spike pierced its brain,
when, of course, it fell down dead.

Ahman was beginning another story descriptive of
a method of killing elephants by a dynamite fuse on the
end of a bamboo pole, when one of the boatmen, a
mannerless cub from Kemaman, interrupted the tale by
bluntly calling him a liar. Ahman was so hurt that he
refused to speak another word. The light was soon put
out, and the men pulling their cotton cloths around them
disposed themselves for the night. I lay awake some
time after they were all asleep. It was an intensely dark,
still night; there was the whisper of the river at the
bows where the boat broke its flow, and its caress at the
side where it ran softly by. Everything was black, but
not undistinguishable: I could see the black-green line
of the great forest standing on the river bank; the river
was one flat dead gleam of bottle-black, and over all
was the hollow black sky. At intervals some night bird
would utter a single mournful note.

We were all awake at early dawn, and when the sun
was showing over the distant mountains Ahman, Sleman,
and I set out to look for fresh tracks. We took a straight
line through the forest for some miles in the direction
which we imagined the elephant to have taken, and then

made a wide sweep round towards the place we had been in the day before. We found nothing, however, and late in the afternoon returned to the house-boat disappointed and weary.

As we appeared upon the bank, we were greeted by a shout from the other boatmen, almost in chorus.

" 'It' fed in Brahim's garden last night".

Poor Brahim! There was something very pathetic in his fate. While we had been running through the forest, like questing hounds, in search of the elephant, he had sat quietly in his house to await its coming.

We unmoored the house-boat, and paddled down-stream to Brahim's house. He was perfectly calm and impersonal, the fact that the damage was in the past instead of being in the future making no difference to him. He took us round his garden as the sun was setting, and, amidst the wreckage of the leaves and branches and the great pit-holes where the enormous feet sunk into the soil, showed us where some twenty fruit-trees had been destroyed.

While we were discussing the probability of the ele-phant's return to the plantation during the night, a couple of rattan-cutters passed by on their way home from their day's work, and informed us that it had in the last hour or two crossed to the other side of the river some three miles lower down. There was little chance of another visit from it, therefore, and we turned in to sleep at an early hour.

At daybreak next morning Ahman, Sleman, and I set off down-stream in a small dug-out. We found the place where the elephant had crossed the river, and landed. The tracks showed that it had fed close to the river bank most of the night: then they led inland, and we followed them for some hours. We were now some miles down-stream of the country in which we had been tracking for the last two days, and were not far from the mangrove belt and the tidal area. The forest was no less heavily timbered than that farther up-stream, and the undergrowth was even more dense and more thickly encumbered with rattans and thorny creepers. The greater part of our way lay through swamp and morass, in which patches of higher ground were interspersed.

At about ten o'clock Ahman kicked a piece of the elephant's dung in half, and felt in its centre with his bare toes to discover some remnant of heat. It was quite cold. "We must hurry", he said; "the elephant is a long way in front of us".

The tracks followed a well-defined animal path through the forest, and it was only necessary to keep to this path and have a watchful eye for any place at which the elephant might have left it. We hurried along, Ahman close behind me and Sleman at his heels. And a few hundred paces farther on, at a place where the path made a sudden bend round the trunk of an old dead tree, I saw lying down on the path, only a few yards away, the Blat Elephant.

It was sound asleep. Flat on its side, it had its head on the ground, and all four feet stretched out. It lay across the path with its back to me, and rattans and forest-creepers so hemmed it in that its head was hidden on one side and its hind-quarters on the other by under-growth and tangled foliage of every description. The two men stood still behind me, while I crept forward a few paces and knelt down under the dead tree to take a steady aim. The animal was not more than fifteen yards away, but the gaunt ridge of its backbone and the nape of its neck were all that I could see. To right and left were great tangled masses of rattans, whose stems were sheathed in great thorny coverings, and whose every delicate tendril carried stems of clinging hooks; and I dared not attempt to make a detour to get a shot at the elephant's forehead. I knew by ex-perience how alert it was, and that I should not be able to move more than a few yards before it would hear me. I took a steady aim, therefore, at the last vertebra at the nape of its neck, expecting the bullet to smash its backbone and perhaps to rake into its brain. I fired, and all was still.

Peering under the smoke of my 10-bore, I saw the animal lying motionless. I waited a few seconds, and then looked round towards the two Malays. The week before, shooting in the Kuantan valley, I had killed a fine tusker elephant with a single bullet in the brain. This made two consecutive elephants with two consecutive bullets; and the second of them was the famous Blat Elephant. Trying to conceal my emotion, I beckoned to the men to come up, saying that the animal was dead. But "dead" had barely crossed my lips when there was a rending of the rattans, and before I could move the elephant was charging straight at me.

A second before, it had been lying on the ground with all four feet stretched out, and with, I believed, a bullet in its brain. An elephant cannot spring to his feet, and a tame animal generally takes some time to rise. The suddenness of this charge may therefore appear exaggerated: I can only say that I was standing within a few yards of the animal, and was not aware of any interval of time between its lying silent on the ground and its charging me. I saw the green rattans tearing asunder to right and to left, away from an enormous brown head—a trunk tightly coiled up and a pair of huge gleaming tusks. It was all high up in the air, and right above me—imminent as a wave that curls before it breaks. With my second barrel I fired into the centre of the enormous brown chest, the head being so high and so close that it was covered by the tightly coiled trunk, and then with an empty rifle I turned and ran down the track up which we had come. The elephant was only a few yards behind me, and I ran for life.

Before I had gone more than fifteen or twenty yards I tripped and fell heavily to the ground, my rifle being flung from my hand. Death seemed certain, and I could only hope that it would be painless. But, to my intense surprise, the elephant had not followed me. Looking over my shoulder, I saw it standing under the great dead tree, from underneath which I had fired both shots. I picked myself up and, not daring to wait to get my rifle which had been thrown into a thicket by my fall, raced down the path again and hid behind the first convenient tree. From this point of comparative safety I saw the elephant still standing under the dead tree. It was fumbling dizzily with its trunk in the heavy smoke of the black powder. The blood was pouring from the wound in its chest in great throbbing jets, and the bright green undergrowth was drenched with heavy red.

After a few seconds the great brute began to scream with rage and pain. How it screamed! As the numbness caused by the shock of the first bullet wore off, the pain of the wound and of the second bullet in its chest drove it to frenzied madness. It trampled over the ground which was already besmeared with its blood, and, with trunk outstretched and ears thrust forward, turned in every direction to seek its assailant. My empty rifle lay between us, and I could not think of attempting to move towards it. Neither dared I move farther away, for any motion on my part might attract its attention. Ahman and Sleman were both unarmed, for in those days I did not own a second rifle, and we all cowered behind our respective trees. Any one of us, of course, could have killed it had he been armed. And each one of us knew that at any minute he might be detected, and then inevitably be killed.

After a time—it may have been only a few minutes, but it seemed like hours—weakened by the loss of blood and convinced perhaps of the futility of its search, it moved slowly away. We came out from our hiding-places, and all were very shaky. I picked up my rifle and reloaded it, and then, after a few minutes' rest to settle our nerves, we set off again after the elephant. When we had gone about a quarter of a mile, Ahman, who followed in my tracks, step for step, tapped my shoulder.

"He is going to plug up his wound", he whispered, pointing to a dwarf palm from which some leaves had been torn. I stared at him without at first taking in his meaning, and then, thinking of his quaint stories, continued my silent tracking without making a reply. A few yards farther on Ahman pointed to a place where the elephant had picked up in its trunk a small quantity of soft oozy mud. "Aih! Is he not clever? There is the poultice". This time I stopped, and asked him what he meant. He replied that the elephant would insert a plug of the palm-leaves into the opening of the wound in its chest, and then cover the whole over with mud. It seemed almost incredible, but the time was not one for arguing about animal intelligence, and I followed the tracks again. And, sure enough, before we had gone much farther the blood that had so plenteously besmeared our path suddenly dwindled to a scanty spinkle, and shortly afterwards to a few thin drops at intervals.

After another hour or so the tracks grew firmer, showing that the animal was staggering less and was recovering its strength. Later we came to a fallen tree some five feet in diameter that lay across a bit of swamp, and saw that the elephant, instead of wading through the swamp, had used the tree as a bridge to walk upon. This was most disheartening, and Ahman, cursing the elephant heartily for a tight-rope dancer, urged me to hasten, saying that the animal was now in all probability going faster than we were. We therefore pushed on as fast as possible, trusting that any sound we might make would be unheard by the elephant in the noise of its own movements.

But we had soon to redouble our caution, for in one place the elephant had taken a sudden loop and turned round to watch its own tracks. This is not unusual with wounded animals whose strength and size makes them dangerous, such as rhinoceroses, sladang, and elephants; and when any animal adopts these tactics, its pursuers are running a very great risk. They see the tracks lying before them, and naturally only look for danger in front. But what has happened is that the animal has all but completed a great letter P. It just stops short of completing the lower part of the loop of the capital letter, and, standing back a few yards from the main line of the letter, watches its pursuers advance. It allows them to pass, and then without warning it charges them from behind.

On this occasion, however, luckily for us, the elephant had for some reason moved on again before we reached the spot which it had been watching.

At about two o'clock in the afternoon the tracks turned towards the river. Our luck here deserted us. The elephant decided to recross, and made for the point at which it had crossed the river the night before. This was the spot at which we had joined the tracks in the morning, and where we had left our boat.

As the elephant stepped down into the river, in a fury at the sight of any implement of man, it seized our craft and swung it out of the way, snapping the iron chain by which we had tied it to a tree, and sending it adrift down the stream.

When we arrived on the scene we only found a few links of a chain on the near bank, and in the distance saw the huge footprints which showed where the elephant had clambered up the farther side. The river was not particularly broad, but it was tidal mangrove water, and infested with crocodiles. To cross it without a boat was out of the question. We had the alternative of taking a path back through the forest, making for Brahim's house, which was some three miles away, or of waiting on the chance that some boat might pass. To return was to give up all hope for the day. We therefore decided to wait; but luck was against us. For nearly three long hours did we wait upon a slimy bank, grilled in the sun and devoured by mosquitoes, mocked by the glitter of undrinkable water and insulted by the footprints fast drying upon the opposite bank. At last, at about five o'clock, a boat came round the bend of the river and took us off. It was too late to follow the tracks farther, and I sadly gave the order to return to the house-boat.

It was not until after dinner that I heard of the accident to which I owe my life. Both Ahman and Sleman swore positively that when I fired my second barrel at the charging elephant an enormous rotten branch, loosened by the concussion of the shots of my heavy rifle, fell from the tree under which I was standing. As the elephant charged down the path, the great branch fell fair upon its back. It was this that had stopped the elephant's charge, and not, as I had imagined, my second barrel. If their story is true, and I see no reason to doubt it, it was a marvellous chance that the branch, which would have killed me had I remained where I was for a moment longer, should have saved my life by falling upon the elephant.

I ordered the house-boat to be taken down to the point where the elephant had crossed and recrossed; and we were drifting lazily with the stream, and consoling ourselves with the day's want of success by an assurance of the certainty of meeting the elephant again on the morrow, when suddenly we were hailed out of the darkness by a police-boat—

"Amok! amok!"

When the boats approached one another a corporal came on board and reported that a Malay had run amok, killing his wife and two men. The scene of the murders was on the sea-coast, not far from the border between my district and an independent native state; and the murderer, who had escaped into the forest, would undoubtedly make for the border. The sergeant and a posse had already left in pursuit.

There was no police inspector in the district, and therefore no option was left me. I took the police crew on my boat, and with a double set of men we paddled hard for the river mouth. By midnight we had transhipped into the Government yawl, and a few hours later were out at sea, skirting the coast-line to make for the Kemaman border.

We eventually caught our man; but it was some time before I could find time to return to the Blat river. It was then, of course. out of the question to follow the tracks that we had left, and all that I could do was to organise parties to search in all directions for any signs that there might be of the elephant's dead body. But all in vain.

The next month I left Kuantan on transfer to another district, and shortly afterwards proceeded on a long leave to England. Soon after my arrival at home I got a letter from Ahman to say that a Malay rattan-cutter had come upon the dead body of the elephant, and had stolen the tusks and sold them to a Chinaman over the Kemaman border. I wrote to my successor about the matter, but the lapse of time made it impossible for him to do anything; and that, I am afraid, is the end of the Blat Elephant.

It is satisfactory so far as Brahim and the cultivators of the Blat and Sol rivers are concerned, for they have, I hope, killed the goats and buffaloes that they vowed to slay; and unless a new elephant has appeared to take the place of the old one, their crops are safe.

But where are the tusks that I should have to grace my story? I sigh to think of them lying in a shop-window, cut up into hair-brushes or frittered away to be the fittings of a dressing-case. For in my dreams I see them as I shall never see them again, gleaming in great curves, with an overpowering bulk of head and body behind them, and framed by a veil of green rattans torn asunder to right and to left.

A TIGER-DRIVE.

It is grey dawn on the banks of the Perak river. The little Malay owl has uttered its last ku-hup; in every tree small birds are twittering and fluffing their feathers to warm themselves, and on all sides the jungle-cocks are shrilling a cheery defiance to one another. Sunken under an accumulation of ghost-like mists, the wide expanse of river lies pallid, drear, and chill. A faint saffron light in the east enables one dimly to discern upon the river bank a number of scattered dwellings, such as constitute a Malay village, and at the water's edge a long line of tethered house-boats, prahus, and dug-outs. One by one Malays rouse themselves from sleep, and, with eyes and brains still heavy with slumber, pull a scanty cotton cloth over shivering, rounded backs, and make their way to the river, where they perform their morning ablutions and repeat the morning prayer of the Muhammadan.

A few minutes later a glory of gold touches the saffron sky, tinges it, suffuses it, absorbs it—and there is day. The sun springs above the horizon, shows his clear disc above the distant forest-covered mountains, and throws long horizontal shafts of light and warmth that dance upon the sparking river, and set coursing anew the blood of man and beast.

The morning breeze blows down the river, and gently wafts to one side the vapours that all night long had lain upon the surface of the water. A great bank of mist—a most beautiful thing—now stands upon the river bank. A cloudy mass, its base rests upon the plain, and its summit makes a straight line against the background of a mountain-range. As the rays of the morning sun permeate it, it gently rises, still one mass, from the plain, and not many minutes later lies half up the mountain-side, horizontal, like a great grey sash that cuts the mountain in two. There it remains a few minutes, rapidly dissolving into thin steaks like wind-blown smoke, and, almost before one realises that it is disappearing, it is gone.

It was known that there was a tiger in the *bluker*, or secondary forest, behind the village. For the past week it had been heard roaring day and night, and the sound had always come not only from one direction, but from one place. The Malay said that it was a tigress which had taken up its abode in one particular part of the forest, under some shady thicket or by some overhanging rock, whence it was calling to a royal wooer. The patch of forest in which it lay was so situated that it could be beaten without much difficulty; and it was in answer to an urgent message from the local chief, who was confident that he could show certainly one and probably two tigers, that the Sultan's son and the District Officer had got up a party of guns, and had made the other necessary arrangements for a drive.

A youth seated himself at a great brass gong hung in the raja's boat, and began to beat the assembly call. Before long a distant boat was seen to shoot out into mid-stream, and to move in the direction of the sound. Then on all sides the bright surface of the water became dotted with black specks of various size that all converged on the one point. The Malays whose houses were near at hand collected in small groups upon the bank, and round the landing-place prahus and dug-outs clustered thick. Some held only a poler and a steersman, while others were laden to the water's edge with a crowd of Malays perched in ungainly bird-like attitudes, but in apparent comfort, upon the bare inch or two of the free-board. By the time that the party, of whom the writer was one, was ready to step on shore, some two hundred Malays had mustered on the bank. In this throng of men there was not one who was not armed. Nearly every man held a spear, many carried a dagger, or *kris*, as well, and not a few showed a waist-belt loaded with an assortment of weapons that would not have disgraced the most piratical of marauders. The spears showed that a tiger-drive was contemplated, for across each, some eighteen inches below the point, a little piece of wood was lashed on at right angles to the shaft. This crossbar is intended to prevent a wounded tiger from clawing its way up the spear-head that transfixes it, to the man that holds the spear. Such men as owned, or had been able to borrow, a small dagger of a peculiar shape known as a *golok rembau*, exhibited their weapons with complacency and pride; for these daggers are supposed by the Malays to possess such extraordinary, even magical, properties that a tiger is powerless against them.

When the local chief announced that everything was ready, an old pawang stepped forward with a bunch of twigs of a tree for which a tiger is thought to have a peculiar dread. Holding this small bundle in both hands, he repeated over it the charm known as "that which closes the tiger's mouth," and then, after another incantation which was intended to prevent the tiger from winding us, proceeded to break the twigs into short fragments, which he distributed first among the shooters, and then among the beaters. The ceremony did not take long, but by the time it was over, and the final words of advice, exhortation, and command had been said on every side, the sun was strong enough to make the shade welcome; and without further delay the old chief led his picturesque throng of beaters down one path, while we set off along a track that took us into another part of the forest.

The line along which the guns were to be stationed had already been cut through the forest. It was broad enough to afford a fair shot, and had been more or less cleared of undergrowth and obstacles.

The party consisted of nine guns—six Europeans and three Malay rajas—and for each there had been erected in a tree a small platform made of lopped branches bound together with green rattans and screened with leafy boughs. The object of the platform is partly to keep the shooter safe above any danger from the tiger, but partly also to enable him to obtain the best possible view of the ground and to prevent the tiger from scenting him.

As soon as we had scrambled into our individual platforms, the Malays who had been our guides swarmed up adjacent trees, and, having first made sure that they had not intruded upon a nest of the great vicious red ants, selected comfortable perches from which to await the result of the drive. The beaters formed into line at a place some two or three miles away from the posts taken up by the guns. The forest that they had to beat out was a strip comparatively narrow in proportion to its length, lying between a Government bridle-path on the one side and a deep swamp on the other. It was most unlikely that the tiger would attempt to break out at the sides of the ground, and therefore no stops were posted.

We had not been long in our places when the pre-concerted signal of a shot announced that the drive had begun. It would, however, be another two hours at least before the men would arrive at the line of guns —for beating in dense forest, if thoroughly carried out, is very slow work. Deep silence reigned throughout the part of the forest in which we were—a silence enhanced by the faint distant sounds of the occasional war-cry of the advancing Malays. A peacock-pheasant, whose persistent scolding clatter, not unlike the note of a cackling barn-door hen, had warned every animal within hearing of our arrival, had ceased its clamour at last and re-commenced its scratching among the fallen leaves. Two little birds—the male a brilliant black with a golden crown, and his mate a sober russet-brown—resumed the labour of feeding their speckled nestlings. A resplendent ground-thrush, gorgeous as a salmon-fly, which on our approach had hidden under some fallen leaves, had now regained its confidence and came hopping out to continue its search for food. The life of every animal seemed to be a silent one. In the distance, it is true, a great rhinoceros-hornbill called from a tree-top to a mate afar off; and high overhead, hidden in the blinding blue, a kite uttered at intervals its shrill, querulous whistle. But these were the exceptions: at all hours and at all seasons the silence of the animals is one with the silence of the forest.

During the whole of the drive no animal larger than a mouse-deer appeared within sight of my platform, and when finally the line of beaters reached the guns we found that the drive was a blank. A sambar and a barking deer or two had been seen by the other guns, but, since a tiger was our object, no one had fired at them.

The Malays were not only disappointed but much surprised at the failure of the drive. Day after day and night after night the tiger had been heard roaring in the area through which they had just beaten, and they could not understand why not a sign of it had been seen. They were positive that, since it was not in the ground which they had just covered, it must be lying up in a smaller strip of forest between the bridle-path and the Perak river.

After some short deliberation and argument they went off without further delay to drive, and we stationed ourselves at intervals through the forest. There was no time to clear any lines nor to erect platforms in the trees. We took up positions on foot, arranging ourselves in such order as we could, and each man knew, though he could not see, the situation of his neighbours on either side. At the place where the beaters formed into line the bridle-path was about a mile from the river;

while at the point where guns were stationed, about a mile farther up-stream, river and path were within three hundred yards of one another. The ground to be beaten was thus a triangle: the beaters were at its base and the guns at the apex. Behind the line of guns river and path diverged again, and between them lay a vast expanse of dense, heavily timbered forest for which it was thought that the tiger would make. We had not been long in our places before the beaters began to advance towards us. I studied the lie of the forest in my vicinity and the approaches by which an animal would be likely to come in my direction, and then fell to watching an interminable string of little black ants at my feet. They were migrating, but I could not see whence they came or whither they were going. The line that they followed was extraordinarily devious: up one side and down the other of a tree-stump, round three sides of a great boulder, over and along surface-roots, under a fallen log the black line twisted and turned. There seemed to be no attempt to shorten or to improve upon the winding path selected by the leaders of the column. The little creatures moved in a line some six or seven deep; and for some reason which it was difficult to discern, a constant succession of ants kept hurrying back through the ranks to communicate with the rear.

Suddenly there was a cry afar off: "Look out! The tiger is here!" How every feeling intensified at the sound! Not a soul was within sight; but one knew that the men who were hidden to right and to left had heard the words, and had thrilled to them no less than oneself. The beaters were yet more than half a mile away, but it was not difficult to imagine the excitement that possessed them. Somewhere in the area encompassed by them and by the gun there was moving silently through the dense forest undergrowth the lithe powerful form of a tiger. We all knew it: it even seemed strange that the long string of ants should fail to know it and should continue their unheeding ceaseless hurrying. Somewhere near us the tiger was or should be.

At the shout ᵗhe men steadied themselves, moving to one side or the other in order to make the line of advance as perfect as possible. There was silence for a moment, and then a great voice shouted, "Selawat!" (prayer.) "Selawat!" shouted every one; and thereupon one of the men in the long line chanted aloud some verses of the Koran, concluding by shouting at the top of his voice the words of the creed of Islam: "La' ila'hu illa' llahu; wa Muhammadu'r—rasulu' llahi" (There is no God but Allah, and Muhammad is the prophet of Allah). And from every voice in the array that was hidden up and down the forest came the roar of the response of the final Allah. Apart from its religious aspect, the use of the "selawat" is to enable the men to know whereabouts in the denseness and tangle of the forest undergrowth the animal is hidden. If a tiger is suddenly disturbed when lying up beside an animal that it has killed, or has cubs, or is wounded, or is for any other reason savage, it often gives utterance to an answering challenge which it not infrequently follows up by charging forthwith upon the men. I have more than once heard a sudden vibrating roar in reply to a cry of "selawat" that has made the blood of the listeners run warm; and more than one Malay has been struck down with the expression of his faith upon his lips.

On this occasion there was no reply to the long-drawn Allah, and after a pause, during which each man assured himself of his position with regard to his neighbours, the array of beaters slowly and carefully moved forward. At intervals the piercing war-cry of the Malays rose and rang up and down the line. Occasionally an order was shouted to close in on the right or to move up faster on the left, but otherwise the advance was made in greater silence than might have been expected. The men worked out the thickets with their spearheads, and rapped their spear-butts upon the tree-trunks with a

steadiness and thoroughness that would have been credit-
able in any pheasant covert in England. They were,
I may say, an exceptionally fine set of men. The Malays
of Saiong are famous throughout Perak for their skill
and daring in a tiger-drive; and on this occasion they
were under the eye both of their Sultan's son and of
the District Officer.

Before long the cry arose again, "Here he is! Here
he is!" Upon this the old chief in charge of the drive
shouted an order, "Tahan, tahan!" (Steady, hold
steady!) Down on a knee dropped every man of the
two hundred that composed the line. Close to his side
each man gripped his spear, with its point thrust upwards into the dark forest undergrowth in front of him.
It was impossible to see the plainest object at a distance
of more than twenty yards, and a tiger might crouch
unseen within three yards of the most vigilant. Little
doubt that each man eyed the crossbar on his spear,
and thought how very small and very near him it looked;
amid the safety of the crowd in the village he had tied
it on with a pleasurable titillation of excitement. But
now its significance was very real and very grim.

The chief shouted his order to the men to stand
steady, because he thought that, as the tiger had not
by this time passed the guns, it must be aware of their
position, and intend to seek safety by breaking back
through the line of beaters. Every one knew what the
chief thought, and waited, peering into the dark forest
in front of him, in readiness for the next word of command. Then the chief shouted again. All leapt to their
feet, ran forward a few yards—five or six, perhaps, or
it may be even less—and then as suddenly stopped and
knelt again. "Steady! Hold steady!" they shouted
up and down the line, while all strained their eyes to
catch a hidden gleam of yellow in the heavy shadows of
the black and green of the forest. Thus they advanced
in short quick rushes with sudden pauses, until they
were within two hundred yards of us. The excitement

by this time was almost overpowering in its intensity. I could not, of course, see the men, but knew by the sound that only this distance separated us, and that on the other side of the thickets and tree-trunks in front of me fierce Malay eyes glared and peered for the hidden tiger. Then suddenly, in a tree half-way between the beaters and the guns, a squirrel raised its chattering note of alarm. Another squirrel immediately took up the cry, and the pair of them kept up such an incessant excited clamour that it was plain that they were scolding an intruder; it was obvious, too, that the intruder was within a few yards of them. The tree from which they uttered their defiance was situated in a ravine-like depression in the forest, exactly the sort of place in which a tiger, or any animal, would seek a refuge from the invasion of the beaters. The chief shouted to the men to move in upon the place, and the long line swept inwards and enclosed it in a semicircle. By this time the length of the line had so contracted that the men were nearly shoulder to shoulder. Only a hundred yards or so separated them from the guns, and it was therefore practically impossible for any animal between them and us to escape. The Malays now advanced foot by foot, and in an almost breathless silence. Then I saw something move stealthily under a fallen tree, whose dead leaves prevented me from getting more than a glimpse of it, and that, too, a glimpse not so much of it as of the place from which it had stirred. It saw me as soon as I saw it, and, knowing itself to have been discovered, a great, gaunt, wild sow rushed out and dashed past me. The nearer of the beaters heard it and dropped on their knees, with their spears thrust forward to receive it. "Here he is! Here he is! Steady! Hold steady!"

For a space not a man moved: probably not a man breathed. Then I shouted that the animal that had come out was only a pig, and that the tiger had not yet shown itself. "Pig", they roared up and down the line, "only a pig"; and again the line moved forward to beat out the few remaining yards that separated them from the guns. But when they reached us not a sign was there anywhere of the tiger.

Excited questions were yelled on every side. No one knew what had happened. What every one failed to understand was why no one had fired. The men thronged round the place where the old sow had passed by me, and leant upon their spears examining the tracks and mournfully shaking their heads. Their heaving chests, twitching muscles, and unnaturally contracted eyelids told of the intense nervous strain which they had undergone.

Had any one seen or heard the tiger, and who had first raised the alarm? In reply to this, several men spoke to having heard the tiger, but no one had actually seen it. Every man of them indignantly repudiated the suggestion that he could have mistaken a pig's grunt for a tiger's growl. Malays know the two sounds so well that such a mistake would be most unlikely. Some pigs had been seen, but no one had taken any notice of them. When we asked the men who declared that they had heard the tiger how they accounted for its having escaped unseen, they pointed out that when the squirrels had given their alarm we had all taken it for granted that they had seen the tiger, whereas it was probably only the sow, and that when the beaters closed in upon the ravine they had left the forest on either side unguarded. This, of course, was perfectly true, and their explanation of our failure was probably the correct one.

Some of the more enthusiastic of the Malays proposed that the ground should at once be beaten over again; but midday was past, and it did not need a second glance at the majority of the men to see that the excitement, rather than their exertions, had so exhausted them that they were not fit to undertake another drive. Moreover, even if the tiger had really been in the ground covered by the first drive, it by no means followed that

it would be there by the time that the beaters were
ready to line up again. We decided, therefore, that
we must give it up. We covered our disappointment
as best we could; but our long high-strung excitement
had had such a miserable ending that one might have
noticed an almost hysterical catch to the laugh of more
than one man.

This was the most sporting tiger-drive that I have
ever seen. The fact that no tiger was seen, and that
possibly no tiger was near us, does not in any way de-
tract from the sport. We all believed that the tiger was
there: the guns thought that a tiger which was aware
of their presence was being forced to come towards
them; and the beaters felt that they were impelling forward an animal whose desire was to charge back through
their ranks. If the drive had ended by a tiger being
shot, it would not in the slightest degree have added
to the excitement that marked the duration of the drive.
I have shot a tiger in a drive that had not a tenth of
the interest of this day. Accompanied only by Malays,
I have occasionally had to follow wounded tigers on foot
through nasty country. As I have said above, I have
heard the "selawat" answered in royal style; but no-
where else have I seen such an intensity of feeling and
excitement. With this the number of men employed had
a great deal to do. It is seldom that one requisitions
more than thirty or forty beaters, whereas in this case
fully two hundred men were engaged. The amount of
magnetic feeling, where the excitement was communicated from unseen unit to unseen unit throughout the forest,
was enormous, and the air vibrated to the unuttered
excitement of the men.

It is in a drive where a line of men armed only with
spears advances thus determinedly upon a tiger, that you
realise how powerful a brute it is that they are assailing.
From the height of a seat in a tree or an elephant's back
you may shoot tigers with safety; but when you come
down to the ground, and either advance on foot to meet

the tiger or wait on foot for it to be driven up, the feeling comes home to you of the marvellous strength and activity that are combined in that beautiful frame. It may be within a few yards of you, perhaps, seeing all that you do, and itself unseen. It can steal noiselessly through the forest where you can only move with crackling of leaves and breaking of twigs. You know that, when the occasion comes, that wonderful lithe body can come with lightning speed through the thick-tangled growth that hampers and impedes your every movement. Finally, you know that at close quarters a man is as a helpless as a child against the overpowering weight and strength of an animal that kills an ox at a blow.

When you are on the ground following up or waiting for a tiger, you realise all this with some vividness. And in this connection I would advance the theory that the curious horror which some people have of cats is not, as is sometimes said, a sixth sense, but merely an instinctive terror, inherited from simian ancestors, of the feline tribe. The instinct has, I suggest, died out in the majority of cases, but exists in occasional individuals in the same manner that simian tricks of raising the ears or eyebrows are sometimes to be seen.

But whatever the average person's feelings may be regarding the race of cats, there is little doubt that almost every one has a peculiar sensation of the almost god-like beauty, power, activity, and strength of a tiger. A tiger will overawe and make conscious of his inferiority a man who would be unaffected by the bulk of an elephant. The feeling is, however, elusive of description, and I can perhaps best explain it in the words of a most charming French gentleman (now dead, alas!) who was once manager of a great tin-mining company in Perak I well remember his coming into the Tapah messroom where the Europeans of the district used in those days to take their meals. We had just finished lunch when he entered in a state of tremendous excitement. Walking alone and unarmed along an unfrequented bridle-path through the forest, he had walked almost on to a tiger. He gave us a most vivid narrative of the encounter: how the tiger had been lying down concealed in some long lalang grass beside the path; how he was within ten yards of it before he saw it; how then it rose and looked at him; how it yawned at him; how it then walked slowly across the path in front of him, and then stopped and looked at him, again yawning; and how it then deliberately walked away into the forest, whose depths finally hid it from view. I cannot attempt to imitate the beautiful and forcible diction that Monsieur C. had at his command, for the plain facts that I have thrown into a single sentence received from the narrator a majesty of style and a wealth of colouring and detail that cannot be reproduced on paper.

Some one asked him whether it was a big tiger. It is his answer that illustrates my meaning.

"Well, Messieurs, I cannot say if he is a big tiger. My eyes see that he is big; but I cannot say how big I see him to be; and if I say how big, it is perhaps that I tell you a lie. But I can tell you, Messieurs, how big I *feel* him to be, and I can tell you the truth. When he is standing there in front of me, I tell you that I feel he is not less than thir-r-ty feet high."

A TALE BY THE WAYSIDE

One of the charms of shooting is that one's wanderings with a gun, be it rifle or smooth-bore, generally take one into the remoter parts of a district where the Malays are still almost unaffected by the progress of civilisation, and where they live very much as their fathers lived before the days of roads and railways. When one rests for a few minutes, or hours, or for a night, in a village, not only does one see the simple and natural side of Malay life, but has a glimpse of the more intimate side; and one becomes acquainted, in a casual way, with much that one would never learn in an official visit. There is something in a gun that is like the incognito of royalty—it shows that the bearer is not on duty; and when a man is in a stained and disreputable old shooting-suit, it is easy for him to forget, and to persuade others to forget, that he is the Judge or the District Officer.

When you listen to Malays talking naturally among themselves, the thing that will most puzzle you will often be the apparent inconsequence of the remarks, the looseness of the argument, and its curious inherent tendency to drift into yet further vagueness. It will not be until you are thoroughly acquainted with the language and with Malay habits of thought, that it will dawn upon you that the thing which is bewildering you is an airy allusiveness, and that you have not got the key to the allusions. You will probably have been some years in the country before you realise that a Malay considers it crude to say outright what he has in his mind, and that he will prefer to let his meaning be known by a reference to a proverb, a quotation of a line of rhymed *pantun,* or a hint at the moral of a folk-tale.

This allusive style of conversation (regarding which I would like to digress for a moment, for I think that it will afford a clue to a riddle that puzzles many people) reaches its most exaggerated and fantastic form in the quotations from the *pantuns,* which are rhymed quatrains whose third and fourth lines alone carry the sense, while the first and second lines supply the rhymes.

Here is an example in which the translation is in the metre of the original:—

> "The fish fry play in the shallows,
>   While the big fish swim without.
> Tell me, beloved, the truth at once,
>   For my heart is tortured with doubt."

It is part of an amatory song, but in a serious discussion among the village elders you may hear a man say slowly and thoughtfully—

> "The fish fry play in the shallows;"

and though, of course, the words convey no meaning to you, unless you are acquainted with the *pantun,* you will see that the meaning that the speaker has intended to convey by the unquoted third and fourth lines has been perfectly appreciated by his audience.

There may be silence for a short space, and then perhaps another man will open his mouth to speak. You will notice that he has carefully considered his words, but

> "White, pure white, are the river sands,"

is all that he will say. However, every one at once understands that his meaning is—

> "You may say too little or say too much,
>   You can remedy one, but never the other."

Overtures, insults, challenges, may in like manner be
conveyed in such lines as —

> "The reed stems sway in the rippling stream."
> "The green pigeons feed on the fig-tree's fruit."
> "The cataract leaps through clouds of spray"

An argument by quotations from *pantuns* partakes,
however, more of the nature of a contest of wit than of
a genuine discussion. Similes and metaphores borrowed
from the proverbs, of which the language has a rich and
varied store, are more common and more easily understood. But the fact that arguments can be carried on
in such a manner shows how apt the Malay is to speak
allusively, and how quick to recognise the allusion. When,
therefore—this is the point to which my digression led
—a Malay is discussing with a European a matter of
considerable importance to one or both of them, the
European will often wonder when on earth his man
is going to come to the point, while the Malay is only
thinking whether he can say any more without being
so brutally direct as to give offence.

The folk-tales, rather than the *pantun* or the proverbs, are the medium by which a Malay loves to make
his meaning known.

In the village council, when weighty matters are
under discussion, many an argument is clinched or moral
pointed by an allusion to a story that in our prosaic
land would come under the half-contemptuous heading
of "children's stories," but which in the East are treated
as parables.

The little wayside tale, to which these remarks must
serve as an introduction, may perhaps gain some dignity
if I mention that many years ago it was told at length
in the Perak State Council, and that a very important
decision was based upon it.

The Malays have a wealth that has been almost
unexploited of folk-tales. There is a number of stories
of which Pa' Musang (Father Civet Cat) is the central
figure; another series is grouped round Pa' Bilalang

(Father Grasshopper); and there is yet another set of
stories about Pa' Pandir (Father Pandir), the typical
buffoon or fool, who invariably does the wrong thing,
manages to twist the most ridiculous meaning out of
the plainest instructions, and always finds some means
to make the most absurd mistakes.

But of all stories, the most numerous, the best known,
and the most popular, are those that have for their hero
the little mouse-deer, whose Malay name is *pelandok*.[1]
It is the smallest of all the deer tribe,—the daintiest and
most exquisitely formed little creature that can be
imagined. A full-grown animal is barely eight inches
high; and so small is the scale upon which it is built that
its feet, with their delicately cloven little hooves, have
not the thickness of the slimmest of penholders.

No one, so far as I am aware, has attempted any
analysis or classification of the mouse-deer stories. They
seem to contain three separate conceptions of the character of the mouse-deer, and though no hard and fast line
of division can be drawn, most of the stories fall into
one of the three classes.

First of all, we have "the wily mouse-deer"—
pelandok jenaka—the trickster, the practical joker, often
the petty cheat. He is the counterpart of Reynard the
Fox in the stories of Central Europe, of the Jackal in
India and in East Africa, and of "B'rer Rabbit" in negro
tales. He escapes from an enemy by his cunning, but he
is generally powerless to destroy his enemy; he contents
himself with mocking at his discomfiture, generally quite
needlessly, rather in *gamin* fashion, and thus only succeeds in whetting a natural desire for revenge.

Of this class are the following stories:—

A mouse-deer one day fell into a trap, and being
unable to get out again waited there until an elephant
happened to pass by. Then the mouse-deer called out—
"Why, brother elephant, what are you doing?" The

[1]. The final *k* is silent: pronounce *pelando*.

Elephant stopped and inquired what the matter was, and what the mouse-deer was doing at the bottom of the pit. The mouse-deer exclaimed—

"What, you foolish elephant, have you not heard that the sky is going to fall? I am staying down here to be out of harm's way."

The elephant replied that he had not heard anything about it, but at the mouse-deer's suggestion he looked up above his head, and there, between the tree-tops and the sky, he saw the clouds scudding by.

"See how the clouds are flying," cried the mouse-deer. "It won't be long now before the sky falls."

The elephant looked again, and then, without further parley, plunged into the pit for safety.

The mouse-deer then managed to get on to the elephant's back, and thence to leap up to the mouth of the pit and to make good his escape.

He was then mean enough to go and tell the man who had made the pit: which is rather disappointing.

Another time the mouse-deer wished to cross a river, but dared not swim it for fear of the crocodiles that infested it. He had therefore to rely upon his cleverness, and accordingly got into conversation with the Crocodile Raja, who lay basking upon the bank, and started a discussion as to whether there were more crocodiles or mouse-deer in the world. In the course of the argument the Crocodile Raja said that there were more than a thousand crocodiles in his river alone, and the mouse-deer expressed his surprise that there should be so many crocodiles in the whole world, and suggested that the Crocodile Raja should call up all the crocodiles of the river, so that the mouse-deer might count them.

This was agreed to, and soon all the crocodiles in the river floated to the surface. At the mouse-deer's suggestion they put themselves in a row, so that they might be more easily counted, and the row extended from one bank to the other. Then the mouse-deer began to count. "One," he called out as he jumped on to the back of the first crocodile; "two," and he jumped on to the back of the next one; "three," and so on until he reached the other side of the river.

When he was safely upon the bank he turned and jeered at the deluded raja in front of all his subjects, and then gleefully continued his way skipping through the forest.

Another time a crocodile caught the mouse-deer by the hind-leg, which is such a marvel of fine-drawn skin and shapely bone. The mouse-deer saw that any struggle to escape would be fatal, and while with his other three legs he endeavoured to maintain his hold upon the bank, he called to the crocodile—

"Ha! you missed me that time."

"I think not," snuffled the crocodile, with his jaws clenced upon the poor little leg; "I've got you by the leg."

"Leg!" laughed the mouse-deer, suppressing the agony he felt; "that is no leg you are biting. You are holding on to an old dry twig."

The little leg that the crocodile held was as fleshless as any twig; and the crocodile believed that he had made a mistake, and opened his mouth, thus allowing the mouse-deer to escape.

On another occasion the mouse-deer challenged the crocodile to a tug-of-war—the crocodile to pull from the water and the mouse-deer from the land. The mouse-deer tied his end of the rope to the top of a coco-nut-tree, and then gave the word to pull. The crocodile tugged with all his might, and the palm-tree swayed to and fro. When the crocodile, swirling in a turmoil of water, pulled his hardest, the palm yielded and bowed towards him; but when he relaxed his efforts for a second, the palm resumed its natural position, and the crocodile lost the few feet that he had gained. So it went on, and after a while the mouse-deer called from the bank, suggesting that they should wait for a breathing-space.

The exhausted crocodile agreed, and the mouse-deer came lightly leaping down the bank.

"That was a splendid pull," he said cheerily to the crocodile. "You are better than I had thought, but I'll get you over easily next time."

The crocodile could hardly speak for lack of breath, and when he saw that the mouse-deer showed no signs of fatigue, he declined to continue the contest, and admitted his inferiority.

But it is not only the crocodile that the mouse-deer scores off in this fashion. He is always getting the better of the tiger, the elephant, and all the other animals, in the same sort of way. The stories are generally very slight, and, as I have said, they do not always show the wily mouse-deer in a very favourable light; but somehow the little creature has a charm that is peculiarly his own. If he is undoubtedly a trickster, he is without doubt a very fascinating little trickster; but the whimsicality that underlies this charm is so evanescent that it will not live in pen and ink. The stories can only be told. When one has committed them to writing, even in their native language, one cannot but look at them with the same rueful feeling that a man has when he has picked a wood-anemone and sees it fade and wilt at his touch; but when one has to translate the story into another language, in which the words have another value and therefore fail to give the true equivalent of the original, the result is no more like the real folk-tale than a flower, dried and pressed between two sheets of paper and labelled wood-anemone, resembles the white star that raises its delicate head above the fallen beech-leaves.

In the second of three divisions into which the pelandok stories may be said to fall, the little mouse-deer appears in the character of an arbitrator or umpire, chosen on account of his acumen to settle disputes and quarrels. In this role he is generally styled *Che Salam di Rimba* (Sir Peace of the Forest), and is addressed by all with respect.

Of this class of story the following will serve as an example.

Two men (men, be it noticed) quarrelled about a loan which one had made to the other. The debtor had promised to repay the loan in two months. (In Malay, moon and month are the same word.) When, upon the expiry of the stipulated time, the creditor demanded repayment, the debtor replied laconically, pointing to the sky, "There is only one moon."

"It is two months since I lent you the money," replied the creditor, "and you promised to pay in two months."

But "there is only one moon" was all that he could get out of the debtor.

So the creditor went home and waited another month. Then he went again to demand his money, but "there is only one moon" was all that the debtor said.

"You said that last time," cried the creditor, "and that was a month ago."

"Only one moon," replied the debtor; "when there are two moons I will pay you." So they quarrelled. Then to settle the dispute they went to Sir Peace of the Forest.

Sir Peace heard both men state their cases, and then, when the sun had set, took them both down to the river-bank. It was a cloudless night, and upon the bosom of the river the full moon shone reflected.

"What is that?" said Sir Peace of the Forest to the debtor, pointing to the golden circle that lay upon the water.

"The moon," replied the debtor.

"And what is that?" said Sir Peace, pointing to the sky.

"The moon also," replied the debtor.

"That makes two," cried Sir Peace. "Two moons, and the time has come for you to pay your debt."

The debtor was silent. He had relied upon a trick, and the same trick had been used against him. He could find nothing to say, and was compelled to repay the loan.

The stories in this second class are not as numerous as the "wily mouse-deer" stories, and that one example will suffice. As a rule, the stories rather remind one of the Arabian tales of the wise Viziers and Kathis.

In the third class of story the mouse-deer has attained to royal rank and power. By his skill and address he has subjected the other animals of the forest, and all of them—elephant and tiger, sladang and rhinoceros—acknowledge him as their king. His title is *Shah Alam di Rimba* (the King of the Forest Universe), and he is addressed in the honorific forms appropriate to a reigning sultan. He has his throne upon a white marble rock under the canopy of a flowering *bungor*-tree, whose flowers nearest approach the colours of royalty; and when he travels, rides either upon a white sladang or a white rhinoceros. He is the champion of all the animals against their external foes.

I should like to tell the story of how he made the peace between the Tigers and the Goats. and constituted himself as their king-paramount; and the story of how he slew the Giant of Lake Tenom, after the giant had defeated the bear and the rhinoceros. But the tales are too long to tell here.

In this third class of story the mouse-deer has a heroic side to his character that is denied to Reynard, "B'rer Rabbit," or the Jackal. The little champion somehow invites comparison with the hero of the Odyssey. The comparison may appear ridiculous, but in justification I would point out the epithets "of many devices" and "rich in counsel," which throughout the Odyssey are applied to its hero, exactly fit, not the mouse-deer in his role of champion, but the mouse-deer of the first and second divisions that I have attempted to make.

I must repeat that the division between the three classes of story is not clearly defined. Some stories fall half-way between one and the other; and the difficulty of attempting to classify them is added to in no inconsiderable measure by the fact that the Malays love the title of "Sir Peace of the Forest," which is appropriate only to the "counsellor" class of story, but at the same time prefer the simpler stories of the "wily mouse-deer" type, and the result is that, whether the story be of the trickster, the counsellor, or the champion, the little mouse-deer generally bears his whimsical title of Sir Peace of the Forest.

When you have a few minutes or half an hour to spare; on a river-bank, while you wait for a dugout to convey you across to a teal pond or to a place where the green pigeons are flighting; under the shade of fruit-trees, besides the snipe-fields, while a boy climbs to get you green coco-nuts; in some way-side shelter from the heat of the sun, while some one runs to call the dog-cart that is waiting farther down the road,—it is easy, if you go the right way about it, to bring into the conversation some allusion to Sir Peace of the Forest, and then, when you have either made some one tell the story or have told it yourself, nothing is easier than to get another man to cap it.

The story which I set out to tell is properly speaking an animal story, pure and simple, and does not belong to the mouse-deer cycle. My preface is intended to explain, firstly, how much a part of a Malay's daily conversation and life these folk-tales are; and secondly, why in this story the little mouse-deer bears, for no apparent reason, his fantastic title.

This is the story. I heard it one day when we were resting in the forest near Teluk Kepaiang after a deer-drive. We had entered the forest early in the morning, and having found fresh deer-tracks, had disposed ourselves along some woodcutters' paths at points where the deer was likely to break out. When we put the dogs in,

a deer had dashed out, affording me a shot which I had
missed. The deer was now some miles away, and while
a couple of men were following the tracks to recall the
dogs, we were lying in the shade of the great dark forest-
trees waiting for them.

There were six of us: my brother Eric; Che Ngah
Durani, the headman; Ali and Sahak, two peasants; my
tracker, Malias; and myself. The Malays were all smoking their native cigarettes or meditatively chewing betel-
leaf.

At intervals one of them would call to the absent
dogs at the top of his voice—

"Doh! Doh! Doh!"

"Oh! Si Nibong!"

"Oh! Si Kumbang! Doh!"

While we were talking, Sahak took up a couple of
fallen twigs, and in an absent-minded way beat on a dead
crisp leaf with them, tapping as one plays a kettle-drum.

"Ah!" chuckled little Che Ngah Durani, "that is
the war-drum of Sir Peace of the Forest."

We all laughed. The mouse-deer call to one another
in the mating season by rapping their hind-feet on the
ground, and the Malays decoy them by imitating the
sound with two sticks in the manner that Sahak was
doing.

"Ha! ha!" Che Ngah Durani laughed on, "and
that is the way that Sir Peace of the Forest beat his war-
drum when he killed the Otter's babies. Tell us the
story, Ali."

And Ali thereupon, without hesitation or demur,
told us the following tale: —

"One morning, Memerang the Otter was going down
to the river to catch fish. She left her family of baby
otters on the bank, and, before she went, begged Sir
Peace of the Forest to look after them for her. This,
of course, was in the days when all the animals spoke a
common language. Nabi Sleman [King Soloman] had,
by appointment from Allah, authority and power over all

created animals, and Nabi Noh [Noah] had charge of all the trees and plants."

"Yes; but," interrupted Che Ngah Durani, "there were some plants that Nabi Noh forgot. Nabi Tuakal [the Chance Prophet] discovered that Nabi Noh had overlooked certain roots, and decided to plant them himself. The whole of the earth had been taken up by Nabi Noh, so Nabi Tuakal had no alternative but to plant these roots upon growing trees. He did so, and the orchids are the result, and they are in the charge of Nabi Tuakal, not of Nabi Noh."

After the interruption Ali continued—

"The Otter plunged into the river, and Sir Peace of the Forest remained on the bank, playing and nibbling the young grass, and keeping an eye on the Otter's babies.

"Suddenly he heard 'tap-a-tap—tap-a-tap—tap—tap —tap.' He listened, and then heard it again, and recognised the notes of the drum of the Woodpecker, and the call was that of the war-alarm.

"You know Blato' the Woodpecker," Ali said, turning to me,—"the bird that lights on the tree-trunks, and drums with his beak upon the bark?

"Well, of the birds of the forest the Woodpecker is the one that may beat the war-drum. And when Sir Peace of the Forest heard the alarm, he knew that somewhere killing was afoot, and he is as skilled at drumming on the ground as the woodpecker is at drumming on a tree, and among the four-footed animals of the forest he is the chief dancer and drum-beater.

"So he proceeded to spread the alarm, and with his little heels he tap-a-tap—tap-a-tapped on the ground, in exactly the way that Sahak played with those two twigs just now. But in his excitement he did not see what he was doing, and, before he realised it, all the Otter's babies lay dead, trodden flat under his prancing hooves.

"Soon the Otter returned, and there was a terrible scene. Sir Peace of the Forest admitted all that he had done, but the Otter would hear nothing in extenuation, and went away to Nabi Sleman to obtain redress. When she reached the presence of the King she made the obeisance [which is made by Malays by raising the two hands, pressed palm to palm, to the level of the eyes] and said—

"'Pardon, O King! Sir Peace of the Forest has killed thy slave's children, and thy slave would hear the order of the King.'

"Nabi Sleman replied: 'Never yet without a father and a mother was child begotten; and without an audience of both the accuser and the accused, never yet was justice done. Go, call Sir Peace of the Forest.'

"Then Nabi Sleman turned to his Bentaras [court officials] and said: 'We will hear this case at the palace by the mouth of the river. Let all the animals attend.'

"Later, in full state, Nabi Sleman repaired to the palace. All the animals were present. On one side of the palace was the sea, thronged with all the sea-fishes; on the other side was the river, full of the river-fishes; on the land side were the forest animals; and the trees were full of birds and butterflies.

"Then Nabi Sleman, ruler under Allah of all the animals, turned to the Otter and said, 'Tell thy story.'

"And the Otter made the obeisance and said; 'Pardon, O King! This morning thy slave, before going down to the river to catch fish, left her children in the charge of Sir Peace of the Forest. On her return she found them dead, trodden to death; and Sir Peace of the Forest admitted having done the deed. Thy slave would hear the order.'

"Nabi Sleman turned to the accused and said, 'Tell thy story.'

"Sir Peace of the Forest made the obeisance and said, 'Pardon, O King! What the Otter has said is true. But soon after thy slave had been left in charge of the children, Blato' the Woodpecker sounded the war alarm. And thy slave, as in duty bound, also sounded the alarm, and, in doing so, unwittingly trod on and killed the

Otter's children. Thy slave only did his duty. The fault is with the Woodpecker for sounding the alarm.'

" 'Let no one be judged in his absence,' said Nabi Sleman. 'Send for the Woodpecker.'

"The Woodpecker came flying through the air [Ali imitated with his hand the undulatory flight of the wood-pecker tribe], rising and falling in lines, like the curves of a kris or a wave of the sea, and entered the presence and made the obeisance.

"Nabi Sleman said, 'Sir Peace of the Forest has killed the Otter's children, and ascribes the fault to thee, saying that the war alarm was sounded by thee. What is the reply to this charge?'

"Pardon, O King,' said the Woodpecker. It is true that thy slave sounded the war alarm. But thy slave saw Tuntong, the River-turtle, leave the river. He was followed by all the river-turtles, and they all wore their coats of armour. As they ascended the banks in their numbers, they presented the appearance of an invasion of the country, and thy slave accordingly sounded the war alarm. The fault is with Tuntong, the River-turtle.'

" 'Because the branch brake when the Hornbill flew by,' said Nabi Sleman, 'who shall say that the Hornbill broke the branch? We would hear the River-turtle.'

"The River-turtle was in the stream amidst the throng of the water-dwellers. He scrambled up the bank, the sand flying to right and to left under his broad flat flippers, and made his way into the presence.

"He made the obeisance, and Nabi Sleman said to him, 'Blato' the Woodpecker has sounded the war alarm, and has given as his excuse the appearance of an invasion of the country by thy kin. What hast thou to say?'

"The River-turtle again made the obeisance and said, 'Pardon, O King! Thy slave saw that the river was full of turmoil and alarm. Udang, the Prawns, were ascending the river in companies and battalions, and all of them carried their long spears between their eyes. Sebarau, the Perches, were swimming up-stream in broad

lines of array, and every one carried his bright war-sash
across his body. And Jenjulong, the Garfishes, dashing
hither and thither, followed close behind, and each
of them carried his terrible pike. When thy slave saw
in the river such signs of war and cruel death, thy slave
and thy slave's kin left the river for the safety of the
banks.'

" 'By the grace of Allah,' said Nabi Sleman, 'a
stream is not without its bends and turnings. Send for
the Prawns, the Perches, and the Garfishes.'

"The creatures named were all in the river in
attendance on the court of the king, and when their
names were called they approached the bank and made
their obeisance. In answer to the questions put by Nabi
Sleman they all replied with one accord, 'Pardon, O
King! the River-turtle has spoken the truth. But no
invasion was it—no array of warriors. It was that thy
slaves were fleeing for their lives from the onslaughts of
Memerang the Otter, who ever kills and harries thy
slaves.'

"Nabi Sleman then turned to the accuser, now the
accused, and said, 'Hah, Memerang the Otter, what sayest
thou to this?'

" 'Pardon, O King!' replied the Otter. 'It is true
that thy slave harried the Prawns, the Perches, and the
Garfishes. It is the nature of thy slave to feed upon
them, and to feed thy slave's children upon them. And,
moreover, it was to seek and to slay them that thy slave
left her children with Sir Peace of the Forest.'

"Then said Nabi Sleman, 'The case is clear. Hear
now our judgment. Learn, O Memerang the Otter, that
is it not the arrow, but he that draws the bow, that slays.
The fault is with thee. Hadst thou not harried the
Prawns, the Perches, and the Garfishes, the River-turtle
had not left the stream, and the Woodpecker had not
sounded the war-drum, and Sir Peace of the Forest had
not, in spreading the alarm, killed thy babies. None but
thyself is to blame, and upon none other can punishment

rightly fall. Let the death of thy babies be sufficient punishment for thee. Go in peace.'

"Nabi Sleman then turned to the Bentaras and said, 'Our judgment is delivered. See that all the animals here present return in peace.' "

As Ali was describing the dispersal of the animals, Nibong, whose name meant "the brindle," burst in upon us.

It acknowledged our greetings with a short wag of a tail, and threw itself down in the dampest and coolest spot to be found, where, with heaving flanks, it gave itself up to the luxury of complete exhaustion.

A moment later we were joined by Kumbang, an old black pariah, whose Malay name meant "the beetle," but a most staunch and excellent hound withal.

When the two dogs had been stroked and patted for a minute or two, to show that we knew what they knew —namely, that the day's failure had been our fault and not theirs,—we made a move, and prepared to go homewards.

As a chance would have it, we had not gone far before Kumbang gave a sudden yelp, and dashed into one side of the path. A moment later I heard a rustle among some dead leaves in the thick growth in front of me, and there under a fallen branch I saw the small form of a pelandok. The descendant of animals that "once upon a time" had held the forest in sway now cowered in apprehension. Its ears were turned back to catch the sound of Kumbang on its track, and its great eyes viewed with terror the open line made by the path on which we stood. At my sign Malias held Nibong, and as the pelandok bounded across the path I had time to rush forward and seize Kumbang.

The Malays all thought that I objected to dogs trained to deer acknowledging the scent of so small an animal as a mouse-deer, and little Che Ngah Durani only half-guessed that he had hit upon the truth when he laughed and said, "It was only right that Sir Peace of the Forest should go free to-day."

TUBA FISHING.

WHEN I was stationed, some years ago, at Kuala Kuantan, I represented throughout a district of many hundreds of square miles, principally forest, all that the Malays understood of British Protection. My nearest European neighbours to the west could only be reached by two days' poling up river; southward, by a two days' journey on foot along the sea-shore. Eastward lay the China Sea, thundering upon a sandy beach within a mile of my door. Northward, over many hundreds of miles, through unprotected native states, there were no Europeans until Siamese territory was reached.

I was therefore fortunate in finding myself among an exceptionally fine set of Malays. One and all they welcomed any sporting expedition, and a whole village would turn out at the shortest notice to join in a deer-drive. So much did they enter into the sport and identify themselves with it, that the idea of being paid for their work never occurred to them. Between associates there is no question of remuneration, and if I had offered them money they would at once have felt that I looked upon them as servants rather than as my fellows. All that they asked was, that if it were necessary for them to sleep away from their homes I should provide them with food. Never, if I had given due notice to the village headmen, had I any lack of men for a deer-drive; the difficulty was generally to turn back the lads whose strength was less than their keenness. But these Malays would work as well as play. One day, on the way to a deer-drive, for which the men of two villages had turned out in force, we had to pass through a deep swamp, three-quarters of a mile long, between the two villages. We had a good day's sport, getting two splendid deer, and when it was over I told the two village headmen that they ought to build a light trestle-bridge across the swamp. They both agreed that it should be done, but all said that it would cost too much. I thereupon proposed that the men of Gebing should make half the bridge and the men of Pengorak the other half, every man in each village making his share, and promised for my part to provide the workers with food. My offer was accepted on the spot. A few months later the bridge was built, and well built, at a cost to the Government of only a few bags of rice. And though it is some years now since I left that district, I am told that the bridge is still known by my name.

I had been an honoured guest at a great seine fishing held out at sea to inaugurate the first wetting of a set of nets, and Ahman, my head boatman, hinted to me that, by way of returning the hospitality, I should hold, for the benefit of the whole district, a tuba fishing of one of the rivers. Tuba is a small wild plant, whose roots contain a vegetable poison that has an extraordinary effect upon fish; and tuba fishing is one of the recognised national pastimes of the Malay Peninsula and of Sarawak. Many a great river is tuba-ed annually on so extensive a scale that at the end of the day one might well believe that it had been depleted of fish. Yet the succeeding year shows no diminution either in the size of the fish or in their numbers.

At Ahman's suggestion I sent for Pawang Duhamat, a recognised expert in all matters relating to tuba and tuba fishing. When he came he gave his opinion in favour of the Blat river as being the most suitable, in its present condition of water, for our object, and said that he had in his house, sorted and ready for use, the quantity of tuba root that we should require, about ten hundredweight.

I bought the root from him, and, when he had selected an auspicious day for the fishing, issued invitations to the chiefs, and proclaimed to the district at large that on that date I should tuba the Blat river.

A few days before the appointed day Pawang Duhamat and Ahman collected four or five Malays, unpaid volunteers, and paddled away up river to make the preliminary arrangements. They took with them a few measures of rice from my store-room, but for the rest depended upon such fish as they could catch, and upon an old gun which I had lent Ahman, nominally as a protection against tigers, but really to enable him to get some jungle-fowl and imperial pigeon. Their object was to erect a barricade across the river at the point that Pawang Duhamat might select as the place for the tuba fishing to end. The building of this barricade was no light task, and upon its stability would depend much of the success of the day.

They were to encamp upon the river-bank while engaged upon this work, and to remain there when it was completed, to see that no harm befell it before we arrived.

Upon the day appointed a great throng of boats of all sizes collected round my landing-stage, and with great booming of gongs, we started up-stream. We found that Ahman had completed the barricade across the river, having left only a small passage for our craft to pass through. When the last boat had squeezed past, the barricade was completely and finally closed, until it was opened or broken, no fish or boat could pass it to go either up-stream or down-stream. We were now in clear, shallow water, and urged by the boat-poles the boats made rapid way up the river. On either bank was great primeval forest. Late in the afternoon we reached the sandy spit which Pawang Duhamat had selected as a favourable spot for the tuba fishing to begin. By sunset we had made all our preparations for the night. The little boat in which I came, my house-boat being too unwieldy, was broad enough to hold a jungle mattress, but the majority of the men had come in light dugouts, in which it was impossible to sleep, and they had to encamp upon the bank. Their preparations were simple: a *kajang* (palm-leaves sewn together with rattan), four posts stuck in the ground, and a couple of boat-poles across them, made in a few minutes an excellent protection against the dew; and a few handfuls of *tepus*-leaves afforded a comfortable and fragrant matting. Three pointed sticks hammered into the ground made a tripod for the rice-pot, and what more does any man want?

At first the moon was overcast with heavy clouds that threatened rain, but the surrounding darkness only set off the cheerful brightness of the camping-ground. The lights of the different fireplaces fell brightly on the forms of the men, their rude lean-to's, the throng of boats, and flickered gaily on the trunks of the great solemn forest trees above and around us. Later the clouds passed away, and the glorious full moon shone upon us.

By seven o'clock all had finished their evening meal, and small woven cases of native cigarettes, and little covered bowls of silver or copper, containing betel-leaf and its accessories, were brought out and passed round. After a while old Pawang Duhamat was seen handling a short thick bludgeon. Similar bludgeons immediately made their appearance on every side, and then we all went down to the water's edge. Ten dugouts lay a little apart from the others: cleaned and washed, stripped of everything, they were mere empty vessels. The tuba root lay in great bales on the bank. Each man picked up as much as he required, and took it to one of the empty boats. After splashing a few gallons of water into the boat, he soaked a piece of the root in the water for a moment, and then began to pound

it with his bludgeon.   As the root abraded, a little milky
juice ran out, and trickled down the side of the boat
into the water at its bottom.   While he pounded the
root, he sprinkled it from time to time with an occasional
splash of water from the river.   Round each of the ten
boats as many Malays as could find a place collected,
each bang-bang-banging away at a piece of root: those
that could find a foothold on the narrow lines of the gun-
wales perched there happily, whilst the others stood
contentedly in the river, despite its coolness.   Above the
din of the pounding bludgeons rose the babble of voices
and laughter.

A wag of a boatman of mine began telling stories—
some of them about Sir Peace of the Forest, the little
mouse-deer that by his cleverness became ruler over all
the other animals, and some of them about the choleric
captain of a local coasting-steamer; and all told with a
wealth of happy imagination and happier mimicry that
convulsed his audience into apoplectic choking.

After a while one of the men burst into a song, of
which the refrain sounds somewhat as follows: —

"Deng—a—deng: —Deng—deng—deng: —Deng—a—deng! —
  Deng—a—deng—deng: —Deng—deng—deng: —dang—
  Deng—a—deng—deng: —Deng—dang—dong."

The Malays call it the "dendang" song, and to a
wild catchy refrain, of which my written characters can
only give a bare idea, they sing impromptu verses.   When
the first singer had finished a stanza, another man
answered it, and then the two sang against one another,
time and time about, each happy turn of a phrase or
trick of a rhyme winning instant appreciation and
applause from a highly critical audience, until one man,
failing of a reply, admitted the other's victory and, with
a laugh at his defeat, handed on the right of contest to a
third party.

By the time that midnight was reached and the
moon was poised overhead, the dug-outs were half filled
with the milky juice of the abraded root; and as there

was no sign of the abatement of the energy of the pounders or the spirit of the singers, I stole away to the bed on my boat.

At the little distance the "dendang" had a lullaby sound, and the soft moonlit streaks of the smoothly flowing water were a restful sight on which to close sleepy eyes. All round us was the great primeval forest, old beyond all knowing, and from age to age but rarely invaded by man; and from the heart of the forest came wafts of night odours, fragrant of rich soil, of leaf-mould, and a strong strenuous tree life—wafts only sensible to man in the hours of darkness.

When we woke the next morning the ten dug-outs lay nearly brimful of the thick milky juice of the tuba poison. A hasty meal, and then on every side fish spears were brought out. The unambitious produced a *serampang*, a three- or four- pronged spear which is useful for any fish up to five pounds; those more hopeful of adventure had a *tempuling*, a spear with a barbed detachable head to which a rope is tied. It will hold anything, and with the bigger fish it is a necessity; but, on the other hand, it misses many of the average-sized fish.

The camp was struck in a few minutes, the palm-leaf coverings rolled up, the boat-poles collected, and the place that had resounded to the song and laughter of the night was abandoned.

When we were all in our sampans and prahus, Pawang Duhamat stepped on the bow of one of the tuba-laden dug-outs, and stood up amidst the silence of the throng. A fine-looking old Malay was he, erect and tall above the average height, with the high-raised cheek-bones of his race, dark expressive eyes, and sad lines round his mouth. A thin grey beard on the point of his chin added to his venerable appearance. He leant on his fish spear, and then uttered the following charm over the tuba water:—

>"Hong! Hak! Tina buih ipong
>Batang ku tarik bulan charan
>Naik segala yang bisa tuba jinul."

When, many weeks later in the privacy of my house, he confided the words of this charm to me (for no one could catch the rapid mutter in which they were uttered), all that he could tell me of the first two lines was that they were in the language of the Jins. With the exception of *jinul*, which is the Jin's word for tuba, the third line is Malay, and means, "Let all that is poisonous in this tuba arise."

He also told me that this charm so increased the efficacy of the poison that one boat-load of the root was, if thus charmed, the equivalent of two boat-loads of uncharmed root. After a few minutes' silence, during which we waited for the poison of the root to assert itself, Pawang Duhamat splashed some of the liquid into the river, and then gave the word for the contents of eight dug-outs to be thrown overboard. The tuba juice in the remaining two boats was reserved for later use.

With one accord the multitude raised the ringing Malay war-cry, and amid shouting and excitement the liquid was flung into the river. The milky juice soon lost itself, and for a space we all kept our positions, while the vessels that had held the poison were washed and cleansed. Then Pawang Duhamat led the way down the stream. For a few hundred yards there was not a sign of a fish; everything had sped away from the first taste of the poisoned water. Then in a little eddy by the side of the river we saw a dazed fish swimming slowly in circles on the water's surface. It had had one taste of the poisoned water, and instead of fleeing down-stream on and on as the other fish had done, it had turned into some hiding-place to wait—under some stump, perhaps, or by the roots of an old tree that had often afforded a refuge from bigger fish or a place of safety in times of floods, but which gave no protection against the insidious tuba. A second taste of the poison and it had floated helpless to the surface.

Pawang Duhamat bade the man who paddled his dug-out to turn towards the fish, and then he slowly and deliberately speared it. He cut it in two, and repeated over it this charm: —

"Pekih! Pekah!
Ayunberdum is my bodyguard!
Jibrail is my weapon!
O Gathering of Angels at the Gate of Earth,
Rise ye up to the Gate of Earth!
O Children of the Gathering of Angels at the Gate of Sky,
Come ye down to the Gate of Sky!
Let us all be joined in a Bond of Union,
Let us all join in one Game;
It is not that I wish to thrust aside all the doings of the Jins,
It is not that I wish to thrust aside all the doings of the Children
    of the Gathering of Men:
It is that I am under the Canopy of Allah!"

If there is not in this invocation, uttered in the midst of the throng that floated on the breast of the stream deep in the recesses of the boundless uninhabited forest, something that touches the imagination, let the fault be ascribed to the translator.

Pawang Duhamat threw one half of the fish on to the right bank as a propitiatory offering to the Jins, and the other half on to the left bank for the Sheitans.

When this was done, all were free to find and spear their fish as best they could; and, with yells from their occupants, the boats darted forward. But the race was not to the swift, for the pace was set by the stream which carries the poison; and when the first excitement had subsided, the boats glided gently and silently forward.

The next few bends of the river presented the sad sight of the day, for here were numbers of fry lying dead on the surface of the water. At the place where the tuba water is poured into the stream, not only is there, of course, enough poison to affect the whole river, but the liquid mixes equally with the surface and the bottom of the river. Later the specific gravity of the tuba water, which is considerably heavier than that of river water, asserts itself, and the poison is carried along the bottom of the river. The small fry that flee for safety to the shallows then escape unharmed; but, at first, a number of them are killed. It is the sight of these poor little dead fishes that is responsible for the general, and totally incorrect, opinion that tuba fishing kills all the fry in the river.

The poison affects different species of fish in different ways. Perches, probably through seeking the shallows with the fry, escape altogether; the mud fish find safety in burying themselves; while the little buntal, a small fish with a peculiar power on inflating itself, floats dead to the surface at the first taste of the poison. But the great majority of the fish seek safety in flight.

Keen eyes in one boat mark, under an over-hanging branch, the lips of a fish which cannot breathe the tainted water breaking the surface of the stream to inhale the freshness of the air. But the fish, though distressed, has not lost its senses, and before the spear can be thrust it has disappeared.

A broad brown back is seen as a temoli swims slowly down the river and two boats dart towards it. Neck and neck they race until they are within a few yards of the fish, when the splashing of their paddles alarms it, and it dives. A hundred yards farther down the river it rises to the surface again, and the race begins anew. Gradually one boat gains on the other, and at last is some three yards ahead. As the occupant of the leading boat raises his arm to stab, the Malay in the other hurls his spear.

Under the steel of the descending spear the point of the long spear of the thrower flashes and then buries itself, quivering, fair between the shoulders of the temoli.

It is a splendid throw, and, despite their discomfiture, the occupants of the first boat join in the applause.

A few minutes later a great belida, that has been skulking under a bank, and hoping perhaps to make a dash up-stream to purer water, is transfixed and held up by an exultant Malay for all to see.

The tuba is doing its work well, and on every side we shout our compliments and congratulations to Pawang Duhamat. We shout because the Malay fully realises that a compliment, like a libel, owes much to its publication.

Some fish are half dead when seen for the first time, and therefore afford no excitement, unless a race is necessary; whilst other fish will keep the occupants of a dozen boats on tenterhooks for a quarter of an hour, and give all the excitement of an otter-hunt. Some fish are so affected by the poison, that it appears to be necessary for them to come to the surface to breathe. Though extremely alert, they cannot stay below the surface for more than a minute or so. When the boats surround a place where one of these fish has been marked down, the men all wait with uplifted arm for it to reappear. Perhaps some one sees its lips at the water's surface by the roots of an old tree: as he hurls his spear the fish dives, and the Malay has to disengage the barbs of the spear-head from the tree-roots with such patience·as he can. Two or three minutes pass and, as the fish does not reappear, there are fears that it may have escaped, until it is seen quietly hiding under the stern of a dug-out. Before the occupant sees it, it is gone again. Eventually, after many misses, a clever thrust, delivered just as it rises to the surface, transfixes it, and amid tumultuous shouts it is lifted into a boat.

The day wears on. Bend after bend the beautiful forest-clad banks open themselves in front of us and close behind us. In each dug-out rises a heap of fish; and an occasional splash, with a lift of the light split-bamboo flooring, tells of an imprisoned monster.

The chief excitement of the day is occasioned by the shout of "Buaia." Buaia, the crocodile, as a rule, is found in Malay rivers only in tidal waters. But, be the reason what it may, not only do a certain number of crocodiles find their way up to the higher reaches of the rivers, but they even dare to leave for miles the safety of the water to seek a way through pathless forests. It may be that the motive is one of direct pressure: or may it be that this chill and repellent saurian is animated by the instinct of the English younger brother, and wanders forth in quest of adventures?

The crocodile is only a small one, some four feet long, and manages to escape unharmed after having caused a ripple of excitement down the length of the river by the mere terror of its dreaded name.

All day long there is nothing to break the continuity of the great virgin forest that clothes either bank. But not for a moment of the long day could one find any degree of monotony in its endless lines and masses. Though the general aspect of the forest is that of great dark-foliaged trees, every turn of the river affords a view that has something in it of individuality, and the variety in the endless succession of views is as delicately marked as their general similarity is broadly outlined. Added to the charm of the beauty of the forest is the charm of its mystery. For mile upon mile, hundreds of miles upon hundreds of miles, it extends north and south and west. All that it holds of life is hidden from our eyes under the heavy screen of foliage. Under any tree that lines the bank a tiger might be lying, or perhaps some shy naked aboriginal, armed with a blow-pipe and poisoned darts, might be peeping to see the passing throng of Malays. But however close we might be to tigers or to Semangs, we should no more see them than we should see the fish in the depths of the pools over which our boats were passing.

Bend after bend of the river now lay behind us. When we were within a mile of Ahman's barricade, where the final scene would be enacted, Pawang Duhamat emptied into the river the two boat loads of tuba water that he had saved in the morning, repeating the same short incantation as he did so.

Then we pressed on to the barricade. This, as I have said, extended across the river. Stout posts had been driven, a few feet apart, deep into the sandy bottom of the river. Between them was supported, from one bank to the other, a framework made of split bamboos so closely laced together with rattans that no fish could pass between the interstices. The bottom of the framework was pegged to the river bottom, and its top rose to a height of some eight feet above the surface. In addition to this framework the posts supported a light platform on which a man might stand. It was about a foot above the level of the river, and was on the up-stream side of the bamboo framework. Some three hundred yards above the barricade, on either bank, a great post with a streamer of red cloth had been erected. This marked the limit below which only the boats of chiefs might pass, and old Ahman and Pawang Duhamat stationed themselves there to see that none should intrude. The four principal chiefs of the district and I took our stand on the narrow gangway of the barricade, and with uplifted spears waited for the coming of the fish. The tuba water was still some way up-stream, but it was driving the fish before it.

In the press of the boats above the line marked by the red flags an occasional spear rose and fell and rose again, but in the open space immediately above the barricade all was still. Suddenly the surface of the water was broken, and a great fish launched itself at the barricade. The gleam of a bar of silver and the twinkle of falling drops, and then the fish hit the bamboo framework some four feet above the level of the river. With a mighty splattering of its tail it managed to maintain its position for a moment, and then it fell on to the platform just in time to escape the thrust of a chief's spear. While the old man was extricating his barb from the bamboo framework the fish leapt free, and, leaving only some glittering scales behind it, fell back into the river. A moment later another huge broad back showed above the surface, and we saw a fish carefully and deliberately trying to find whether, in the length and breadth of the barricade, there was not some loophole of escape. A steady hand drove the spear, and after a struggle a young chief laid the fish on the platform.

Soon the fish came in numbers, and we were thrusting and stabbing on every side, now at one as it hit the barricade, now at another in the water; now at one as it fell on the platform; sometimes at one as it flashed through the air. While we thrust at one, another would leap up beside us, and before we could turn it two would fall back into the water. Beside each of us there grew up a pile of splendid fish.

One magnificent fish—a great temoli, weighing perhaps sixty pounds—twice launched itself at the barricade, and twice escaped in safety back into the water; but each time it fell back on the up-stream side, and safety from the tuba only lay in flight and access to the down-stream side.

Then, during a lull, while all were waiting, the great fish broke the surface of the water some eight feet away from the barricade, and, cleaving through the air like a broad spear-head, rose up to the top of the bamboo framework. It hit the barricade some few inches below its summit, and hung balanced for a moment. Two men thrust at it and missed it, and then the framework bent back under the great weight, and the noble fish fell into the water on the down-stream side—safe.

This was one of the last fish of the day, and before long all was over. We made our way to a sandy spit where the day's catch was exhibited.

Here Malay women were waiting beside great steaming cauldrons of rice and many bowls of the ingredients of feast which only awaited the arrival of our fish. Other women had huge earthern-ware jars for pickling fish for future use.

But of all the day's strange sights the strangest sight is to see the fish fry playing and splashing for the rice grains that fall from the plates on the scene where all the great fish had been speared a short hour before.

Except where it is first poured into the water, and where the poison permeates top and bottom of the river, tuba does not kill the fry. The fry, keeping to the surface, escapes the tuba, which follows the bottom.

Some years ago I was present at a tuba fishing party given by His Highness the Sultan of Pahang to the British Resident and the District Officers. When we were at lunch in the Sultan's boat, after a tremendous catch of fish at the barricade, His Highness pointed to the swarms of fry that surrounded the kitchen boats, and, inverting the Malay proverb, "Big fish eat little fish," said "Big fish die, but little fish eat."

A   WERE - TIGER.

SOME years ago I was travelling on a somewhat delicate
mission in one of the petty sultanates of the Malay
Peninsula that lie to the north of the federated states
administered under British protection.   The state is a
long narrow strip of land lying on the east coast, and is
traversed by a number of rivers that run parallel to one
another from their source in the main range of the
peninsula to the China Sea.   The area of the district
watered by each of these rivers is perhaps 500 square
miles, of which at least 495 are forest.   At the mouth of
every river a few hundred Malays collect and make a
living by fishing; while, scattered up and down the
stream, separated from one another by distances varying
from one to five miles, are small clearings containing
ten, twenty, or even fifty families, who are dependent
upon an annual crop of padi and the collection of various
forest products, such as rubber, gutta, and rattans.   As
against the rest of mankind, the Malays say that the land
is theirs; but no one knows better than themselves that
the real lord and master of the country is the forest.
Each clearing has been hacked out of the primeval forest
with infinite trouble; the period of its possession is
marked by one continuous fight against aggression by
forest seeds and creepers and weeds of every description,
and when, finally, it is abandoned, it is covered within
a few months by a dense and almost impenetrable scrub
that will eventually grow up to become forest.   My only
companion was To'Kaya, an important and influential
chief of one of the districts of the state, and our following

consisted of a few Malay boatmen. To'Kaya was a fine specimen of a Malay of the last generation. He was some fifty years old, but time had had little apparent effect upon his wiry agile frame. He was a short man, not more than five feet four inches in height, of neat trim build, with square shoulders and small hands and feet. He had little superfluous flesh, but the curves of his arms and chest showed a muscular development considerably greater than would have been expected. His head was small and well shaped, its poorest feature being a broad and somewhat flat nose. The whole of his scalp was clean shaven, and chin and cheeks were kept free of occasional hairs by the use of tweezers. The striking feature of his face was a small, fierce, closely-cropped moustache of rather coarse bristly hairs, whose almost snowy whiteness afforded a brilliant contrast to the smoothness of his face and head, and to the rich olive-brown of his complexion. His eyes were somewhat sunken, with an expression of suffering and patience, but the crow's feet at their corners often curved into unexpected lines of humour. In every expression the old man showed the quiet dignity and self-respect of the true Malay.

Round his waist he wore the national garment— a sarong, which is in shape like a somewhat wide sack with the bottom cut off. His coat was nearly as primitive, for it was innocent of buttons, and could only be put on and taken off by being pulled over the head. A big coloured handkerchief was tied round his forehead, with a fantastic peak carefully arranged in front. Sarong, coat, and handkerchief were all of Malay weaving and coloured with native dyes, and nothing could be more simple or more effective and becoming to the wearer.

We took boat at the mouth of one of the rivers, the Malays at first using their paddles in the tidal waters where the inflowing tide bore us swiftly past densely timbered banks, and afterwards exchanging their paddles for poles when at last a sandy bottom was reached. We

poled slowly against a strong current until the river became so narrow and so shallow that farther progress by
boat was difficult. Then we left the river, and struck
inland at right angles to it. For a whole day we made
our way along a narrow track through heavy forest, where
the great trees afforded shade and coolness even at midday. At sunset we camped on a ridge that formed the
watershed between the river we had left and the one for
which we were making. An armful of leaves was thrown
down to make a bed for each, and a deftly plaited screen
of wild palm-leaves was placed over the beds to keep off
the dew.

During the night at intervals "the spirits of the
semambu" called to one another in a little ravine below
us. The semambu is the Malacca cane of commerce, and
the Malays imagine that each plant has a spirit. At
night-time, they say, spirit calls to spirit, making inquiry
as to the length of the cane between the joints: *panjang*?
belum? "is it long? not yet?" cries a high resonant voice,
throwing the accent of the question sharply on the second
syllable of each word; then, after a pause, another voice
is raised in a different key, and with the accent and falling
intonation of the sad response, *panjang, belum:* "it is
long, not yet."

The call is really that of an insect, but the sound is
weirdly voice-like, and the vibrations of the question
and reply awake a corresponding thrill in the listener.

We also heard, two or three times during the night,
the trumpeting of some wild elephants that had been
alarmed by meeting our tracks. The next morning we
continued our journey, which lay through dense forest
the whole day, and emerged at nightfall upon a little
village on the bank of the river we sought. Here I met
the man whom I had come to see. When my business
was finished, I hired a dug-out, and To'Kaya and I
started down-stream.

The pleasant easy progress of the boat, which was
carried by the swift current and only required the gentlest

paddling to give it steering way, was a welcome rest after laborious poling and travelling. To'Kaya and I sat under a little awning made of palm-leaves sewn together and talked the long day away, while reach after reach the bends of the river opened a gleaming way before us, and reach after reach the forest-clad banks closed in behind us. The small Malay clearings that appeared at intervals on the banks only accentuated the sense of the overpowering dominion and vastness of the all-encompassing forest. Its mastery held us, and our conversation for the most part turned upon its inhabitants, both animal and supernatural. Thus we came to the discussion of were-tigers, which are in the Malay Peninsula the counterpart of the were-wolves of Europe. That were-tigers exist no Malay doubts; and the popular belief is that the men from the district of Korinchi in Sumatra have the power of assuming the form of a tiger at will, and that in this guise they range the forest, hunting the wild game and occasionally killing mankind.

The Korinchi men, who are mostly pedlars of cloths, naturally resent the imputation, and contend that it is only some of the men of Chenaku, a sub-district of Korinchi, who have this unholy power. But as the contention admits the existence of the power amongst certain of the suspected class, the Malays of the Peninsula are only strengthened in their opinion, and believe the charge to be true of all Korinchis. To'Kaya told me of a village where, for some months, the fowls had been harried by a tiger or panther, both of which are known to the Malays by the same generic term, and where one day a Korinchi man lying sick with fever in the house of the headman, who had had pity on him, had vomited quantities of undigested chickens' feathers. I, in my turn, told him a story that I had heard in the reaches near the source of the Slim river. There, in an isolated hill-padi clearing, lived a Malay, his wife, and their two children, young boys of the age when they learn to read the Koran. One night came a rap at the door of the house, which, like all Malay dwellings, was built upon posts some ten feet above the ground. In answer to a demand from the father as to who was at the door and what was wanted, a voice replied, "We ask for a light, our torches are extinguished, and we have still some distance to go to the house where we are expected." Now, it is well known that this is a common device of jins and evil spirits to obtain admission to a house, and one should always beware of opening the door to give a light to a stranger who pretends to be belated. Well, the two boys, while the father was questioning and cross-questioning the stranger, slipped out of the house by the ladder behind the kitchen. Excited by the visit of a stranger at such an hour, they moved silently along the ground under the bamboo flooring to peep upwards at the threshold. There, on the rung of the ladder next below the door, stood a man talking to their father; but even while he spoke a tail striped in black and yellow dropped down behind his legs, and then up and down his lower limbs ran successive ripples of change and colour. The toes became talons, the feet turned to paws, and the knee-joints, already striped with the awful black and yellow, were turning from front to back.

And all the time the human face of the creature was giving specious explanations to the questions of the master of the house. Half in fascination, half in desperation, the two boys seized the tail that dangled before them, and shouted to their father to kill the thing. But before he could reach for his spear the animal, now nearly all tiger, tore itself from the puny grasp of the youngsters and fled into the darkness of the forest. Though I did not tell the story as a true one, To'Kaya shook his head and said, "That was a narrow escape. But it is fitting that we should talk of were-tigers, for here in the village of Bentong which we are approaching there was a were-tiger not many years ago."

This is the story: not, it will be seen, as To'Kaya told it, but as I have reconstructed it from what he told me.

A few years ago Bentong, a village of considerable importance in a sparsely-populated district, for it consisted of some fifty houses, had suffered much from the depredations of a tiger. Scarcely a month passed without a buffalo or two being taken, and the Malays were in despair. They had tied up goats with spring-guns set over them, and they had made elaborate traps, like gigantic mouse-traps, baited with dogs. But the tiger would have none of them, and the Malays were beginning to talk of abandoning the village, for they depended upon the buffaloes to plough the padi-fields, and the possible extermination of the herd meant nothing less than utter ruin.

Such was the state of things in Bentong when late one afternoon, in drenching rain and growing darkness, an old Korinchi pedlar named Haji Brahim was hastening towards the village, where he intended to spend the night. He had a regular round through the district, in which he had been known for years, and the next day would peddle cloths and silks to the women-folk, collect his small debts, and then move on to the next village. The inclement weather and slippery path had made him much later than he had expected, for, like every one else in the district, he had heard of the Bentong tiger. He was making his way somewhat nervously, therefore, hoping that every turn in the narrow forest-track would disclose the village clearing, when he was panic-stricken to hear the tiger roar within a short distance of him. Shaking with fear, he ran for his life towards the village. He had not gone far before he came on a tiger-trap built at the side of the track, ready set with its bait of village cur, and with the door wide open. Struck by the idea that the timbers which would keep a tiger in would also keep one out, he dropped on his hands and knees, crawled in, and let the heavy door fall behind him. And when the tiger roared again in still closer proximity, on one occasion within a few feet of him, and continued to roar in the vicinity at intervals throughout the night, he forgave the presence of the unclean dog that cowered beside him, and blessed the thought that had led him to seek such a refuge.

When morning broke it found him stiff and shivering from the effects of the night's rain, the exposure, and the cramped position; but it found him alive, and for that he added special thanksgiving to the morning prayer of every Muhammadan believer. He discovered that from the inside of the trap he was unable to raise the heavy falling door, but remained where he was, content with the knowledge that before long some one would certainly pass along the track. In this he was not disappointed, for soon he heard a man approaching, and shouted to him for assistance. The man looked round him on all sides, but failed to discover whence the voice came.

"Where are you?" he replied.

"Here! Here in the tiger-trap!"

The Malay came up and, peering into the darkness of the trap, cried, "Who are you? What is it?"

"It is I, Haji Brahim," was the answer. "I am in the tiger-trap."

The man peered yet closer, his somewhat dull wits puzzled by the strangeness of the situation, and then suddenly recognised the features of the captive. As suddenly a light struck him. "It is Haji Brahim, *the Korinchi*," he yelled in an access of terror. He forgot the helpless position of the inmate of the trap: he could only realise one fact, that the tiger, which for so long had been the pest of Bentong, was a were-tiger; and without another word he turned and ran down the track as though he ran for his life.

The boom of the mosque-drum soon reverberated through the village, and in answer to its summons every able-bodied Malay thronged to the house of the chief, Raja Alang. The man who had given the alarm told his story, and then, after due deliberation and consultation, the men proceeded to the tiger-trap. The raja led the

way, and behind him crowded the Malays, each armed
with a spear, and with a belt full of krises and daggers.
As they left the cultivated area and entered the forest
they strung out into single line upon the narrow track,
again massing in thick array behind the raja when they
reached the trap. Raja Alang stepped up to the door
and demanded of the prisoner—

"What is the name of this work?"

The old man's heart sank at the tone of the stern
inquiry. During the long weary vigil of the night it
had not occurred to him to connect his nationality with
the fact of his entering the trap: the villager's alarm had
been a shock to him, but he had persuaded himself that
it was the mere temporary panic of an ignorant clown.
But he now saw that he was on his trial.

"Let me out," he pleaded. "Let me out, and I will
explain everything."

"That cannot be," replied the raja. "First you must
explain how you came to be in this trap."

"Yes," agreed the voices in the background, "for
who would release a tiger when once it is caught?"

"How came you here? Was it not you whom we
heard roaring last night?" demanded the raja.

"No raja, no," answered the old pedlar; "the tiger,
which is always here, roared close to me last night, and
it was to save my life that I ran into this trap."

"How can any one believe such a story?" murmured
the crowd.

"The sole of your foot on the crown of my head,
raja; have not you and all these men known me for
many years? Am I not an old man and feeble, and could
I do such a thing as this that you think of me?"

"But who ever heard of an honest man in a tiger-
trap?" reiterated with dull persistency the voices behind
the raja.

"The tracks will prove the truth of what I say,"
cried the pedlar.

The justice of the contention appealed to all, and the ground was carefully examined. But the crowd had obliterated the footprints round the trap, and all that could be seen were the tiger's tracks following a wild-game path to its junction with the main forest path, and then losing themselves in the trampled ground around the trap.

The inspection was carried out thoroughly and impartially, and its result, which of course tended to confirm the suspicions of the Malays, was communicated to the trembling captive.

"But I can prove that I left the village of Siputeh yesterday afternoon to come to Bentong. Every one saw me there," wept the old man.

"That may be true," retorted some one in the crowd with relentless logic, "but it is of last night that we talk. The tiger was here last night, and you are in the tiger-trap this morning."

The pedlar, who throughout had been on his hands and knees, the only position of which the cramped space of the trap would permit, seeing the futility of argument, turned his face up to the judges who stood massed in front of the trap and tried through his tears to recognise them.

He called to the village imaum, and offered to swear on the Koran of the mosque in any form of oath that might be imposed that his story was true. But though the Malays are, as a rule, in favour of the ordeal by oath, they felt at once that there was an obvious objection to its use in this case. The question which they had to decide was whether their captive was an ordinary Malay like themselves, or that awful horror, a were-tiger. It was plain that a creature so unnatural as that they imagined their prisoner to be would not hesitate to forswear itself in order to attain its liberty: not only then would the oath fail in its effect, but their mosque and Koran would have been polluted by the presence and touch of the unclean thing. When this last resource failed him the poor old man cried to those who had known him longest and best, and begged for his life for pity's sake. He promised to do anything that was asked of him, and, if necessary, to leave the country for ever. But the Malays did not dare to let themselves be influenced by any thoughts of pity or compassion. They had to decide a question upon which their herds, their crops, and their very lives depended, and that question was put to them with Malay terseness and directness by the raja.

"If we open the trap-door," he said, turning to the men who leant upon their spears behind him "and let this that we have here now go loose, what is our position?"

What was their position? One must realise how the little village was isolated in the midst of a vast forest, how exposed the inhabitants were to any attack from it, how powerless to retaliate upon any man-eating or cattle-eating tiger, which had such easy access and such safe retreat, and how sick with helpless misery they must have felt at the mere idea that they were at the mercy of something that was partly tiger, partly demon. It is easy to imagine their fierce exultation at the thought of having trapped so awful a creature.

The raja repeated his question.

In answer a Malay, whose chief wealth lay in his diminishing herd of buffaloes, stood forth.

"Who of us has not lost one or more of his buffaloes? Who does not know that these Korinchis can turn themselves into tigers? Did we not all hear the tiger roar last night? Have we not got his tracks here? And here, where the tracks lead up to the trap, have we not, by the grace of Allah ,got the Korinchi trapped? What more?"

"What more?" said old To'Kaya, turning to me. At the sign from the raja one of the men stepped up to the trap, and, thrusting through the open bars of the woodwork, drove his spear through the old man's side.

For a moment I was silent with horror, and then said, "Pity on an old man to die in such a manner!"

"What pity does a tiger show?" retorted To'Kaya; "and what pity can it expect? Was it not clearly proved that this man was a were-tiger? It was not that he was unjustly or unfairly tried. The men of Bentong had known Haji Brahim for many years, and against him, as a man, they had no ill-feeling. The raja—Raja Alang, whom we shall see in the village if we stop the boat and call in—is both mild and just. Could he have decided otherwise?

"If a woman is accused of sin, or a man of murder, and evidence not half so strong as that in this case is advanced against them in the justice halls of the states under British rule,—nay, even in the Great Court-house of Singapore,—does not the judge convict them?"

I made an expostulation, and was painfully aware that I was begging the question. To'Kaya politely, but firmly, pointed this out, and I then attacked the evidence, saying that it was merely circumstantial.

To'Kaya bowed and said, "That may be; but have not men been hanged on slighter evidence?"

I could not think of a suitable reply: and it must be remembered that I was on a somewhat delicate mission in a state of which To'Kaya was one of the principal chiefs. There was, therefore, silence for a space as our little boat broke the sparkle of the river. We were now passing the village: the banks were covered with green turf cropped close by buffaloes, a few of whom—animals that perhaps had often seen the tiger which poor Haji Brahim had met—raised their heads to stare at us. Farther back from the river was a grove of coco-nut palms, whose slender heads and graceful curves were outlined against the blue sky; and at their feet, dotted at intervals, were the Malay houses, which are built of bamboo and plaited bertam palm-fronds, and whose colour is that of ripe dead leaves. A woman was pounding rice with a pestle worked by her foot, and in the river a number of children were playing and splashing; but the men were for the most part in their houses seeking a refuge from the heat of the day. Then suddenly a little dug-out shot forth from the bank to cross the river. One man poled, another steered with a paddle, and in the centre sat a fine-looking old Malay.

"It is Raja Alang," said To'Kaya.

We stopped for a while to exchange the greetings and the courtesies due to, and expected from, our various ranks. Then we parted, and at the next bend of the river the great forest swept down again to the bank on either side, shutting us off from the view of aught else, and telling us that the little village of Bentong now lay behind us.

CROCODILE SHOOTING.

THE vast dense forest that covers the length and breadth of the Malay Peninsula generally changes its character before it reaches the coast-line. In places, it is true, one may find a rocky headland covered with heavy timber running out to sea until the waves break at its feet; but for the most part, on the east coast the forest is cut off from the sea by an open foreshore of rank wind-swept grass, between which and a shallow sandy beach grows a narrow fringe of casuarina trees, through which the sea-wind whispers, sighs, and murmurs day and night; while on the west coast, where the land falls to the sea level, a mangrove forest growing on alluvial mud takes the place of the trees of the interior.

On part of the Perak coast the mangrove forest is intersected by channels formed by joint actions of the rise and fall of the tide and of the currents of the inland streams. The effect of these channels is to cut the forest up into numerous islands of varying size, and a launch can make its journey by these back ways from end to end of the forest without being seen from the sea. In the old days before British protection, many were the exciting games of hide-and-seek played up and down these by-ways between the Chinese boats that carried the tin of the alluvial fields of Larut and the pirate prahus of the Malays.

The channels vary in width from a hundred to three hundred yards: at high tide one sees nothing on either bank but the mangrove-trees growing out of the water and occasional patches of nipah palms. At low tide the mangroves are left high and dry above the expanse of a slimy foreshore of evil-smelling mud. One notices that a line, that might have been drawn with a ruler, runs along the foot of the row of mangroves, and marks the high-water limit below which the leaves of the trees cannot live.

Above this line all is green, below it there is nothing but bare trunk. On the mud the crocodiles that infest the channels come out to bask when the tide is low.

Some months ago my tracker Manap and I were in the mangrove swamps of Larut trying to shoot a tiger that had been taking off the Chinese wood-cutters on the coast. As we were returning to my launch at sunrise, after one of many fruitless night-long vigils in a mosquito-infested forest, it occurred to me to take advantage of the low tide and to paddle along the banks of the back-waters and inlets of the mangrove forest in order to pick up a crocodile or two. We left the launch to follow us at a discreet distance, and set off in a little dug-out canoe. The tide was running out fast, and long stretches of bare mud were exposed.

In the distance these flat expanses glistened in the morning sun like molten gold; but when seen close at hand, on either side, they resolved into a horrible blue-brown slimy mass.

Crabs of weird shapes and colours thronged the flats. Great ugly green crabs crept sluggishly over the mangrove roots, or climbed, with the appearance of painful movement, up the slime-covered snags and dead branches that jutted up abruptly above the level of the mud. With jerky efforts hermit-crabs dragged along their whelk-shell homes, and upon any alarm withdrew into the farthest recesses of their shells, which fell over backwards with horrible deathlike suddenness, and which then lay until the danger was past, as apparently tenant-less as any of the empty shells that were scattered over the surface of the mud. Brown crabs scuttled towards their holes, and then, having made safe their line of retreat, stared with beady, expressionless eyes at the passing boat.

In strong contrast with these ungainly varieties, and with the surrounding of the mangrove swamps, were the little crabs: some of the brightest vermilion, others of the most perfect turquoise.

One tiny creature—a miniature in purest enamel— which had found a delicacy, plied two claws, enormous in proportion to its body, to convey infinitesimal morsels to an invisible mouth; and the claws worked alternately with the speed and clicking regularity of knitting-needles. Never was greed more prettily served. Pugnacious little creatures were they too; and each stood by its hole and waved a claw in the air on the alert for love or war.

We slowly paddled along with the ebbing tide, and soon disturbed a small crocodile—a youngster some four feet long. It had been hidden from sight by a dip in the bank, and we were upon it before it knew its danger. Its efforts to reach the water and safety were frantic. All its four legs clawed madly and splutteringly at the yielding mud, and its tail swung wildly from side to side as if to help it on its way. But, for all its ungainly appearance, it covered the ground at an extraordinary pace. The first bullet struck the bank just below it, and plastered it with driven splashes of mud; the second hit it fairly behind the shoulder just as it reached the water, and turned it over on its back. The head and body disappeared under water, and only the tail remained on the bank: a hind-leg waved convulsively in the air. "Mampus!" cried Manap—a contemptuous expression, of which "dead as mutton" is a fair rendering; and he paddled on slowly and with the deliberation that befitted a man who was going to pick up something barely worth the shooting. But "mampus" the crocodile was not, for, as we came up, the leg that had appealed to high heaven assumed a more natural position, and with a desperate effort the animal righted itself and managed to slide down into the muddy stream. Manap dug his paddle deep into the water, and put all the strength of his broad back into his stroke. As the dugout shot up to the spot where the stirred-up mud marked the course taken by the wounded animal, Manap groped in the shallow water to find it with his paddle. He touched it once, but another dying effort enabled it to wriggle into deeper water where the paddle could not touch bottom. We had therefore to leave it, and after marking the spot with a pole paddled on again.

There were birds on every side: kingfishers of several species, some as big as jackdaws (one of them cursed with a maniac laugh), the smallest a purple gem, even smaller and more resplendent than the brilliantly-coloured bird of the English rivers. On the mud were padi-birds—a species of crane, the perfect and absolute whiteness of whose plumage was in as strong contrast with the sombre background as the blue of the tiny crabs. With bowed neck and abstracted mien, a marabout stork took long slow strides in search of incautious fish. Brown Brahminy kites wheeled in circles overhead. Then, in our silent approach, we disturbed a sea-eagle: sitting in a mangrove-tree on the water's-edge, it allowed us to approach within a few yards before it deigned to fly. As it launched itself forth from the tree it dropped down a foot or two before its powerful pinions had sufficient spread to bear the weight of the heavy body. Then it flapped slowly in front of us over the surface of the mud-banks. Suddenly, as if to show that it was not afraid of us, it let drop two enormous taloned legs and seized a luckless fish; crooked claws and curved beak met, and without a break in the flight the captive was swallowed. In a dead tree, standing white and gaunt against the blue sky, two other sea-eagles wrangled and screamed in discordant tones. At the water's-edge sandpipers tripped with dainty feet along the mud, and rose to take short flights as we approached too close. Their call "kĕ-dî-dî —kĕ-dî-dî" (whence they get their Malay name) was the same as that of the English sandpiper, and the clear fresh notes were reminiscent of a cooler clime and a softer scene. Green pigeons—some of the most lovely birds that fly—fluttered from tree to tree in search of fruit; and, unseen in a mangrove-tree, an imperial wood-pigeon called to its mate. No thin "coo" like that of the English bird was his note, but a deep "boom" that resounded far through the forest.

Before long we saw a crocodile floating in the stream. It was close to the edge of the mud, probably making up its mind to crawl up the bank, and taking a look round before it did so. Only the tip of its snout and its eyes appeared above the surface, but the distance between these three points showed it to be a big one.

The slanting rays of the sun shone on it, and we could see the outline of its body in the water. It was probably some sixteen or seventeen feet long; but it had not grown to that length without learning wisdom, and, as it saw us, it gently sank out of sight. There was no hurry, no alarm or excitement. It merely subsided, and let the water rise over it and hide it. And when the crocodile had gone there was not a ripple anywhere to show the place where it had been.

A couple of hundred yards farther on we marked a crocodile stretched in sleep on the mud. At this distance it was peculiarly inconspicuous, despite the serrated outline of its back and tail. Branches of trees, nipah palm-leaves, with wreckage and detritus of all sorts, are always scattered about the mud-flats, and it is difficult to say whether they or the crocodile succeed the better in their mimicry of one another. Time after time the broad back and jagged fronds of a nipah leaf will make one tighten the grasp on the rifle, and I well remember that the first time an excited Malay pointed out a crocodile to me I could see nothing but an old log. We drifted slowly towards the sleeping crocodile, and though it is not, I admit, a high form of sport, still it was exciting, for one could not tell when the animal would wake. It might only be half asleep, or not even asleep at all, and might at any moment make a dash for the water. When a crocodile does awake to realise its danger, there is such a rush and such a swirl, and the flying mud is so much the colour of the animal, that to put a bullet through its heart or head cannot but be more a matter of luck than skill. Every yard that brings the boat closer to the animal of course increases the danger of its waking; and added to the thrill of the lessening distance is the difficulty of deciding whether to take one's shot while yet one may or whether to try and get a little closer, and thus, if the animal does not first take alarm, make certain of it. Slowly and silently we drifted on until we were within twenty yards of the crocodile. Its whole side was then exposed, and I got an easy shot at its heart. I fired, and the animal did not move. At the moment that the bullet struck it, the jaws opened to their full extent, showing every pointed tooth in the serried rank that filled the hideous mouth, remained at their widest gape for a frac-tion of a second, and then closed with a snap like that of a springing rat-trap. There was not another move-ment of the body, but the brute lay stone-dead. Had any particle of life remained in it, it would have struggled to the water; but this snapping of the jaws, which is an involuntary muscular effort, is an infallible sign that the animal has been killed on the spot. Manap paddled to the water's-edge, struggled nearly waist-deep through the semi-liquid mud towards the brute, and, slipping a rattan round its body, tied it to a pole, which he stuck in the mud. It was a brute some ten feet long, but heavy for its length, and capable of taking off a man with ease. We signalled to the launch, which followed about a quarter of a mile behind us, to pick up the carcass as soon as we had passed on, and continued to paddle slowly down the tide. The next crocodile that we saw had apparently not yet disposed itself for its siesta, for before we approached within range it started up, whirled round, and dashed into the water. Farther on we saw another crocodile floating high in the water, with its head and body above the surface. We approached to within thirty yards before it moved. It then began slowly to subside in the same manner as the one that we had seen before. I fired at the diminishing target, and in a second transformed the phlegmatic saurian into a raging monster. In fury, surprise, and pain it lashed the water with its powerful tail, turning and twisting its body until the churned up water hid it from view. I fired my second barrel into the turmoil of spray and water, and the brute plunged below the surface. As soon as it had disappeared from sight, Manap's quick eyes discerned on the mud-flats the track by which the crocodile had just come down to the water.

"See," he cried, "it has not been basking; there is its wallow.

"Have you not seen a crocodile's wallow?" he asked me as he paddled on with long easy strokes, letting the tide do its full share of the work. "This is how he makes it. When the tide is at its full he comes up over the water-covered bank, and lies down on the mud close by the mangrove trees. He twists and turns himself in the ooze until he has hollowed out a shallow pit, in which he lies. Then the tide turns to run out, and the mud and silt carried down by the stream settle in the wallow and on the crocodile's back and round his sides, until, by the time that the retreating tide has left the mud-flats, bare, a thick layer of mud covers the crocodile, and nothing is seen to break the level expanse of ooze. The crocodile's nostrils and his eyes are, however, just above the level of the mud, though the keenest eye could not detect them. Thus he lies concealed until a family of monkeys comes chattering, playing, and scrambling over the mud to look for crabs or shellfish.

"If one of them happens to come too close to the hidden watcher there is an upheaval of the mud, and, *bap!* the monkey is in the crocodile's jaws; and for all its screams and all its companions' cries it is carried off towards the water, to be devoured at leisure. Sometimes it is not a monkey but a man that is taken."

This is unfortunately only too true, and I well remember hearing at an official inquiry a Malay's horribly vivid description of his companion's death in this manner. They had been cutting nipah palm-leaves together, and were loading their canoe with the fronds that they had collected, when a crocodile make a dash out of a wallow at one of the men and seized him above the knee. Neither man had a knife in his hand, and all that Awang, the wretched man who had been seized, could do was to throw both his arms round a tree and attempt to hold on. The other man, Saleh, ran to fetch his knife, he had left in his boat, but even as he turned to run Awang had been torn from the tree and carried towards the water. Twice again did Awang momentarily check the brute's course by seizing and holding on to a tree or branch, but each time the weight and strength of the crocodile wrenched him from his support, and before Saleh returned with his knife Awang had been torn from the last tree on the river-bank, and was carried screaming to his death.

"But it is not every one," said Manap continuing his story, "who is aware that both crocodiles and tigers are forbidden to kill mankind, and that every time one of them kills a man it breaks one of the great laws imposed by Nabi Sleman [King Solomon] upon the animals. Every animal knows what it may do and what it may not do. The deer may live on the forest foliage and grass; the tigers may kill the deer; the various kinds of fish have their peculiar food; the crocodiles may feed on the fish and on such four-footed animals as chance may bring in their way: but no animal may wantonly attack mankind. That is the first law of Nabi Sleman; and if any animal kills a man Nabi forthwith drives it out of his fold. Thenceforth it lives apart from its fellows, an outcast and an accursed thing.

"When, therefore, a crocodile has killed a man, it tries to evade the punishment of its offence. It buries the body in the mud, and then after three days floats to the surface with it, pretending that it has just found it. It calls out over the water—

> "'It was not I, O sun!
> Not I, O Moon!
> Not I, O Stars!
> Bear witness all that it was not I,
> Not, I that killed this man:
> The Water killed him.'

and this is partly true, for the crocodile kills a man by drowning him. Then as the sun and moon and stars hold their peace, the crocodile thinks that it has freed itself of guilt, and sinks again to the river-bottom to devour the body at its leisure."

"The water killed him," Manap murmured two or three times to himself; and any one who has experience of the hair-splitting quibbles in which Muhammadan jurisconsults delight, will understand his appreciation, even relish, of the ingenuity of the imaginary appeal.

It was nearly the ebb-tide, and the channel grew narrow. Small fry leapt out of the water in terror at our approach, and now and again some large fish surged past between our canoe and the bank, its broad back driving a curling wave before it. To see the size and swiftness and silent strength of these great fishes made it a joy to think of the feel of a salmon-rod bending to the weight of one of them.

Playing and feeding near the surface of the water was a shoal of extraordinary small fish with long pointed snouts like those of the English garfish. But the fishes were not confined to the water,—they were crawling all over the mud-banks in every direction. Look at this fish, the *ikan blachak*, whose pectoral fins appears to have developed into jointed legs: it walks sturdily and determinedly over the mud, with its dorsal fin erect from the back of its neck to the base of its tail; and very imposing

it looks to any fish that has not attained the dignity of its
six inches. This panoply is intended to strike terror
into beholders; but the *ikan blachak* knows its limita-
tions, and the kites that wheel overhead will not be
intimidated by any dorsal fin however stiff: so when the
little fish stops, it sinks its fin and lies as close and as
flat as it can to the mud its colour resembles. But should
any other *blachak* come straying too close, at once it
leaps up and with open mouth stands ready to fight if
the intruder will not retreat. When thus excited it erects
not only the dorsal fin, but the smaller fins that run down
the back to the tip of the tail. Another extraordinary
occupant of the flats is the *ikan tembakul*: it lies on the
mud like a narrow wedge of wood, with a length of
about ten inches and a base of about two inches. The
base of the wedge is the *tembakul's* head, and on the top
of this square-cut head is a pair of gigantic goggle eyes
which stare at the world in blank surprise. It has short,
powerful, bandy-legged fins with which it "hunches"
itself forward over the mud. If, however, it is frightened or excited, a sideways stroke of its powerful tail
sends it in flying leaps on its way. It swims in the
water, too, in a weird manner, with its misshapen head
and monstrous eyes high above the surface. It moves
slowly and deliberately, but if startled rushes forward
with more than half of its body out of water, and then
suddenly bobs its head under the surface and disappears
from view.

"Quick, quick, fire."

A crocodile we had not seen was rushing down the
bank some twenty-five yards ahead of us. I fired, and
the first bullet broke its spine and knocked it on to its
side, but only stopped it for a second. It quickly righted
itself, and with its two fore-feet continued to claw its
way towards the water. The second bullet hit it in the
shoulder, but did not stop it. By the time that I had
reloaded the canoe had dashed up alongside the crocodile,
whose dying struggles had brought it to within a few

feet of the water. With marvellous quickness and dex-
terity Manap dropped his paddle, picked up a rope noose
and slipped it over the crocodile's head. The brute was
now half in the stream, and though it was to all intents
dead it continued blindly to struggle towards the water.
It made no effort to bite or to use its powerful tail, its
one idea being to reach its natural element. "Take the
paddle and strike it on the body. Don't fire." I dropped
the rifle and hit the brute over the body and head until
the struggles ceased, and, save for muscular contractions
that rippled over its skin, it lay still.

It was a small brute, between six and seven feet
long, and leaving it for the launch to pick up, we paddled
on. The next crocodile we saw was a little creature, not
more than two feet long, that was learning to bask like
its elders. Both my bullets flew over its back, and it
escaped in safety.

"Do you see the patch of lalang grass by the point
in front of us? Last year I found a crocodile's nest there:
three-and-sixty eggs there were in it, and the clerk at the
police station gave me ten cents apiece for them. Six
dollars and thirty cents I got, but one does not find a nest
every day. You do not know how a crocodile makes its
nest? The mother selects a spot, open to the sun, on
some dry sandy soil; often, as in the case of yonder nest,
it is in a patch of lalang grass, often in the *piai* fern.
She collects grass and dry fern in her mouth, and heaps
them up until she has formed a pile as broad as three
men can stretch from finger-tip to finger-tip, and in height
midway between the man's knee and his hip. In this
nest she lays fifty or sixty eggs, and covers them over
with dry grass. She then makes two wallows by the
nest, one on the side by the rising sun, the other towards
the setting sun, and prepares to guard the nest against
all possible enemies. Of these the worst is he who
ought to give her most assistance: the male crocodile
not only does not help her in collecting the grass and
making the two wallows, but if not repelled by her will

destroy the nest and eat the eggs. A tiger, too, loves
crocodiles' eggs as he does turtles' eggs, and against him
also the mother crocodile has continually to be on her
guard. She sometimes will even face a man, barking
and showing her teeth at him like a savage dog. She
allows the sun to hatch out the eggs, as the Chinese do
with ducks' eggs. Ah, she is very clever! as the Malays
say, she has 'a long mind'; for should the day be cloudy
and the sun's power be weak, she removes the covering
of grass from the eggs, and at night-time, or when the
rain falls, she replaces it. And if it is a hot day, not
only are the eggs covered, but with her tail she sprinkles
water from the wallows over the eggs. Yes, truly, she
has a very 'long mind.' And the reason that she makes
her wallows to eastward and to westward of the nest is in
order that she may be able to interpose her body, if
the day should be too hot, between the nest and the rays
of the morning sun and of the afternoon sun. No, I
myself have not seen all this, but I have seen many nests
with their wallows, and what I have said as to the rest
is what men who know about these things have told to
me. And they say, furthermore, that when the eggs are
hatched out all the little animals that run towards the
water become *buaia*, the crocodile, whilst those that run
towards the land become *biaua*, the iguana. But I do not
believe that: it is a story we tell our children just as our
fathers told it to us."

"Ha! listen to that."

A magnificent sea-eagle, white and grey, and resplendent in the sun, sitting on the topmost branch of a
dead tree, where all might see him, had uttered two clear
high notes. His ordinary call is like the mewing of a
cat, but these two notes, "Hoo" "Hoo," rang out like a
bugle-call.

"That means that at the river-mouth the tide has
turned, and that now it is *bunga pasang*—'the flower of
the rising tide.' The sea-eagle is the king of all the birds
in the forest, and he tells them all of the turn of the tide.

With the rising tide the fish will come in from the sea, and the crocodiles will soon wake up and return to the water to seek their food. But there on the bank is one still asleep."

It was an animal some eight feet long, and it lay sound asleep with that ludicrously amiable smile at the corners of its mouth that is far more characteristic of a crocodile than are any tears. It is impossible to imagine tears in such an eye: a lifeless snaky yellow, with a narrow black slit down its centre, and devoid of every feeling but that of a bitter frozen hatred of every living creature. When the eyes are closed one can see in the animal's smile a trace of the creature that was once the happy innocent plaything of the Prophet's daughter. But when the eyelids open the only expression is that of eternal rancour and eternal resentment of her blighting curse.

The sleeping crocodile allowed us to approach within easy distance, and I was able to kill it on the spot. We did not see another for some time, and then I only got a difficult shot, which I missed. The tide was now running in fast, and in more than one place there were some tracks to show where a crocodile had returned to the water.

It was time to stop, and in answer to a signal the launch steamed up alongside and took us on board. We had done fairly well, and the three crocodiles represented a total length of twenty-four feet. The Government pays a reward of twenty-five cents a foot, and as this was Manap's perquisite, the morning's work meant six dollars to him, or about the cost of the living of himself and his family for a month.

While lunch was being prepared I stood in the bows of the launch and took in all that I could of the scene I have attempted to describe: the colours of the water, of the mud, and of the mangroves; the varied multitude

---

[1] The Malay story of the creation of he first crocodile is told on page 52.

of the birds, the fishes, and the crabs that crowded the
foreground. In a few minutes we came to a bend of
the stream and the sea lay in front of us, a broad expanse
of blue, with waves all laughing in the sun and twinkling
into golden dimples; the breath of the south-west mon-
soon blew in fresh and salt from over Sumatra and the
ocean beyond, and the little launch with her propeller
racing at full speed left the narrow discoloured waters
of the mangrove swamps and breasted the incoming tide
and freshening breeze, and headed for the open sea.

THE PAWANG.

WHEN a man, and more especially when a nation, is converted, it is not a question of the exchange of one religion for another. The new belief forms a stratum that covers, more or less deeply, the old one. The teachers of the new beliefs refer, with pity or contempt, to the convert's old beliefs as his *superstitions*—something, they say, that stands upon his religion; and thereby go as far wrong as it is possible to do, inasmuch as the truth, which they fail to see or refuse to admit, is that the things which they term a superstition are really a substratum.

When a nation accepts a third religion, the three strata of beliefs may sometimes be discerned; and of this formation, if I may so call it, an excellent example is found in the Malays of the Malay Peninsula. Until perhaps six or seven hundred years ago they were nature- and spirit-worshippers, holding beliefs very similar to those of the Dyaks of Borneo at the present day. Then a wave of Hinduism swept down from India over Sumatra and Java. It reached the Malay Peninsula, but with such greatly diminished force that its traces there are but faintly discernible; whereas it has left its mark deeply and permanently in Java, and still survives in the islands of Bali and Lombok on the Javanese coast. A few centuries later a far greater wave of religion came surging down from India over the same course: Islam, which had invaded India from the North-West in the eleventh century, reached Java, Sumatra, and the Malay Peninsula about the fifteenth century.

The Malays of the Peninsula became ready converts, and are now without an exception followers of the Prophet—decidedly unorthodox in many ways, it is true, but unshakable in their adherence to what they consider to be the essentials of their religion; recognising the claim of the "Law of the Custom," the *Hukum Adat*, the traditions of many centuries of paganism and Hinduism, on the one hand, and on the other hand the often conflicting claim of the "Law of the Prophet," the *Hukum Shara*, their more recently acquired code; and always ready to make a compromise between them. In certain parts of the Malay Peninsula the pre-Muhammadan customary laws of debt, land tenure, and inheritance have prevailed over the Muhammadan code, and have recently in some instances been perpetuated by judicial decisions and by statutes.

It is often said that the Malay of the Peninsula is a bad Muhammadan, because he has retained so much of his pre-Muhammadan beliefs. The truth more really is that he is an imperfect Muhammadan: he certainly is not an indifferent one, for even his severest critics will admit that he would die rather than willingly do what he believes to be forbidden. If he is told that his habitual omission to say the five daily prayers, for instance, will ensure his eternal damnation, he will be greatly distressed to hear it; but he will probably contend that this is not the law as he knows it, and thence proceed to try to persuade his critic, as he has persuaded himself, that a man should be judged not by the law, but by the law as he knows it.

Of the old pagan religion the *pawang*, or sorcerer, is the priest. He still survives in nearly every village in the Malay Peninsula, and is the counterpart of the *manang* of Borneo and *shaman* of the Mongolian tribes. Although a sorcerer, he is, like every one else in the community, a Muhammadan; and he defends himself, his practices, and beliefs from the attacks of the orthodox followers of the Prophet by claiming for his craft the sanction of the *adat*, the immemorial custom of the country.

The following beliefs are represented by the *pawangs*, and survive to-day from the old pagan times. A belief

  (i)   in certain great and powerful spirits called the *Jin Tanah* and *Jin Laut*, the "Spirits of the Earth" and the "Spirits of the Sea";

  (ii) in innumerable lesser spirits of the mountains, rivers, and forests, and even of particular rocks, rapids, and trees;

 (iii) in familiar spirits created by the *pawangs*, and ordered to obey their commands;

 (iv) in the animistic properties of plants and trees (of this idea, the best known example is the annual ceremony of tending the soul of the rice crops);

  (v) in were-tigers;

 (vi) in invisible folk;

 (vii) in death-avenging influences;

(viii) in a spectral huntsman;

 (ix) in innumerable spooks, goblins, bogeys, and weird apparitions of various kinds.

There still survives a pagan tradition of the creation of the world by the first *pawang* and a bird. This most extraordinary story is not considered in any way incompatible with the Muhammadan tradition of the creation, with which the Malays are of course perfectly familiar.

During the period of Hinduism the *pawangs* borrowed largely from the Hindu mythology. The very word for the spells or charms which they repeat to propitiate the spirits is pure Sanskrit (*mantra*); and in the *mantras* there still survive to this day the names of Siva, Vishnu, Rama, Ganesha, Hanuman, and Arjuna. There are memories of heavenly creatures like the *dewa*, *dewata*, *chandra*, and *bidadari*; of demons like the Indian *bhuts*, which the Malays call Bota; of ogres (*gergasi*), and of giants (*raksasa*). There has been a tendency—which was very natural perhaps—to degrade the Hindu gods to the level of mere forest spirits.

When Muhammadanism swept Hinduism away before it, the *pawang* turned eagerly to the new religion to borrow what he could. The only spirits lower than the angels of which the Koran admits the existence are the Genii (Jin) and Fairies (Peri), some of whom are said to be believers and some unbelievers. They are imagined to be created of pure fire, to be of both sexes, to propagate their species, and to eat and drink. They were at once accepted and introduced into the *mantras*. So also were the archangels Jibrail (Gabriel), Mikail (Michael), Azrael, and Israfil. One is not surprised to find their names; but one may own to a feeling of awe at finding in the mouth of a *pawang* in the Malay Peninsula the name of Azazel, the *pre-Mosaic* demon of the wilderness, to whom the scapegoats of Leviticus xvi. were sent as an offering.[1]

Actuated, perhaps, by a desire to show that their old beliefs were in no way incompatible with their new religion, the *pawangs* also freely introduced the Muhammadan Prophets into their *mantras*. Nabi Noh (Noah, who is supposed to have charge of all the plants and trees), Nabi Sleman (Solomon, who rules over all the animals), Nabi Musa (Moses), and Nabi Muhammad himself, are frequently invoked; and the *mantras* often begin with the words, "In the name of Allah, the All-Compassionate and All-Merciful," and end with the words, "There is no God but Allah, and Muhammad is the Prophet of Allah."

But this is not the whole of the borrowings of the *pawangs*. The Siamese, who are the neighbours of the Malays on the north of the Peninsula, were, like the Malays, at first nature- and spirit-worshippers. When they were converted to Buddhism their old beliefs

[1] It is only right to say that D'Herbelot gives another account of Azazel in his 'Bibliothèque Orientale.'

found in the new religion an attitude so gently tolerant, and even so kindly disposed, that the old beliefs continued to flourish to an extent impossible under Muhammad's stern creed of "There is no God but Allah." The Siamese are more skilled than the Malays in the use of charms, spells, and herbs; and the Malays so readily admit the superiority that in many a Malay village one may find an old Siamese man who has established himself there as the local *pawang*. Neither the Malays nor the Siamese, the Muhammadans nor the Buddhists, seem to consider the position in any way remarkable: more or less unconsciously they recognise the fact that they meet on common ground in the beliefs that both nations shared before their religions took them along different paths. As an example of the extent to which the Malay *pawangs* are indebted to the Siamese, I may refer to an article in Journal No. 45 of the Royal Asiatic Society (Straits Branch), to which I have contributed an account of the *mantras* used by the Malays in catching wild elephants. The charms have been in use for many generations, and the Malays have little knowledge of their origin other than that there is a tradition that it is Siamese. The language is certainly not Malay, and is either some exceedingly corrupt form of Siamese, or else some tongue that is no longer known in the Peninsula. The influence of the Siamese *pawangs* is also seen in the frequent reference in the *mantras* to the *Maha Rishi*, the Great Sagas of Buddhism.

Such, then, are the sources from which the *pawang* has derived his present knowledge of charms, spells, and medicines. His services are requisitioned at every birth and death (not at a wedding, a social contract of distinctly religious aspect, where the *kathis* and *imaums* will not brook his interference), at every sowing and reaping of the rice-crop, and at every accident or illness. The opening of a tin-mine, the construction of a dam, or the erection of a fishing-stake, always call for his attendance.

The functions of a *pawang* are roughly divided into spirit-raising and spirit-propitiation. Spirit-raising, the coercion of spirits, is known by the Malays as *ber-hantu*. It is the pure undiluted *shamanism* of the Mongolians; and upon the exercise of the power every Malay looks with considerable dread, and even the least orthodox shakes his head when it is mentioned. It is seldom attempted, and every year is becoming more rare. I have only twice attended a *séance*,—once on the occasion described in "The Pinjih Rhino," and once when a chief was about to perform the long and dangerous pilgrimage to Mecca (its use on such an occasion shows how deeply rooted the belief is), and his relatives were anxious to know what the future might have in store for him. On both occasions I particularly noticed that the *pawang* and the audience, for no other reason than that they knew that they were about to do something which the law of Muhammad held to be wrong, made a special point of commencing the proceedings with a recitation from the Koran. Spirit-propitiation is considered a far less serious matter, the reason perhaps being that the offering of small gifts, such as eggs, limes, or a bowl of rice, and the repetition of *mantras*, is a simple and apparently innocuous thing, very different from participation in the wild scenes where in successive ravings, ecstasies, and collapses the *pawangs* are possessed of demons.

The collection of *mantras* given in the article "A Deer-Drive" is a fair example of a *pawang's* lore. A similar set, with appropriate ceremonies and due offerings, would be used at the opening of a new clearing in the forest or any similar enterprise. In the case of sickness, the *pawang* adds a potion or poultice, or perhaps a pill of paper upon which weird figures have been traced. Often he will insist upon the person or persons interested keeping some peculiar observances which generally take the form of something *not* to be done rather than something to be done. This is known as *pantang*, and corresponds to the well known *tapu* or *taboo*.

The Malays believe that the power lies in the *mantra* itself, not in the man that repeats it. The Hindus have the same idea, but amongst them the use of the *mantras* is confined to the Brahmins: they have a proverb—

"The earth is subject to the gods:
　　The gods are subject to the *mantras:*
　　The *mantras* are subject to the Brahmins:
　　Therefore the earth is subject to he Brahmins."

The Malays admit of no caste restrictions; and the *pawang* from whom I learned the *mantras* set forth in the article "Tuba Fishing" assured me that, when I had committed them to memory, they would be as effectual in my mouth as they were in his own.

The *pawangs* (like the *manangs* of Borneo) are not a hereditary class, though, as one would expect, a son often follows in his father's footsteps in the same way that in England a gamekeeper or a sexton succeeds his father. Any man who has shown a little aptitude may learn from a *pawang* all that he has to teach, if the application for tuition is made with due deference and in proper form. There are certain (often many) observances to be kept, and some services to be rendered; and there is a recognised fee,—so many lengths of cloth, so many measures of rice, and so many pieces of silver. The fact that the *pawang's* craft does not necessarily descend from father to son is interesting, for among most of the Mongolian tribes the *shaman* priesthood is strictly hereditary. There, in fact, so much is the profession confined to certain families that the *shaman* priests pretend to derive their power from the spirits of their deceased ancestors. Such an idea is unknown to the Malay.

When a man's skill has made him famous, the word *pawang* is prefixed to his name as a title; and even in official documents, such as the grants issued by the Land Offices, one may find such names as Pawang Duhamat or Pawang Glam.

Only a small percentage of the *pawangs* attempt spirit-raising. The majority confine themselves to the *mantras*, offerings, and medicaments. They specialise very considerably. One man will devote himself to the lore regarding the spirits and influences connected tin-mines; another to those attendant on rubber-collecting or camphor-hunting expeditions; while a third, in whose special care the rice-fields or fishing-stakes may be, will probably be entirely ignorant of the charms and spells used by the other two men.

The *pawangs* are dying out. It is not that the civilisation of British rule exercises a direct influence upon the native belief in this respect, but that this civil-isation is making the inhabitant of the Peninsula more of a Muhammadan and less of a Malay. The more he learns of his religion the more he realises how impossible is the compromise that has been allowed to exist for the last four or five centuries between his pre-Muhammadan beliefs and the precepts of the Prophet.

He has only to open his Koran, and turn to the seventy-second chapter, which entitled the Genii, to find a severe condemnation of those who, in fear of any spirits or in the hope of propitiating them or of appeasing their wrath, make any application or petition to such spirits instead of making their prayer to Allah, who alone is God, and to whom all things in heaven and earth are subject. No hair-splitting, no quibble of the wiliest of *pawangs*, can evade this uncompromising denunciation; and the alien Muhammadans, whom the rapid develop-ment of the Malay Peninsula has brought into the country within the last ten or fifteen years, are not slow to press home the charge of apostasy against the *parang*. The Javanese and Sumatra-men, earnest, narrow-minded fol-lowers of the law, the Indians, who are even more strict, and the Arabs, who are the sternest of bigots, have no sympathy for the *pawang*; they have nothing in their blood that cries out for the old aboriginal beliefs: and in the mosques and village deliberations, at all times and at all seasons, they denounce him and all his works. The Malays, too, perform the pilgrimage to Mecca in larger numbers every year, and each man upon his return, when he has donned the *haji's* turban and frock, feels constrained to conform to a stricter observance of the faith, and therefore to frown upon the poor *pawang* as savouring unduly of heathendom.

It is the alien Muhammadan immigration, not British civilisation, that is the enemy of the *pawang;* and as the *pawangs* of the present generation, who still hold their position by their personal influence, die off, there will, except in the more remote districts and villages, probably be but few men of the younger generation to take their place.

APPENDIX I.

THE MANTRAS.

THE FOREST. Page 9.

As salam aleikom,
Aku datang ini bersahabat sehaja,
Sehaja na' menchari hal Kahidupan,
Janganlah angkau mengaru-ngaru ku,
Dan anak istri ku,
Dan rumah tangga ku,
Dan segala kampong laman ku,
Aku yang na' tumpang bersahabat ini,
Mintalah selamat pulang balik.

Page 9.

Hei! Salam aleikom,
Kita na' tumpang tambat
Pada sa' rimbun daun
Sri bergenta sa' panjang lampei.

A DEER-DRIVE. Page 42.

As salam aleikom,
Beribu ka bumi,
Bapa ka langit,
Sudara ka ayer,
Aku na' tumpang tambat
Pada sa' rimbun daun
Sri bergenta sa' panjang lampei.

Page 43.

Ah gana! Mah gana!
Turun gana angkau, naik gana aku;
Turun jinggi angkau, naik jinggi aku;

Jinggi sa' ratus sembilan puloh;
Sah pindahlah angkau,
Ka cherang tiada berburong,
Ka laut tiada berikan,
Ka padang tiada berrumput,
Sah pindahlah angkau dengan kuasa Allah.

Page 43.

Hei! Salam aleikom,
Serjang bumi sa' kilat lalu,
Kalau angkau lalu ujong,
Ka lautan yang besar,
Nempoh pangkal, ka gunong api yang besar,
Angkau ikut sa' denai raia,
Permatang yang panjang,
Sinilah tampat angkau ikut,
Balik ka kandang nabi slêman.

Page 44.

Hei! Salam aleikom,
Sri bergenta sa' panjang lampei.
Lalu dua, angkau pegang dua.
Lalu sa', sa angkau pegang,
Lalu besar, besar angkau pegang,
Lalu kechil, kechil angkau pegang,
Aku ta' tahu-kan jahat, tahu kan baik.
Putus, aku ta' chakap mengganti
Hilang, aku ta' chakap menchari.

Page 45.

Hei! tejah jantan di ujong sidin aku.
Ru tunggal di pangkal sidin aku,
Tinggallah mu, aku na' pergi menghambat
Segala raiat nabi slêman.

Page 46.

Si panji lela nama anjing aku,
Si panji ladang nama anjing aku,
Angkau hambatlah raiat nabi slêman
Yang sa' kilat lalu, serjang bumi,
Yang bersubang mas,
Yang berchaping mas,
Yang diluar kandang nabi slêman.

Page 46.

Tu- u- u- u- u-
Telekul lam telekul,
Sanggana dewerna,
Raja Una punya pegang.
Tu- u- u- u-.

Page 48.

Ah bahdi, Mah bahdi,
Aku tahu asal angkau bahdi,
Sa' kling mas tuli,
Sa' pancha mas buta.
Demaga Adam asal angkau bahdi.
Aku tahu k' asal angkau membuang bahdi
Aku tahu k' asal angkau membuang genaling,
Gempa chahia membuang angkau bahdi,
Gempah pakoh membuang angkau genaling.

Hei! Malik Zabaniah!
Bukakan pintu yang sulit,
Aku endah membuang seklian bahdi,
Bukakan tampat yang lepas,
Na' membuang seklian genaling.
Jangan bri tuntut daua kapada aku,
Kapada rumah dan tangga aku,
Kapada kawan dan teman aku,
Kapada rodong sain aku
Kapada anjing pemburu aku,
Jangan angkau tuntut daua.
Kalau angkau tuntut daua
Angkau neraka kapada Allah
Angkau neraka kapada Raja Yang Brahi.

Crocodile Catching. Page 57.

Sang Raga, Sang Ragai
Sambutlah perkiriman Siti Fatimah.
Kalau Angkau ta' makan,
Mati di pengkalan ayer,
Mati di pengkalan tulang,
Mati di pengkalan darah.

Tuba Fishing. Page 191.

Pekih, pekah.
Korinchi nama yang bersi,
Ayun berdum hulubalang ku,

Jibrail akan senjata ku,
Hei! sidang maleikat di pintu bumi,
Naik angkau ka pintu bumi.
Hei! anak sidang maleikat di pintu langit,
Turun angkau ka pintu langit.
Mari kita sa-rêkat-êkat,
Mari kita sa' permainan,
Aku tiada akan tolak segala perbuatan jin,
Aku tadia akan tolak segala perbuatan sheitan,
Aku tiada akan tolak segala perbuatan anak sidang
  manusia,
Karana aku berpaiong Allah.

CROCODILE SHOOTING. Page 218.

Hei!matahari, bukanlah aku,
Bukanlah aku, bulan
Bukanlah aku, bintang,
Saksi-lah kamu yang bukanlah aku,
Bukanlah aku yang membunoh orang ini,
Ayer yang membunoh.

APPENDIX II

THE END

APPENDIX II.

THE LIGHTS OF CHANGKAT ASAH.

THE first two editions of this book contain the following
footnote at the end of the article on "The Lights of Changkat
Asah": —

Since writing the above I have seen the following account by Mr. Andrew Lang in the 'Illustrated London
News': —

"I am well acquainted with the set of lights which are
often seen by the people of Ballachulish and Glencoe,
villages on the south side of the salt-water Loch Leven (not
Queen Mary's fresh-water Loch Leven), on the west coast
of Argyllshire. They are bright lights which disport themselves on the north side of the loch, where steep hills
descend to the level, and to the road along the level, leading to the head of the loch. They rush, as it were, along
the road, then up the hill, then down to the water edge,
and so on, and are visible not only to the Celtic natives but
to the English tourist. The ground is not marshy, even on
the level, and the phenomena, though doubtless natural and
normal, have not yet found a scientific explanation. They
are not what people call 'corpse candles,' and a local myth
used to attribute them to the agency of a dead laird—an
explanation in itself improbable, and now abandoned as
inadequate to the facts of the case."

These Loch Leven light would appear to be the same thing
as the lights of Changkat Asah.

From time to time I have received letters from people in
Siberia, Russia, Germany, Finland, Norway, Scotland, and South
America, with accounts of their experiences with these flying
balls of light, and with their theories and suggestions. These
letters were, of course, not written for publication.

238 APPENDIX II

In conclusion, I may say that the virgin forest which surrounded Changkat Asah in 1895 has now been felled, cleared and to a certain extent replaced by rubber, but that the "lights" on the hill top have been seen from time to time by the Europeans on the rubber estates at the foot of the hill.

THE END.